Spiritual
Seasons

To
my wife, Jane,
and our children, Stephen, Amy, Jeffrey,
with whom I've had the joy of traveling
through my many years of Spiritual Seasons.

Spiritual
Seasons

Discover *God's* purpose
for *each* stage of *your* life

Thomas A. Vaughn

Chosen
Grand Rapids, Michigan

© 2005 Thomas A. Vaughn

Published by Chosen Books
A division of Baker Publishing Group
P.O. Box 6287, Grand Rapids, MI 49516-6287
www.chosenbooks.com

Printed in the United States of America

Library of Congress Cataloging-in-Publication Data
Vaughn, Thomas A., 1935-
  Spiritual seasons : discover God's purpose for each stage of your life / Thomas A. Vaughn.
      p.   cm.
  Includes bibliographical references. (p.   ).
  ISBN 0-8007-9379-X (pbk.)
  1. David, King of Israel. 2. Christian life—Biblical teaching. I. Title.
BS580.D3V38 2005
248.4—dc22   2004017461

CONTENTS

Prologue   7

Section 1 Spiritual Seasons Are Divinely Determined Times

1. Types of Seasons   15
2. Natural Seasons and Spiritual Seasons   21

Section 2 Foundation: The Season of Beginnings

3. God's Choice   35
4. Foundation Building   39
5. Time for School   47

Section 3 Fighting: The Season of Battle

6. Dreams and Remembrances   67
7. God's Instructions   74
8. The Battle   88

Section 4 Futility: The Season of Barrenness

9. Our Thoughts versus God's Thoughts   99
10. The Start of God's Lessons   103
11. When the Going Gets Tough   110
12. His Priceless Providence and Protection   127

Section 5 Favor: The Season of Blessing

13. A Moment of Crisis   143
14. Putting God First   150
15. The "God Kind" of Kindness   163
16. Blessing, Warfare and Work   168
17. The Monarch's Mistakes   176

Section 6 Failure: The Season of Backsliding

18. The Traps of Temptation   183
19. The Seeds of Sin   189
20. The Quicksand of a Quandary   197

Section 7 Forgiveness: The Season of Brokenness

21. Confrontation   209
22. Hard Lessons   214
23. Bitter Harvests   224
24. Grace in the Midst of a Storm   233

Section 8 Finality: The Season of Begetting

25. God Chooses Again   245
26. Never-Ending Blessings   249
27. David's Legacy   252
28. Leaving Our Legacy   260

    Epilogue   265
    Principles   268
    Abbreviations   270
    Notes   271

PROLOGUE

My wife and I walked into the Atlanta airport on a delightful day in late April, relaxed and refreshed from a much-needed vacation spent on the South Carolina coast. Our pleasant chatter ground to a halt when we looked at the large information screen announcing flight arrivals and departures. No departure time was listed for our flight to Chicago's O'Hare Airport—only the word "Delayed."

The clerk at the ticket counter gave us an unwelcome explanation: "A sudden snowstorm moved into the Chicago area and all flights into O'Hare have been cancelled for the time being. We've been advised the delay may be a couple of hours or so."

A late April snowstorm. My wife and I shared a rueful look. Suddenly neither of us looked forward to our arrival at O'Hare.

When we began our trip ten days earlier, spring seemed to have arrived in Chicago, with all of its welcome warmth and sunshine. We left home wearing and carrying only the light clothing suitable for enjoying the soft breezes and warm climate of our South Carolina destination. I then compounded the problem by leaving our car in the long-term parking lot, meaning that it was outside and located some distance from the terminal, thereby allowing it to catch the full brunt of the weather.

The bright sun and blue sky that greeted us when we finally arrived at O'Hare belied a strong and bitterly cold north wind. It sliced through our thin clothing as we struggled to carry our suitcases over the several inches of snow that had fallen in the parking lot. Our car was blanketed with a combination of ice and snow. Removing it was an added bit of agony, since the ice scraper and snow brush I normally carried in the car throughout the winter had been left in our garage. *After all,* I had reasoned, *it's springtime, isn't it?*

We had spent all of our married years in the Chicago area and should have learned by this time one of the immutable facts about living there: The spring season in this locale brings a wide range of weather conditions, from arctic cold to Florida-style heat and humidity. But because of our overly optimistic and unrealistic assumptions, we had not made proper preparations for an all-too-typical spring in the Windy City.

What my wife and I experienced on this occasion occurs all too frequently for many Christians. I do not mean that they misjudge the weather, but that they fail to understand the seasons in their spiritual lives. Many people are unaware of the changing times and seasons that God brings into their lives, and some appear oblivious to the fact that spiritual seasons even exist!

This oversight or ignorance can prove to be dangerous. The seasons we experience in the spiritual realm have a much more profound effect on our behavior and lifestyle than any winter blizzard, summer heat wave, tornado or hurricane. How often are Christians baffled by an unexpected turn of events, distraught and discouraged over a lengthy period of trials or surprised and bewildered over a sudden shower of blessings? How often have we asked ourselves questions that begin "Why is God letting . . . " or "Where is God when . . . " or "When will this end . . . " or "How did this happen . . . ?"

This book has grown out of a season that my wife and I had been experiencing for two years when I began writing. It was proving to be the most difficult and confused period of our entire spiritual lives. We prayed diligently, studied and meditated on God's Word. We fasted, sought the Lord, counseled with mature Christian friends and devoured numbers of fine Christian books. In the course of this struggle, I sensed God leading me to undertake an intense study of David's life.

Having been a student of the Bible for many years, I considered myself fairly familiar with this subject. My wife and I had even acquired and read for our home library a number of fine books on various Old Testament periods in Israel's history, including a number about David and his rule.[1]

It was not long after beginning this in-depth study that I discovered just how far down on "God's learning curve" I really was, in terms of discovering the many lessons God taught David, and how many of these same lessons should be applied to my own daily situations.

As I followed David from his earliest recorded days in Scripture—the young shepherd boy alone on the barren Judean hillsides—to his final hours as an aged and bedridden king, I saw that David's life is unique in all of Scripture. The Bible presents his story in unprecedented detail, and with fewer gaps than any other person's history in the Old Testament. The lives of some of the Bible's "giants of faith" are chronicled from their early years until death, but in each of their lives, there are periods of years during which nothing was recorded. In Joseph's case, for example, nothing is recorded about the many decades that elapsed between the events immediately following his father Jacob's death until his own death, except for the mention that he lived to see his great-grandchildren and the oath he took from his descendants.[2] Even in the record of our Lord Jesus Christ's time on this earth, we are given only one instance in His life between the almost three decades from when He was a small child until the moment He began His public ministry.[3]

It was the detail with which Scripture describes David's life that first opened my eyes to the truth of spiritual seasons. I found that David's story displays a pattern that can be divided into very definite segments or periods of time. While similar patterns can be seen in the lives of other scriptural characters, David's seasons are more numerous and more developed than the seasons of other great men and women in the Bible. Each segment of his colorful career is distinct from the others—in many instances as distinct as summer is from winter. His seasons differ in terms of major events, relationships and, most importantly, God's dealings with David. The transition from one season to the next is noticeably sharp, so there is little question as to which season David is in at any moment.

David's life began to show me that while God can work in our lives through single events, He most often deals with us over periods of time. This understanding helped me to recognize how the seasons of our spiritual lives differ, what the characteristics of these seasons are and the ways our Lord uses them to mold and shape our characters and lives for His purpose and glory.

This study also helped me to become more aware of three traps into which we Christians are prone to fall. I have become increasingly convinced that these are the pitfalls that keep Christians from experiencing more of our Lord's daily presence and power, and from coming into an awareness of His plans for them:

One trap is the tendency to "compartmentalize" our lives by dividing them into separate sections. We give one part of our lives to our jobs, another to our families, a third to recreation and so on. Sunday morning is the spiritual segment, the hour (or two) Christians give to God. Many born-again believers see nothing wrong or harmful in keeping these compartments separate from one another. The world certainly encourages us to act in this manner. "Don't try to bring your Christianity into the workplace" is one of society's frequent admonishments.

The Bible's view of the nature of mankind is holistic, however. In other words, God created us each with a body, mind and spirit, and these three aspects are to function as a unified whole. The Old Testament Jews made no distinction between the secular and spiritual spheres of their lives. Every part of their existence on this earth—home life, occupation and relationships with others—was governed by their interaction with God. Jesus Himself validated this lifestyle when He said in Matthew 22:37, "You shall love the LORD your God with all your heart, with all your soul, and with all your mind." We may pay lip service to this command on Sunday morning, but many of us return the rest of the week to loving and worshiping the gods of mammon and pleasure. Compartmentalizing our lives in this way is not scriptural. In so doing we fail to understand the critical linkage between the secular and the spiritual; that the things we are experiencing in our everyday lives are an integral part of God's work in us.

This trap of compartmentalization leads to a second and equally dangerous deception. We have a tendency to feel that either "the age of miracles is past" or that "God only works miraculously in the lives of well-known Christian leaders." Jesus, however, is "the same yesterday, today, and forever" (Hebrews 13:8), and He "shows personal favoritism to no man [or woman]" (see Galatians 2:6; Acts 10:34). We need to start believing that He can and will operate miraculously in our own lives!

Over both these deceptions (or perhaps underneath, as their root) is our tendency to view our lives as a long series of isolated and unrelated happenings. We believe in a sovereign and loving God, yet live as though all our experiences come about through chance! Brennan Manning makes the following observation about this type of mind-set:

> Treating life as a series of disconnected episodes is a habit deeply rooted in many of us. We discern no pattern in the experiences and events coming from outside ourselves. Life seems as disjointed as the morning news.[4]

This outlook reflects the influence of Darwinism on modern-day thinking and behavior. If we believe that our existence is the product of chance and random happenings, then we will fail to acknowledge our God as the "Blessed Controller of all things" and will not respond correctly to His working in our lives.

The song "In His Time" contains a line from Ecclesiastes 3:11 that states: "He makes all things beautiful in His time." God has begun, in His time, to meet my wife and me in the midst of our searching and to answer the questions that have plagued us. He has not used a cosmic remote-control to change the channel on our season, but He is providing us with greater insight and revelation, enabling us to see from His perspective.

I have learned a lot of lessons from David, many having to do with how a man after God's own heart responds to difficult seasons. But in the course of my study I also gained a much clearer picture of David's spiritual foundation. While seasons and storms cycled around him, David's faith rested on an underpinning of principles that apply to every believer regardless of situation.

I want my readers to discover these principles as I did, in the organic context of David's life, so I have not organized them into their own topical section or into a list that you can memorize. Instead you will find them here and there along the way (they are numbered sequentially to make reference easier). I hope that when you find them, you will allow yourself to be interrupted—to meditate as I have on the underlying truths of David's life.

And so this book comes to be written. For those who have never considered the truth of spiritual seasons, I hope it will serve as an introduction to their reality and the vital impact they can have on our lives. For others, who are only too aware of these changing times, I pray this book will give added enlightenment. May we all be encouraged to obediently receive the full purpose of every spiritual season, those divinely determined times our loving and gracious heavenly Father brings to each of His children.

Black Mountain, North Carolina

SPIRITUAL SEASONS ARE DIVINELY DETERMINED TIMES

"The church's singular failure in recent decades has been the failure to see Christianity as a life system, or worldview, that governs every area of existence."

—CHARLES COLSON

TYPES OF SEASONS

In the prologue, we discussed how spiritual seasons really are divinely determined times. In fact, understanding spiritual seasons can help us understand the primary way God works in our daily lives. This first section of our study will consider, compare and contrast the various kinds of seasons.

Types of Earthly Seasons

The word *season* can be defined in a number of ways. Most people living in the earth's temperate zone think of this word as referring to the yearly cycle of changes in temperature that causes spring, summer, fall and winter. Persons in the tropical zone do not experience much variation in temperature but they do in moisture, so they divide their year into a wet season and a dry season.

Seasons also can be defined in terms of activities. Sports fans speak about the seasons of football, baseball, basketball and hockey. Outdoors enthusiasts count the passing of the hunting and fishing seasons. (Our family lived for a time in southern Missouri. The start of the deer-

15

hunting season considerably reduced the working population in those communities for at least a day or two.)

Then there are the age-related seasons. This category has taken on a greater importance and variety in recent years. Barna and Hatch refer to such seasons as "life stages." They define a life stage as "a period of time we all go through, usually during a certain age range or family cycle, that dictates how we think and act."[1] They include periods such as adolescence, single and searching, newly married, parenting and empty nesters.

From this brief listing, it is apparent *season* is a word used to describe the many varied aspects of our natural human existence. Then how can a season be *spiritual*? Most importantly, is this concept a scriptural one? Where does the Bible refer to the idea of spiritual seasons?

Ecclesiastes—Seldom Read but Spiritually Significant

A season in the spiritual realm is most definitely scriptural. While several Bible passages deal with this concept, the key text we will be using in our study is found in Ecclesiastes 3:1 and reads as follows:

> To everything there is a season,
> a time for every purpose under heaven.

The succeeding verses, 2–8, list the many types of times and experiences humans undergo throughout life from birth to death—tearing down and building up, sorrow and laughter, acquiring and sacrificing, silence and speech. This section of Scripture conveys a principle taught throughout the book of Ecclesiastes:

Principle #1: **God is the controller of all things, and we are to live our lives in the recognition that He has a specific time, plan and purpose for every one of our life experiences and accomplishments.**

Consequently, all of us are responsible to discern the right times for the right actions so we do not miss or waste the times and seasons our Lord gives us.

The truth presented here seldom is seen by Christians since Ecclesiastes is a part of the Bible they often avoid reading. Ecclesiastes is a seldom-read portion of Scripture, probably because it is also one of the most misunderstood.[2] Solomon is generally credited as its author. As the richest and most renowned monarch of the known world, he had the power and wealth to gratify his every desire and whim. Ecclesiastes recounts his wide-ranging search for meaning and satisfaction in life but contains his admission of finding only futility and emptiness. While his statements appear pessimistic on the surface, the key point to remember is that these are Solomon's observations on how *not* to live our lives. He also presents an alternative to this futility, to his vain and fruitless search for something of value. This alternative is a God-centered life. His conclusion is simple and straightforward: When man is in right relationship with God, then and only then does human life become truly meaningful.[3]

Besides being viewed as pessimistic, Ecclesiastes is often mistakenly seen as fatalistic. Fatalism, the philosophy that the events of our lives are inexorably ordered according to some unknown cosmic force or process, "has no place in Christianity, but is commonly encountered in Oriental religions."[4] A popular song of the 1950s was entitled "Que Será, Será," which can be loosely translated, "Whatever will be, will be." This type of outlook on life has, sadly, become much more prevalent today than it was half a century ago, even among Christians.

Ecclesiastes 3:1 is not a fatalistic statement! Solomon is communicating, simply and directly, that the Lord has a beautiful plan for every one of us in all of our life situations in all times.[5] No matter what the time or season, neither our lives nor the events we encounter are the result of chance or happenstance, good luck or bad luck, fate or fortune, the law of large numbers or Murphy's Law.[6]

The Meaning of Season and Time

The Hebrew word for *time* in this verse is *'et*. It's the most common Old Testament expression for time and is usually joined to specific events. The basic meaning of this word relates to time conceived as an opportunity or season.[7] The word translated *season* is the Aramaic loan-word *zeman* and carries a very similar meaning, although it refers in each instance to an "appointed time."[8]

Reflect for just a moment on the meaning of these two words: a season of opportunity and a time God has appointed just for you. Together these words convey a wonderful truth: God is at work in our lives, constantly offering us divinely determined times and seasons of opportunities. One commentator says of this passage, "To everything there is a season, a fixed time, a predetermined purpose (of God) on which everything depends. There is a season for every work of God."[9]

A spiritual season is a distinct, identifiable period of time during which the Lord works through particular people, events and/or circumstances to

- *Produce* a greater degree of spiritual growth and maturity in us
- *Prepare* us for a future task or ministry to which He is calling us
- *Promote* us to positions where we can be used to achieve victories over the forces of darkness and extend God's Kingdom

Our responsibility is to emulate the sons of Issachar (see 1 Chronicles 12:32) and gain a proper understanding of the times in which we live and what we ought to do. While it is true that God can and does use single events in His process of shaping us, these events are almost always part of a larger, ongoing process. Very few people have a Damascus Road experience like Saul of Tarsus—a happening so dramatic and overwhelming that it permanently changes the course of their lives in a single moment. For most of us, God is the Master Potter, slowly but surely fashioning the clay of our bodies, souls and spirits, by taking us through a variety of spiritual seasons. If we cooperate with God, doing what He has called us to do, then we will find He makes "everything beautiful in its time," as Ecclesiastes 3:11 promises.

Your Present Season

In light of these divine truths, can we truly say that we are really aware of the season God has brought into our lives at this moment, and the purpose He has for us? Do we have an understanding of the times we are currently experiencing? Are we able to interpret our present circumstances from God's standpoint? Do we even recognize the sovereignty of God in the world, much less in our lives? Or have we given over to the pessimistic and fatalistic thinking of modern culture with its attitude of "What's the use?" and the passive, catch-all response of "Whatever"?

The inability of many Christians to answer such questions from a biblical perspective of faith and hope shows that they know *about* God, but do not have a vital and intimate relationship with their Lord. Henry Blackaby says, "Really knowing God only comes through experience as He reveals Himself to you. Throughout the Bible God took the initiative to reveal Himself to people by experience."[10] Brennan Manning echoes the same truth as Blackaby:

> Perhaps we think that because we are Christians and read the Bible and know a great deal *about* God, that therefore we know God. Nothing could be further from the truth. It does us little good to memorize chapter and verse, to master the language of the Bible, if we have nothing to share in that language, no *experiential knowledge* of God in our lives.[11]

And so it is with us. One of the major ways God reveals Himself is through the spiritual seasons we experience. That is why it is so important for us to cooperate with Him—fully absorbing the experiences and lessons He uses during these "appointed times" to fashion the clay of our lives into a vessel for His glory. David Wilkerson, the founder of Teen Challenge, states this fact very bluntly:

> You'll never get true spirituality from someone or something else. If you're going to taste God's glory, it is going to have to come to you right where you are—in your present circumstances, pleasant or unpleasant.[12]

David: Our Model

Throughout the following chapters we will endeavor to answer the question, "What are the spiritual seasons Christians may experience and what practical impact do they have on our daily lives?" To find our answers, we will examine seven seasons in David's life and the profound impact they had on him, his family and his nation. Then we will be able to better recognize how these same seasons can relate to us today.

Why David? Well, why not David? After all, he is the only person in the Bible to be called "a man after [God's] own heart" (Acts 13:22). Anyone who is given this kind of appellation deserves to be used as a model for present-day Christians!

By relating the experiences of David to our own lives, we can begin to see them not as dry, old historical events of three thousand years ago, but as spiritual seasons that the Lord is reproducing in our lives today or may bring to us at some future time. Christians should not be surprised when they find themselves going through several of the same seasons and being taught some of the similar lessons David learned.

Most of us will not experience all of the seasons David went through, and God may determine to introduce us to an entirely new and different season or two. But the key point is this: All of us *will* go through spiritual seasons on this earth.

2

NATURAL SEASONS AND
SPIRITUAL SEASONS

Y ou and I have been, are now and will be experiencing seasons (appointed times) in our spiritual lives. While these seasons and times
are spiritual, they share certain characteristics with the seasons in
nature. Christians need to recognize and accept this fact. Otherwise, we
run the risk of either missing the particular teachings and opportunities the Lord has for us in each season, or becoming resentful and bitter
against God because our lives do not go as we had hoped or planned.
To aid us in focusing on this matter, let's consider the several ways in
which spiritual and natural seasons are similar.

Seasons End

No season lasts indefinitely. Spiritual seasons pass through our lives
just as we experience the different seasons in nature. How unrealistic
would it be for a person living in Chicago to expect summer to last

year-round? Yet how many Christians become agitated and distressed when God begins to change their spiritual summer of physical comfort and financial prosperity to the chill, rainy autumn of unexpected tests and trials! What is the all-too-common reaction to this turn of seasons? We begin to pout, complain and become discouraged about how hard it is to live the Christian life. We run to our pastors for counseling or to our friends for sympathy. Sometimes we start to berate God with our prayers about how unfair and unkind He is being to us after we have tried so hard to live for Him.

Our carnal selves, the flesh, certainly prefer those times when we seem to live in God's blessings and victories on an almost daily basis. This kind of season is like a long, languorous summer marked by bright and cloudless skies. (After all, who wants rain on the day of a picnic?)

In the mid-1960s, a documentary movie entitled *The Endless Summer* gained popularity with the younger generation. The movie recorded the worldwide search undertaken by some young surfers who wanted to find the ideal beach location. They dreamed that it would produce perfect waves for surfing all year long, day after day. Their trek led them from California to Hawaii, Australia and the shores of Africa. Searching for the perfect never-ending spiritual season is an equally useless endeavor.

Even if someone thought that he or she had actually discovered such a season, it would contain the seeds of its own problems. An old Arab proverb states, "All sunshine makes a desert." Likewise, so will a too-lengthy spiritual season devoid of testing, trials and temptations. The history of Israel, particularly as recorded in the book of Judges, provides a sobering illustration of the dangers such fat and comfortable times can bring to God's people.

Alert for Signposts

Since no season lasts indefinitely, Christians must be alert to recognize the signs pointing to a coming change from one spiritual season to the next. This requires making certain preparations and adjustments, just as we observe and plan for the cycle of seasons in nature. The cliché "If we fail to plan, we plan to fail" applies here.

Imagine for a moment a Chicago resident who becomes so comfortable with the pleasant and colorful early fall season he is experiencing that he makes no preparations for the soon-coming winter. As foolish as this appears, how often do we seem oblivious to those approaching changes in our appointed spiritual times?

The Lord does not want us to be surprised and unprepared for these seasonal changes. The Bible contains numerous verses emphasizing God's desire for His people to grow in knowledge and understanding of all spiritual things, including His will.[1] Later on we will discuss some of the specific things He uses to alert and prepare us, as we study His dealings with David.

Blessings from Each Season

Every season has its special blessings and beauty. This statement holds true even for your least favorite season—the one you definitely could do without! Winter always had been the least favorite season for my wife and me, until we moved into our new home in the mountains of western North Carolina one early spring. My wife wrote a description of our introduction to the seasons in the Smoky Mountains. Here is a brief excerpt:

Our house is on a mountain ridge at an altitude of 3,500 feet, a thousand feet above the valley floor. The mountainsides are covered with evergreen mountain laurels and wild rhododendrons, stately oaks and maples, sourwoods, hemlocks and dogwoods—all native to the area. From late spring until early fall, the forests are so thick with greenery that you can see only a short distance into them. As fall arrived, I began enjoying the rich hues of the leaves changing colors: deep crimsons and burgundies, burnt and red oranges, pale and golden yellows. The season was so lovely I hated to see it pass. I was almost dreading the barrenness and "death" of winter. Snow and ice can make mountain driving a treacherous event.

As I started down our road into town one October day, I suddenly realized that I could see the large reservoir-lake that services the nearby metropolitan area. The shining water, peeking through the now partially barren trees, was a beautiful sight. As the days progressed and more of the leaves fell, new vistas opened up before me—the pasturelands on the valley floor and the highest peak in the Eastern United States, Mount Mitchell. I became more and more impressed by what I could see this month that I had been unable to see since spring.

The Lord seized this opportunity to speak clearly to me. He showed me that when the leaves, the foliage—the "stuff"—is stripped away from our lives, He is able to reveal some things that were always there, but that we couldn't see because of all the "stuff" that was hanging on us. Our "stuff" can hinder our ability to see clearly—to see Him clearly.

He showed me something else about the "winter" of our lives. The thick growth of summer not only hides the views in the distance, it also can hide some things in the forest itself, rotting logs or trash, left and forgotten and hidden by the "stuff." In God's timing, the forest comes to a new winter season and many of the things inside it are revealed. And so it is in our lives. If we never come to a winter time where we stand naked before the Lord, we may never deal with the old trash in our lives. We can try to go somewhere to escape the winter, and we can put off cleaning out our woods. But what a waste of God's timing, plan and seasons!

God wastes nothing in our lives! Those spiritual winter seasons—those dull, monotonous, iron-gray, bone-chilling times that appear to our natural eyes to be so bleak, so barren, so devoid of real purpose, so lacking in victories and the joy of the Lord—are exactly the periods that He takes to prepare us so we can be launched into a greater sphere of service and usefulness for His Kingdom. David Wilkerson offers a telling observation on this truth:

> In all my years of walking with the Lord, I've rarely seen an increase in my spirituality during good times. Rather, any such increases usually took place as I endured hard places, agonies, testing—all of which the Lord allowed. I know the same is true for most of the truly spiritual people I've known over the years.[2]

Remember that even in the most pleasant of seasons we can experience some strong storms. Just as hurricane season in the southeastern United States runs from the warm and sunny days of June through October, we may find a test or trial in the midst of an extended period of blessing and prosperity.

No matter what season we are in, Christians should learn to find the fulfillment and enjoyment the Lord has for them. We often miss the small blessings and pleasures scattered throughout each of our days. Many of us tend to focus on the negatives of life—for example, the "half-empty glass." "Take time to stop and smell the roses" may be a well-worn expression; it carries sound advice nonetheless. God has placed roses in all our days, but we are often too busy, hurried and hassled, too prone to grumble, complain and criticize—too wrapped up in ourselves—to notice His roses.

Francis Mayes wrote a book about a home she and her husband purchased in rural Italy. She describes in minute detail the numerous trials and tribulations of renovating this centuries-old house and tiny farm. I found one of the most telling aspects of this fine book to be her frequent descriptions of the pure pleasures she discovered in the seemingly simple experiences of daily routine—the taste of fruits and vegetables purchased that morning at the local farmers' market, the sunrises and sunsets over the hills and valleys of the region, watching local artisans at work and even the muscle-numbing labor of rehabbing an old home. She speaks of learning to develop the Italian perspective of "the quality of becoming involved in the moment."[3]

We Christians would do well to develop this kind of outlook. Ecclesiastes admonishes us to take delight in and enjoy not only the great pleasures and victories of life, but the things He gives us in the ordinary course of our daily routine—food, employment and so on.[4] Furthermore, Christ has called us to be overcomers in spite of the daily demands and discouragements we all encounter, in spite of whatever season He has dropped in our lives.[5]

A Difference in Duration

At least three differences exist between natural and spiritual seasons. The first difference involves their length. *Spiritual seasons have no definite duration.* Our natural seasons have fairly predictable time spans. Summer may seem to start a bit earlier than normal one year, or perhaps to last a little longer compared to past years. But it does not continue for a whole twelve months or longer (at least not in western North Carolina!). Spiritual seasons, on the other hand, have no normal length and their time spans can vary greatly. The spiritual seasons of my own life, and my observations of those experienced by Christian friends, clearly indicate that our spiritual seasons normally last considerably longer than our traditional spring, summer, fall and winter.

A Difference in Description

Spiritual seasons come in a variety of shapes and sizes, so do not be surprised if the particular season you are going through fails to exactly match the ones described in this book. The reason for this is quite simple. God works through our lives in ways best suited to our uniqueness and personality, and to the call He has placed on our lives. As a result, your Foundation Season (which we will be discussing later) may be different from the one experienced by another Christian. Furthermore you may go through a lesser or greater number of seasons than the seven presented in this book. I believe, however, that the seven major seasons David went through on his life's spiritual journey include several of those that many Christians will experience at some point in their lives.

A Difference in Dynamics

The third difference between natural and spiritual seasons is especially crucial for us to grasp, in light of the popular mind-set in today's Church. While the changing of seasons is common in both the natural and spiritual realms, *spiritual seasons do not recur in a regular cycle* as do seasons in nature. The Lord in His wisdom may take us from a summer rich with fruitfulness in spiritual and material blessings and transport us into a winter filled with trials, upheavals and uncertainties. We do not have the luxury of selecting only those parts of each season that we want while we discard the rest. This kind of spiritual selectivity would be akin to an avid skier who lives in the northern U.S. snow belt saying, "I want a lot of snow this winter so I can ski to my heart's content, but I don't want any blizzards, extremely cold weather or snow on my driveway."

The statements concerning this last difference may appear too self-evident to warrant further discussion. Unfortunately, this is not the case because of one very unpleasant fact: Much of what we see, hear and experience in the Christian Church today is not biblical Christianity. Charles Colson terms it "Salad-Bar Christianity." He has observed increasing numbers of believers who seem determined to build their own personal styles of Christianity. Consequently, they are unwilling to let either the Bible or the Church tell them what to do. He says:

> Some Christians tend to substitute feelings for objective reality, seeking self-centered spirituality over the structured demands of organized religion. With self-fulfillment their standard, they pick and choose, as if at a salad bar, from any belief system that provides comfort or meaning. . . .

On any Sunday morning, an alarming number who fill our pews are either Biblically illiterate or, worse, syncretists.[6]

The Danger of Syncretism

Syncretism, the bringing together of two things that originally were different, was the major cause of backsliding among the Israelites from the time they entered the Promised Land until the Babylonian captivity. During these centuries, the Israelites never totally forgot or abandoned their worship and service toward the one true God. Rather, they simply grafted onto Judaism many of the pagan religious practices of the Canaanites and other surrounding nations. The Lord strongly condemned this syncretistic religion of His chosen people, particularly through the messages given by His prophets. But the Israelites continued in their apostasy despite generations of warnings from the Lord. Eventually, this gross disobedience led to both the Assyrian and Babylonian conquests and exiles of Israel (the northern kingdom) and Judah (the southern kingdom).

Syncretism is really a form of incomplete obedience. And syncretism/incomplete obedience is pervasive in today's Church! While we do not bring the worship of pagan gods into our Christianity, many of us fervently serve the idol of rampant individualism in all areas of our lives. The mind-sets of "Do your own thing" and "I want my rights no matter what" seem to be as common among believers as in the secular world.

So Christians decide which parts of the Bible they will accept (the love of God, for example) and which parts they disagree with and reject (like God's condemning of pre-marital sex, abortion, homosexuality and so on). Their obedience to God's Word is dependent solely upon whether or not it suits their personal desires or goals. Such reasoning is highly dangerous because it runs totally counter to a basic principle seen throughout the pages of Scripture:

Principle #2: **Incomplete or partial obedience is disobedience.**

A good illustration of this principle is found in 1 Samuel 15. God, through the prophet Samuel, told King Saul to totally destroy the Amalekites for what they had done many years earlier to the children of Israel. This destruction was to be complete—all of the people from the youngest to the oldest, and all of the animals. Many Christians are appalled by this seemingly merciless and barbaric command of God, an action that appears diametrically opposed to the Bible's depiction of Him as a God of love (see 1 John 4:8), mercy and grace (see Exodus 34:6). (See the following endnote for an explanation of this apparent contradiction.[7])

Although Saul killed the Amalekite people, he spared Agag, their king, and the choicest of the animals. God told Samuel that Saul's action amounted to disobedience and that, by his disobedience, he had separated himself from God and forfeited the kingship.

When Samuel brought this message to Saul, the king found it difficult to believe he had done anything wrong. Similarly, many people reading this account today may find it difficult to understand why the Lord would deal so harshly with Saul. We are far too used to taking poetic license with God's Word! The lesson to be learned from this episode is the spiritual principle regarding obedience: It is of the highest importance in God's sight.

As we grow from childhood to adulthood, we discover certain laws of nature, like the law of gravity, to which we must adjust. The Lord has principles that are equally fundamental in the spiritual realm. A number of these principles will be presented in the following sections and are an integral part of our spiritual seasons. If we are unaware of them or ignore them, we will suffer the natural consequences. J. W. Follette emphasizes the need for believers to recognize and adjust to God's laws and principles:

> Many Christians seem to think that the realm of the Spirit is a kind of "happy hunting ground" in which we may run around as we please, regardless of spiritual laws, and then expect to have an orderly, well-balanced Christian experience. They are mistaken. In the spiritual order God has principles which are as basic and real as are the principles in the natural world . . . and are just as demanding as the others and require a like obedience.[8]

One subtle form of syncretism is the way people often manipulate words in their attempts to get what they want, or to justify and rationalize their attitudes and behavior. In recent years, the idea has grown that our language is "open-textured" and "indeterminate." According to this kind of reasoning, we can have great latitude in our use of words and infuse them with our own personal meaning.[9] Examples of such word gymnastics are becoming more and more common. The word *sin* has been replaced by terms such as *mistake* or *error*. *Fornication* and *adultery* have been eliminated by the use of softer words and phrases like *love relationship* and *private affair*. This way of dealing with language can allow a person to formulate his or her own personal code of ethics and actually develop a religion suited to one's own desired lifestyle. The comic strip "Kudzu" carried a telling comment on this trend in language. Minister Will B. Dunne is shown preaching to his congregation from a modern translation of the Old Testament he calls the "Retro Testament." His sermon is on "The Ten Requests" and includes such points as "Thank you for not killing" and "Thank you for not stealing."[10]

Caution and Consolation

Allow me to close this introductory section on spiritual seasons with a caution and an encouragement. Both are needed because change is always involved when moving from one season or time to another, and change can be difficult and unwelcome, particularly as we grow older.

On the caution side: We need to guard against the mistake of living in the past by too frequently reminiscing about and desiring a return of the good old days—those past seasons and times that we remember so fondly. In actuality, the advantages and pleasures we recall are probably part real and part imaginary—as much fantasy as fact. Ecclesiastes 7:10 warns us against this kind of unrealistic backward-gazing: "Do not say, 'Why were the former days better than these?' For you do not inquire wisely concerning this."

Certainly it is enjoyable to look at the pictures of a wonderful vacation trip and remember again some of those pleasurable experiences. Similarly, we can have joy and blessing in recalling the marvelous things the Lord has accomplished in our lives in the years since we became Christians. Remembering such experiences and events helps to build and strengthen our faith and trust in the Lord. At Mount Sinai, the Lord gave Moses instructions for various sacred times and feasts that were to be continually observed by the children of Israel and their descendants. Through these means, God's people would always be reminded of His miraculous works and blessings. In addition, the Israelites built stone pillars and memorials from time to time. These "stones of remembrance" testified to the victories, deliverances and blessings that the Israelites had enjoyed. We, too, need to keep such memories fresh in our minds and not allow them to fade into forgetfulness.

But we should not attempt to return to a season that is already past! The danger for both individuals and churches is that living in the past allows "traditions" to develop. Dr. Fuchsia Pickett has said at many Christian conferences, "The greatest enemy of the next move of God is the last move of God." Management books often contain the admonition that the last seven words of a dying business or organization are "We've never done it that way before." Change is a vital part of the fabric of life, and we need to accept it and embrace it.

On the consolation side: Be encouraged and understand that spiritual seasons are not just a matter of change for the sake of change. Our Lord is a God of infinite creativity and variety. There is always a newness, a freshness and a sense of anticipation and wonder as we walk the path of life with Jesus. Do not be too quick to hurry God and yourself through any spiritual season. Remember that true joy and satisfaction is found in the journey, not only in the arrival at your final destination.

Jim Jackson, the president of Christian Believers United, often tells his audiences to trust our loving and almighty God because "the best is yet to come." That is sound advice. So do not be afraid to step out in faith and experience the wonderful spiritual seasons that the Lord has planned for you. David Wilkerson writes:

> Many believers are satisfied with what I call an initial, one-time revelation of Christ's saving power and grace. Every true believer experiences this wonderful, life-changing revelation. Yet that's only the first step. What lies ahead is a lifetime of deeper, more glorious revelations of Christ.[11]

Some Final Suggestions

Before we begin our journey through these spiritual seasons, here is a word of advice: As you read the following chapters, take time to consider and pray as to how you could begin to apply these lessons and principles to the situations you face in your own life. Do not be a Christian who is full of Bible knowledge but poor in its application. As the great nineteenth-century evangelist D. L. Moody remarked, "God didn't give us the Bible just to increase our knowledge but to change our lives."

The events David experienced in each of his seasons provide living illustrations of the wonderful ways God can work in all of the times He sends to us. Consequently, I strongly urge you to also read the corresponding account of David's times directly from your Bible. His life story covers more chapters in the Old Testament than any other person's, so no book can hope to cover in breadth and depth all of the happenings, large and small, of his extraordinary career. Reading the appropriate sections of Scripture in 1 and 2 Samuel, 1 Kings, 1 Chronicles, and the Psalms will enhance your understanding of these spiritual seasons.

And now let's begin our journey into the first of the spiritual seasons the Lord had for David—the one every Christian must also experience personally.

FOUNDATION

The Season of Beginnings
(1 Samuel 16)

"The issue is not how many people are attending church, but how many are becoming Christlike, how Christlike we are on Monday morning when we're in the world."

—FRANCIS FRANGIPANE

3

GOD'S CHOICE

The residents of Bethlehem are nervous and confused, while the town leaders are downright fearful. Samuel, Israel's mighty prophet and judge, has arrived unexpectedly in their little community. Why has he come? Bethlehem is not a normal part of the annual circuit Samuel makes to carry out his ministry of judgeship.[1] Have they done something to incur God's wrath? Perhaps he is bringing stern words of judgment against them!

"Is your visit a peaceful one?" they ask him with a mixture of hope and anxiety.

Samuel assures them it is, saying he has come for a special sacrifice to which only the elders of Bethlehem, Jesse and his sons will be invited (see 1 Samuel 16:5).

As the small group gathers at Jesse's home, Samuel's gaze scans each person with utmost care and discernment. The Lord has sent him on a vital and critical mission—a mission to anoint the one He Himself has already chosen to be Israel's next king, the one who will succeed Saul, who is the nation's current leader. As Samuel's eyes fall upon Eliab, Jesse's eldest son, the old prophet feels certain this young man has to be God's choice. Why, he even looks the part of a king as he stands there—physically imposing, handsome and self-assured. The obvious choice![2] Samuel walks over and faces Eliab as he begins to open the horn of oil in his hand.

Then Samuel hears the still, small voice. It is the same voice he first heard one night several decades earlier as a child serving the high priest Eli in the sanctuary at Shiloh. It is the voice he has heard countless times over the many succeeding years as he prophesied and judged in the nation of Israel. It is the voice he knows beyond any doubt, the voice he has always obeyed, no matter what the circumstances might be or the cost to himself. "Don't judge by the outward appearance," God instructs His old servant. "That is man's method of discernment. I look upon a person's inner makeup."

In obedience, Samuel instructs Eliab to stand aside. Both the young man and those in the room are surprised. No one yet knows for certain what is Samuel's real purpose for coming to Bethlehem, but it seems likely to be some honor or appointment that the aged prophet and judge is going to bestow on Jesse's household. Eliab is the "heir apparent" to rule the family when Jesse is gone, so he must be the one Samuel has come to bless. Yet Samuel tells him to step aside and asks for Jesse's second oldest son, Abinadab, to be called forward. God's voice once again instructs His prophet that the number-two son is not His choice either. So Samuel dutifully but bluntly tells the young man, "You're not the one the Lord has selected either."

Surprise and bewilderment begin to build in the small crowd. And when the third son, Shammah, also is told he is not the one God has selected, a murmur of anger starts to surface both in the three oldest sons and among some of the onlookers.

Why this rejection by God? What are He and Samuel looking for? By the time all seven[3] of Jesse's sons have failed to be selected for whatever it is Samuel has come to announce, the entire group has become visibly upset by these strange proceedings. Even though Samuel is the revered spiritual leader of the nation, everyone feels that he not only has been acting in a most unusual manner but that his treatment of these seven fine, strong sons of Jesse appears almost insulting.

Samuel quietly ponders the situation. He knows with absolute certainty that the Lord has sent him to anoint one of Jesse's sons to be Israel's king. Yet he seems to be at an impasse. There has to be an answer, a solution to this peculiar dilemma.

(Do you find it interesting that when God commissioned Samuel for this assignment, He did not tell the prophet the name of the man He had already chosen? There is a not-so-small truth in this incident. All of God's people are called to walk step by step in faith. Even those we consider to be His great, anointed leaders are not exempt from this responsibility! As each of us obeys the Lord and takes the first step in faith, God will then show us what our second step is to be.)

And so it is with Samuel. He does not allow the circumstances to cause him frustration or confusion, nor does he begin to doubt God's leading. Instead, he exercises godly wisdom, the wisdom that often looks quite elementary but yet is so profound. The old prophet asks a question, but not just any question. It has been said that 75 percent of finding the right solution to a problem is simply asking the right question. Samuel asks the right question and discovers that Jesse has one more son, his youngest.

David is called in from the fields where he has been shepherding the family's flocks, and as David stands before Samuel, all who are in Jesse's home on this fateful day wonder why Samuel has summoned this teenager to their meeting. From a human perspective, he is only a youth (perhaps about fifteen years old), the youngest and least regarded of Jesse's children, and has spent the majority of his young years serving as a shepherd. It is true that he makes a good initial impression with his handsome features, bright eyes and ruddy appearance (light-complexioned in contrast with his fellow countrymen). Yes, he does have some musical ability and has proven to be a dedicated and courageous shepherd. But he is still a boy and does not appear to have any really outstanding qualities or talents. He certainly pales in comparison with his older brothers.

God's command comes quickly and clearly to Samuel. "This is the one. Anoint him!" Samuel obeys without hesitation. As he pours the oil upon the head of God's chosen one, David feels more than just the oil. He senses the presence of God in a way he has never before experienced. The oil will soon wear off or be washed off, but this divine presence will remain with him throughout his life. He will come to know it as the Spirit of God.

Samuel speaks softly but authoritatively, declaring the purpose for this anointing in the hearing of both David and the audience. This boy in his mid-teens is being anointed king, and so there must be witnesses.[4] Everyone appears dumbstruck, especially the brothers. They can hardly believe what is happening before their amazed eyes! Their little kid brother, the one they have teased and mocked and ridiculed, the one who is usually given the menial jobs, the one the whole family considers the least important member—this one is going to be the next king?! Amazement and wonder will soon turn to envy and jealousy, especially for Eliab.

Had any of us been in Jesse's home that day, we more than likely would have reacted in a similar manner. We need to recognize, however, an important fact about the people God selects. As Chafin writes:

> The choice of the least likely person, from a human perspective, is a theme found throughout the Bible. The apostle Paul . . . contends that God has always made choices that have surprised the world (1 Corinthians 1:26–28). The study of church history or the study of the history of any congregation will usually reveal that God has often worked His purpose through some very unlikely choices.[5]

David's Forgotten Years

God's selection of David was neither arbitrary nor haphazard. Although he appeared to be very young and inexperienced by human standards, David had already attained a remarkable level of spiritual growth for one simple reason: This teenage shepherd had faithfully and obediently allowed the Lord to take him through a period of time I call the *Foundation Season* or *Season of Beginnings*.

These early years in David's life are very seldom given any thought or attention. Most Christians only read and study his outstanding career. Yet this almost forgotten time contained a great many experiences that were crucial to David's development and maturity, both spiritually and physically. Without this divine preparation, he never would have been able to fulfill the remarkable future God had planned for him.

Likewise our spiritual futures are dependent upon our willingness to allow the Lord to prepare us through our own individual Foundation Seasons. Preparation is a key component of this season. Experienced carpenters recognize the need for proper preparation as they begin a job, and so they always follow the dictum "Measure twice, cut once." Our Lord Jesus Christ, who was an earthly carpenter and is now our heavenly builder (see 1 Corinthians 3:9), is measuring and shaping us in preparation for our being fitted perfectly into the exact place we are to occupy in the holy temple, the dwelling place of God in the Spirit (see Ephesians 2:20–22).

4

FOUNDATION BUILDING

The Most Important Season

B efore discussing this particular spiritual season, it is critically important to make a clear and unmistakable distinction between the true foundation of every born-again believer, which is the Lord Jesus Christ, and the term *Foundation Season*. First Corinthians 3:11 states, "For no one can lay any other foundation than the one we already have—Jesus Christ" (NLT). Paul felt the need to remind the members of the Corinthian church exactly what their foundation was. Even though they subsequently may have had many "builders" (e. g., pastors, teachers, etc.), their Christian foundation was and would always remain Jesus Christ.

In contrast, the term *Foundation Season*, as used in this book, is that period of time when we allow the Lord to begin the process of growing and maturing us spiritually, conforming us as born-again believers to the image of Christ. I use the phrase *begin the process* because the process in its entirety is called *sanctification*. Sanctification is "the continuing work of God in the life of a believer, making him or her actually holy."[1] It is a progressive work of the Holy Spirit that will continue in our lives until death, when we pass into the presence of the Lord. Consequently, the Foundation Season covers the early time period of our lifelong sanctification process.

One vital fact concerning this period of time must be clearly understood: *The benefits and blessings contained in this season do not automatically follow our conversion experience.* A person can truly be born-again, be baptized in water, join a Bible-believing church and still not go through his Foundation Season. Although the Lord brings this season to every new Christian, each person must *choose* to faithfully enter into this beginning stage of the lifelong journey to "grow in the grace and knowledge of our Lord and Savior Jesus Christ" (2 Peter 3:18). Sadly, many believers refuse to cooperate with God during their own Foundation Seasons.

An Absolute Necessity

Some readers may ask, "Is this season really necessary?" My experiences and observations over the past three decades of serving the Lord as both layman and pastor have convinced me that the answer to this question must be an emphatic YES! Consequently we ignore the following principle at our peril:

Principle #3: **The Foundation Season is the first and most important of all our spiritual seasons.**

Consider this fact: Every one of God's mighty servants, from Abraham to Paul, were at one time required to go through a Foundation Season. The people God has used in mighty ways have all started at the same spiritual "level" that you and I are at right now! David allowed the Lord to take him through this season and others from his youth to his old age. Thus God was able to make David into a choice vessel for His service, "a man after His own heart."[2] The first and most necessary of David's seasons was his Foundation Season. The same is true for Christians today.

The Christian Church Today

Have you ever spent time reflecting on the state of the Christian Church in the Western world today—compared with the days of the apostles and the New Testament Church, or the times of great revival movements? Have you wondered why the Church appears to have such a limited impact on our society despite the numbers of people who call themselves born-again Christians[3] and the widespread availability of Christian television, radio, books, magazines, video and audio tapes, conferences, schools and colleges, vacation Bible schools, youth camps and so on?

Actually, I believe that ours *is* a New Testament Church, but of the wrong kind. The Christian Church in the United States during these early years of the 21st century is certainly far from the picture presented of the early Church in the book of Acts. Instead many of today's congregations resemble the Laodicean church of Revelation 3:14–22, as the studies of pollster George Barna indicate.

The Barna Research Group conducts ongoing surveys and analyses of trends and developments within the Christian population and churches of the United States. The picture Barna presents about Christianity in the U.S. should be a sobering one to every sincere, committed believer in Jesus Christ. His annual State of the Church survey for the year 2000 gave this summary:

> The nation seems mired in spiritual complacency. America certainly did not experience the spiritual revival many Christians hoped would emerge as the new millennium began. In fact, Americans seem to have become almost inoculated to spiritual events, outreach efforts, and the quest for personal spiritual development. There are magnificent exceptions . . . but overall, Christian ministry is stuck in a deep rut. Our research continues to point out the need for . . . a more urgent reliance upon God to change people's lives. Like the churches of Laodicea and Sardis, described in the Bible as distasteful to God because of their complacency and spiritual deadness, too many Christians and churches in America have traded in spiritual passion for empty rituals, clever methods and mindless practices. The challenge to today's church is not methodological. It is a challenge to resuscitate the spiritual passion and fervor of the nation's Christians.[4]

The Answer to the Problem

The Church has failed to impact American culture because so many people who claim to be born-again believers have had little real influence on the part of the world in which they live, work and play. Why this lack of influence? I believe it is due to their failure in learning the basics of Christian doctrine and in applying this knowledge in a lifestyle requiring the sacrifices and commitment of true Christianity. The vast majority of today's Christians are spiritually stagnant because they have not been willing to pay the price of becoming true disciples of Jesus Christ.

Author Charles Colson notes, "We cannot give what we do not have. We cannot impart values we do not hold. We cannot *do* until we *are*"[5] (emphasis mine). Or to quote a phrase popular among the younger generation of a few years ago, "If you talk the talk, you'd better walk the walk!" Our conduct and behavior, not our words and talk, will reveal to others both our concept of God and our true devotion to Him.

The unwillingness of many Christians to go beyond their salvation experience and enter into a life of discipleship, and the failure of many churches to encourage and help them in this endeavor, is indeed tragic. Many of us can paraphrase Jesus' Great Commission in Matthew 28:19–20, but far fewer of us actually live by it.

In my opinion, the Foundation Season is really the opening phase of discipleship training. Colson stresses the importance of discipleship and the responsibility of the Church to carry out Christ's mandate:

> "Making disciples" involves more than evangelism. Though the church must be passionate in its duty to introduce people to Jesus Christ . . . that is only the beginning, only a part of God's commission to us. Evangelism must be fully integrated with discipleship in order for the church to be fully obedient to Scripture.[6]

David's life is a mirror for us today. He had to allow God to take him through this first season of discipleship. Even though David had no idea what lay ahead for him, he emerged from his Foundation Season wonderfully equipped and empowered by the Holy Spirit. So when the Lord promoted him into the next season, the Season of Battle, David did not hesitate to confront and conquer a gigantic soldier, a behemoth who was probably the best and most feared warrior in the world at that time.

Practice and Preparation

While the Lord treats each of us as individuals, working in every person according to his or her unique makeup, two aspects of the Foundation Season seem common to nearly everyone who goes through this entire season.

First of all, this season provides the needed support and preparation for future calling and ministry. My dictionary defines the word *foundation* as "the basis on which something stands or is supported." The Foundation Season provides the support for all that follows in our spiritual lives. It will also have a profound effect on things in our temporal lives.

David's Foundation Season occurred during his pre-teen and teenage years. Throughout this time the Lord was at work laying an amazingly strong and secure spiritual foundation in this shepherd boy. Its strength and durability undergirded David for over half a century as he successfully fought mighty battles, composed psalms that have brought comfort, joy and hope to millions, endured unwarranted rejection and even persecution from close associates and gave us some of the finest examples in Scripture of repentance and forgiveness toward our enemies. Can anyone suppose that David could possibly have accomplished such great exploits, penned such inspiring Scripture or enjoyed such an intimate, personal relationship with almighty God without having experienced an extraordinary period of spiritual teaching and training during his formative years?

The Skyscraper Illustration

A skyscraper requires an exceptionally strong, stable foundation to support the superstructure that towers above street level. I worked in Chicago's downtown business district, the so-called "Loop," during the late 1960s and early 1970s. Several of the mega-skyscrapers were being built then, including the John Hancock Building (termed "Big John") and the Sears Tower (the world's tallest structure at the time).

I frequently passed these and other construction sites on my way to work. The length of time and the great effort it took the workers to construct the buildings' foundations were a constant source of amazement to me. It seemed to take as long for the foundations to be built up to ground level as it did to erect the superstructure. Part of the reason was that these buildings were being built on landfill or soft soil. Consequently, massive caissons and piles had to be sunk many feet into the ground to reach bedrock, the solid rock layer beneath the softer upper soil. (One of the caissons for "Big John" actually reaches 191 feet below the surface!)[7] Then several heavily reinforced subfloors had to be built to complete a strong, stable foundation for the many-storied superstructure it would have to support.

Our firm and eternal bedrock is Jesus Christ, the Rock of our salvation. Unless we have made Him our personal Savior and Lord, our foundation, we will only be building on sand and loose soil. But with the Lord as our bedrock and having completed a solid Foundation Season, we are ready for God to begin putting up the superstructure of our spiritual lives.

Unfortunately far too many people in the modern Church attempt doing things in ministry for which they have neither the training nor the spiritual maturity. The observation deck of a fifty-story skyscraper cannot be designed and built before the other parts of the building. But Christians often try to rush into some ministry before they have been sufficiently grounded in the Word of God and discipled under the oversight of some God-appointed leadership. While their eagerness to serve the Lord is commendable, it can result in errors in doctrine and problems in practice, both for themselves and for those to whom they are attempting to minister. Paul addressed a matter of this nature in 1 Corinthians 3:1-3, calling such people "babes in Christ" who still needed to be fed with spiritual milk and not solid food because they were still "carnal and behaving like mere men."

This situation was not confined to the early New Testament Church. Somehow people get the idea that a kind of "spiritual osmosis" is at work in Christianity.[8] Their belief system tells them that all they have to do is attend Sunday morning services fairly regularly, put a few dollars in the collection plate, perhaps watch a bit of Christian television, occasionally play some Christian music in the background at home, read a few pages of the latest Christian self-fulfillment book on "why God wants you to go first class" and *voila*! The spiritual atmosphere they have exposed themselves to will miraculously sink into their inner beings and make them good, mature Christians. This attitude is the reason there are two nurseries in the typical American church. The smaller one is usually located in a little side room and contains cribs, diaper-changing tables and rocking chairs where a few faithful, caring women can watch over and minister to their charges. The much larger nursery meets in the church's main sanctuary.

The Price of Preparation

A second aspect of the Foundation Season must be recognized and accepted if we are to successfully go through this season. But it is often the one that causes Christians to quit before the Lord has fully completed their training. You see, a degree of unpleasantness is necessary to this season. Anyone who has played competitive sports knows about *training* and *practice*. American football players go through grueling two-a-day workouts in the heat and humidity of late summer, swimmers log thousands of laps in a pool and basketball players spend countless hours trying to perfect their shot-making skills—all in the hope of getting a few fleeting moments of satisfaction and glory from playing (and hopefully winning) a game or competition. Practice is a vital part of preparation. It is the price athletes know they must be willing to pay if they want a chance to succeed, and the price is usually difficult, expensive or both.

Bobby Wilkerson was a member of the undefeated Indiana University basketball team that won the national championship in 1976. That team was coached by Bobby Knight, a highly successful but notoriously hard and demanding coach. Many years later Wilkerson recounted the incredibly tough practices and preparations Knight put his team through for their games: "I'll tell you part of the reason we were so good. Under Coach Knight, the games seemed like a vacation."[9]

I recall reading years ago a story about Ignace Jan Paderewski, who was a world-renowned concert pianist during the latter part of the nineteenth century and the first decades of the twentieth. As I remember, it told of a newspaper interview he gave at the height of his career.

The reporter asked Paderewski, "Maestro, how often and how long do you practice?"

"At least six to eight hours a day, every day," replied Paderewski.

"Every day?" asked the surprised reporter.

"Every day," Paderewski firmly stated.

"But Maestro," the reporter asked half-seriously, "what harm could there possibly be if you took two or three days off from your practice now and then?"

"I'll tell you what would happen," said the great pianist. "If I didn't practice for one day, I would know it. And if I didn't practice the second day, the critics would know it. And if I failed to practice for the third day, the world would know it!"

Right and Wrong Priorities

By and large, though, Christians seem unwilling to endure the commitment to discipline, self-control and (surprise!) inconvenience to their lifestyles that the Lord requires of us during this season. I am puzzled by how many believers adopt this mind-set. We realize that success in any of the secular world's occupations demands serious commitment and much hard work. Yet numbers of believers seem to think that because salvation is a free, unmerited gift from God, He will provide them with a free ride in all other aspects of life.

This unwillingness to put up with any problems, hardships or (heaven forbid!) trials in any part of our Christianity seems to be a growing one today. Jim Cymbala summarizes this tendency briefly but boldly:

> We have all met more than a few Christians who expect their trip to heaven to be one smooth ride from the time they accepted Christ straight to the pearly gates—especially here in America, where the culture is overwhelmingly pleasure-oriented. As a result, believers in Christ have lost their bearings about what a godly life is all about. Unfortunately, a lot of gospel preaching adds to the problem, since it conveniently omits the hard facts of spiritual life.[10]

A "microwave" mentality has affected a large segment of our population. As a result of the many people who want instant solutions to their problems, we are inundated with books, advertisements and infomercials offering products and services guaranteed to make us rich, thin, healthy and stress-free—in only a few hours a week! Despite such claims, most of us realize that it takes a great deal of preparation and perseverance to achieve worldly success—or even a trim physique! In like manner, much spiritual preparation and perseverance is needed for us to reach spiritual maturity. God's way is not quick by human standards, but it most definitely is sure.

5

TIME FOR SCHOOL

The Foundation Season has some hallmarks, certain distinguishing characteristics, of which we need to be aware. They appear regularly because this is a schooling season, a time for taking God's truth to heart. So do not be surprised when these characteristics appear in your own experience!

Obscurity: The First Hallmark

David was born in obscurity, the eighth son of a man named Jesse living in the small town of Bethlehem. Today Bethlehem is known around the world, but such was not the case at the time of David's birth in the eleventh century B.C. Scripture does record several events that occurred in and around this little community in the centuries before David came on the scene.[1] On the whole, however, Bethlehem at the time of David's youth was a simple, humble community. Its only real importance was due to the town's location on a rocky spur of the Judean mountains just off the main road running from Bethel to Jerusalem, Hebron and Egypt.[2]

The "Hindrance" of Obscurity

Obscurity is one of the major hindrances to our willingness to undergo the necessary learning and training processes in any job, ministry or activity. The clichés of "starting at the bottom" and "learning the ropes" do not appeal to us because they usually involve (at least in our minds) doing menial things in insignificant areas away from the spotlight where our talents and abilities can be noticed and applauded (and our egos will be nourished). The Kingdom of God operates on a far different set of principles, however. Being in an obscure and overlooked situation is not an obstacle to recognition but the only way to promotion.

God found Joseph in a dungeon, Moses on the backside of a desert, Gideon threshing grain in a hidden location, the widow Ruth in a pagan land, the barren and humiliated Hannah weeping outside the Tabernacle, Elisha plowing his father's fields, Amos tending sheep in the tiny town of Tekoa, Jonah in the belly of a whale and some grubby fishermen working by the Sea of Galilee. People living and serving in out-of-the-way places, no matter how insignificant from our human perspective, are never in a place so small, unknown or distant that they escape God's ability to find, bless and prepare them for His service.

Obscurity is never a negative from God's standpoint and can be a great positive. It presents us with a fine opportunity to trust Him in the midst of apparently negative circumstances, thereby helping to build our faith. It also sets a stage upon which God can demonstrate His power and greatness when He does raise us up to places of honor and prominence.

A Modern-Day Example

In 1945 a young Indian man and his wife opened their little rented home to begin a church in the small town of Itarsi, located in the central state of India. Although this godly couple prayed fervently and the husband preached faithfully each Sunday morning, his "congregation" for many months consisted only of his wife and baby son. Talk about obscurity—a church that was nothing more than a small family gathering, in a tiny, mostly Hindu town with no electricity or water system, in a dusty corner of a third world nation!

Yet this couple refused to be discouraged or deterred from what they knew to be God's call for their lives, and He rewarded their faithfulness. The small church in their home finally began to grow, slowly at first, but steadily and surely as God prospered it and opened new areas of opportunity. So when this man, Dr. Kurien Thomas, went to be with the Lord in the year 2000, the tiny church had exploded into a ministry responsible for birthing over one thousand churches throughout India and founding several Bible schools that have trained thousands of Indian men for the ministry. God also enabled Dr. Thomas to travel and preach all over the world for nearly forty years. Today this couple's eldest son is the senior pastor of a large, dynamic church in a suburb of Chicago. Another son now heads his father's ministry, and the other three sons and a daughter all live in the United States and are actively serving the Lord.[3] Obscurity will never stop God from fulfilling His plans for your life. Only you can prevent it by a lack of faith and stubborn resistance to His leading.

Humility: The Second Hallmark

Humility—the quality of being humble and submissive—is not a popular thing in today's Western world. It is, however, a matter that is very important to God. A number of Bible verses remind us that the Lord threatens to bring down those who are proud and haughty but promises to bless and promote those who will walk humbly before Him.[4] David learned the hard lesson of humility through two circumstances in his life. He was the youngest of Jesse's eight sons, perhaps the last of all ten children in the family, and he spent much of his early life serving as the family's shepherd.

Being the baby of the household, however, was far from the some-times pampered position of the youngest child in modern-day homes. Correct or not, a general perception exists that adults tend to spoil the youngest child. (My two oldest children, who are grown and married, remain convinced that my wife and I were much more lenient toward our third and youngest child in terms of discipline, responsibility and chores than we were with them.) In the agricultural society of David's time, however, the lot of the youngest boy was probably not an easy one. All of the children were given chores at fairly early ages, a custom still existing among many farm families today. One of those tasks involved tending the sheep. This responsibility would be given first to the oldest boy as soon as he was considered able to handle it. As this boy grew older and stronger, he would be called upon to begin helping his father with the more significant farm duties of plowing, planting, cultivating and harvesting. So the job of shepherding the sheep would then be given to the next oldest child. As time went on, the task was passed from older to younger until the youngest finally became the family shepherd.[5]

David's Dilemma

David had a unique problem when his next oldest brother passed him the job of caring for the family's sheep. Being the youngest, he had no one to whom he could give this lonely and lowly responsibility. As a result David may have spent more years as a shepherd than any of his older siblings. When we first meet him in 1 Samuel 16, he most likely was in his mid-teens and probably had served as shepherd for nearly half of his young years.

What thoughts might have gone through our minds if we had been in David's place at that time? Would we have grown resentful and bitter toward our older siblings and parents for dumping this miserable situation on us? Or would we have given ourselves over to feelings of despair and hopelessness, thinking we were doomed to have this job for years into the future? Scripture gives us not the slightest shred of evidence David harbored any unhappiness, bitterness or despondency over his position in Jesse's family.

Solitude: The Third Hallmark

Solitude is another unwelcome word in our noisy, frantic, adrenaline-charged 21st-century world. It conjures up negative images in our minds—monks in cold, lonely monastery cells who have taken vows of silence, or hermits living in caves and mountaintops in wilderness regions. Many people act as if *solitude* is a synonym for loneliness, boredom and inactivity.

We live at a time and in a place where being alone and quiet feels unnatural. Richard Foster writes, "The fear of being left alone petrifies people . . . [and] drives us to noise and crowds."[6] Noise seems to be everywhere: music piped into elevators, stores and workplaces, portable CDs and cassette players and radios so everyone can get their quota of noise while they walk, ride bikes or weed their gardens. People get uncomfortable when faced with too long a period of silence. Have you ever been at some event where the audience was asked to stand and observe a moment of silence? Moment of silence? Hardly! The usual length of these moments of silence is about twenty to thirty seconds. Few in such crowds would be able to endure a whole minute of total silence.

God sees solitude much differently than we do. He offers it as one of His main tools in training and developing Christians for service. He did so with David and He will do it with each of us. By taking David through frequent times of solitude, the Lord formed a trait in this boy that would be absolutely vital to his success later in life. That trait was the powerful, personal and intimate relationship David experienced and enjoyed with God for over half a century. The Lord knew David would need an intense and unbreakable personal relationship with Him for the later seasons in his life when he would face a constant stream of dangers, decisions and discouragements. So He brought the young boy out into the barren Judean hillsides. Here he would be away from the distractions and diversions of everyday life. Here he could begin to listen for and recognize the still, small voice of his God.

Jesse's Problem Family

The Lord began the process of providing David with solitude by removing him from the household of a dysfunctional family. Several Bible verses present glimpses into the complex and contentious relationships that probably existed in Jesse's home. Jesse himself was "old, advanced in years" (1 Samuel 17:12). It appears that he married again late in life to a woman who was either a widow or concubine of a man named Nahash, and who brought with her two daughters, Abigail and Zeruiah. [7]

The segment of chapter 16 we have already discussed reveals in a sharp and telling way Jesse's failure as a father. When Samuel, the nation's great spiritual leader, paid a sudden visit to this modest community, he invited Jesse and his sons to join him and the town elders in a sacrifice to the Lord. What an honor and unique opportunity this was for such a poor, obscure family! If you were in Jesse's place, wouldn't you have wanted all of your children to have the privilege and blessing of being a part of this important event? Yet Jesse thought so little of his youngest boy that he did not bother to bring him home from his shepherding duties.

In a parent/child relationship, two of the most important aspects are acceptance and appreciation. When a parent provides a child with acceptance, it gives the child a sense of security. In a similar manner, showing appreciation to the child conveys a sense of significance.[8] Jesse did neither of these things. His actions said that all of the older sons were more important (accepted) while David's role in the family was ignored (not appreciated).

God saw Jesse's older boys in a completely different light. He knew that character flaws existed in each one. These flaws were serious enough to disqualify any of them from being chosen as the next king, notwithstanding the fine outward appearance they projected. What was it these older brothers lacked? Scripture does not specifically tell us, but we can surmise the probable cause from two things. One is seen in the words of Eliab, the oldest brother, toward David in 1 Samuel 17:28 (which will be discussed in greater detail in the next section).

Children are quick to pick up the parents' attitudes toward one of their brothers or sisters. Jesus tells us that "out of the abundance of the heart the mouth speaks." Eliab's heated outburst revealed an angry, critical spirit and a demeaning, insulting attitude toward his youngest brother. So it is quite possible Eliab was influenced by his parents' treatment of David and their failure to curb the sibling rivalry and conflict that may have existed in their home.

It is also telling that none of David's brothers ever had a significant leadership role in David's kingdom.[9] Was this David's way of exacting revenge on his brothers for their cruel treatment of him as a youth? Not likely. Scripture shows David to be a forgiving person, a man like Joseph, who understood how God used the evil designs of family members for His perfect plan. The character faults and flaws lay within the inner makeup of the brothers themselves. David must have recognized their shortcomings and knew such things would preclude them from being effective leaders.

This picture of David's family background is certainly not one of home, sweet home. With an elderly father who seems to have given him little attention, a group of older and domineering brothers whose characters left much to be desired, a couple of older stepsisters and their children[10] and a stepmother, David was the proverbial "low man on the totem pole." In such surroundings Jesse's youngest son could easily have become a defiant and disturbed delinquent, a veritable gold mine of analysis for a modern-day psychiatrist. Instead, he yielded to God's presence and call, permitting the Lord to take him out into the shepherds' fields and be his companion and instructor.

Alone with God

The next part of God's process to bring David into a place of solitude was to confine him to the lonely task of shepherd for many of his youthful years. A mature person does not normally perceive a year as being a long period of time. For youngsters in the period of life surrounding puberty, however, it can seem like an eternity. Young David was alone tending the sheep many days and nights during these early years, except for the infrequent times he would return home for food and other necessities. He seldom would have had opportunities to "hang out" with other young people, enjoying their friendship and participating in their activities. As noted earlier in this section, there is absolutely no indication in Scripture that David ever became resentful or bitter toward his family for his lot in life nor toward God for allowing it. Instead he must have eagerly responded to God's call and presence just as the young Samuel had answered many years before.

So although David lived and worked in fields uninhabited and silent from a human standpoint, the Lord was always with David, and He was not silent. As David began to welcome the presence of the Lord, response turned to friendship and friendship developed into the deep trust and faith that guided and sustained David through one of the most event-filled lives recorded in the Bible. As we read about the succeeding years in his life, one almost gets the sense that David recognized God's voice and presence as well as he knew the voices of any of the people around him, whether they were the leading priests and worship leaders, military aides, advisors or even family members.

Jesus made a regular practice of going to solitary places to spend time alone in His Father's presence. Christians who truly are serious about growing in spiritual maturity need to follow His example "in order to hear the divine Whisper better."[11] Old-time Holiness believers used to talk about "being shut in with God." That is what David elected to do, and his long times alone with God were to produce remarkable results in the years ahead.

Trust: The Fourth Hallmark

The Hebrew uses two words in the Old Testament to convey the concept of trust. *Batah* "expresses the sense of well-being and security resulting from having something or someone in which to place confidence."[12] The other Hebrew word is *hasa* and carries the meaning "to seek refuge, flee for protection (and thus figuratively) put trust in God."[13] It stresses our insecurity and helplessness in time of need.

While David exhibited magnificent trust and confidence in the Lord from his early days till the end of his life, trust certainly was not a character trait he was born with. His trust in God grew over the years, but it was birthed and first began to develop during the Foundation Season. God took David through a series of experiences to bring about this development.

In the beginning there was the loneliness, uncertainty and worry of a young boy saddled many days and nights with great responsibility but with no human to turn to for counsel and friendship. No adult was available when new and unforeseen difficulties arose, or when fear gripped his mind and body from the sudden appearance of danger. No one was nearby, except the One whom David needed above all else and at all times.

David's First Battles

We should not be surprised, then, to read of David's great exploits, even those he performed at a young age. The shepherd's life was more than merely one of isolation; it could involve considerable danger as well. Wild animals were prevalent in that land—lions, bears, wolves, hyenas and jackals.[14] Many of them would come from their lairs in the thick undergrowth along the Jordan River to hunt in the pasturelands of the Judean hills. The shepherd was responsible for protecting his flock from these predators. But the weapons at his disposal appear awfully flimsy to us today—just a heavy club and a sling. Furthermore the shepherd normally worked alone, far from any other human assistance. Imagine yourself going alone against a lion or bear with only a club and a sling as David did.

A bear has been described as "a very sensitive nose attached to a very large stomach." It is said to be able to eat almost anything and to eat continually. Have you ever tried to get a choice bone away from a hungry dog? Imagine attempting to rescue a lamb from the mouth of a hungry bear as the Bible reports David doing—or to get it away from the jaws of a lion!

And Speaking of Bears . . .

Our former home site in the western North Carolina mountains borders a large wilderness area where the wildlife is protected from hunting.

Consequently, the population of wild turkeys, deer, bobcat and bears is quite large. A 1998 report by the North Carolina Wildlife Resources Commission indicated that the density of the black bear population in this area is among the highest in the United States.[15] As a result, our "neighbors" include black bears—lots of black bears. They have been known to climb through the open windows of unoccupied houses if they smelled food inside. They have also broken into parked cars and trucks because someone had inadvertently left a few bits of food or drink in the vehicles. So would I try to take a meal away from a hungry bear? Not on your life! But David did, and on more than one occasion, as the Hebrew text indicates.

A Critical Test of Trust and Faith

These are some of the most vital experiences in David's life. Their importance should never be underestimated. For had he been unwilling or unable to stand against and kill these fierce predators, he never would have been able to challenge and conquer Goliath! Read David's testimony to Saul in 1 Samuel 17:34–37. He could testify of God's protection and power on his behalf because he had personally seen and experienced it on past occasions. David undoubtedly had heard and/or read the Pentateuch, the five books of Moses, and he had heard God's voice out in the still, desolate shepherds' fields. But these things, even though wonderful and blessed, were not enough. He needed to appropriate and fully experience the written and spoken Word of God by going through the actual trials and battles of life. So God gave him that opportunity by bringing him face to face with some powerful adversaries.

Let's apply this lesson to our own lives. Go into a Christian bookstore and note all the books on faith and trusting in God. Perhaps you have some of these titles in your own home. Most believers do. Isn't it curious, however, that we see so few demonstrations of faith in our lives? The reason is that most of us are unwilling to act on the faith we read about. Ours too often is "a faith without works," to paraphrase the book of James. Rick Howard makes a telling observation concerning our need to put our faith through the crucible of experience:

> Most of us do not learn a great deal from the classroom experience. We generally learn out of circumstances . . . out of necessary actions and responses. Here is where we learn things about God and His character.[16]

David learned. After experiencing God's protection and empower-
ment as he confronted and slew the bears and lions who attacked his
father's sheep, David viewed Goliath as merely a human predator who
was attacking his Father God's sheep, the army of Israel.

Our Own Battles

Is a bear or a lion confronting you at this moment? I am not speaking
about a literal animal but of spiritual bears and lions. I firmly believe
that the vast majority of Christians I have encountered are unwilling to
exercise their faith and trust in the Lord by confronting and gaining the
victory over the beasts that are attacking and destroying the relationships
and opportunities in their lives.

Who and what are these predators? They can be any one of a number
of things. Maybe a secret lust for pornographic material has gripped
your spirit for years. Or maybe a deep root of bitterness and unforgive-
ness is growing in your heart toward a person. Or maybe a relationship
with your spouse, child or other family member has become so soured
and fractured that you barely ever speak with the person. Or maybe you
harbor a deeply concealed anger and frustration toward God who, in
your thinking, has failed to keep His promises to you, has favored others over you in both temporal and spiritual blessings and is constantly
insensitive to your prayers, problems and priorities.

The Importance of This Battle

This explains one of the major reasons why the Foundation Season is
so important in our lives. Had David not stepped out in faith and done
battle with these wild animals, it is highly doubtful he would have trusted
God enough to face the Philistine giant, and the course of his life would
have been radically altered. His willingness to confront such predators
constituted the significant "spiritual proving ground" of his young life.
God's people most often have faced such times of crisis early in their
walks with God. Joseph's refusal to enter into an adulterous relationship
with Potiphar's wife is one example.

Unless we are willing to trust God and exercise faith in spiritual warfare
against the lion and bear who have invaded our lives, we will forfeit the
opportunities to gain future victories and the accompanying blessings that

the Lord desires to bring into our lives. Our growth in Christian maturity and service will be stunted, and the abundant life that the Bible promises us will fail to materialize in either the spiritual or the temporal realms. This battle can be a lonely one. Just as David fought these predators alone, away from the cheering crowds and the limelight, we, too, must face our bears and lions alone and unobserved, relying on our faith and trust in the Lord to provide us with His protection and power. When we gain the victory, no one may ever know it except the One who is omniscient, and He will reward us in ways no human ever could.

Servant Leadership: The Fifth Hallmark

The fifth significant lesson God gave to David during these years involved the principles of servant leadership, a term that the world might consider contradictory. While superficial similarities do exist between the world's definition of leadership and God's system of authority, the two are actually opposed. Jesus pointed out the major difference in Matthew 20:25–28.

The world's brand of leadership too often depends upon intimidation and fear. But Psalm 78 contains several revealing insights concerning the character the Lord wants in His leaders. In verse 70, He gave David a high honor by calling him "His servant." Referring to someone as a servant would certainly not be considered a compliment today. But God views servanthood quite differently from the 21st century's perspective. He calls only a relatively few people in Scripture His "servants," including Moses and Joshua, two of the Israelites' greatest leaders. Jamie Buckingham says:

> Jesus' lifestyle and lessons establish the mode for a new kind of leader—the servant leader. [The true servant leader knows] whom God has made him or her to be and [rests] in the peaceful awareness and confidence that God's hand is ordering his or her personal security.[17]

Noted author John Maxwell has written a number of articles and books on the topic of leadership. It is interesting to compare the principles of leadership that Maxwell cites in his writings with the leadership characteristics David learned from the Lord during this season of his life. Maxwell believes that leaders' attitudes are their most important assets and claims, "Leadership has less to do with position than it does with disposition [and] . . . the leader's disposition is important because it will influence the way the followers think and feel."[18] David displayed in these early years the kind of disposition that must have been pleasing to God and attractive to others. Scripture pictures him as being obedient to his parents, humble despite great honors, even-tempered in the face of criticism and brave and resourceful.

Leadership Training under God

God developed in David the principles of servant leadership by making him a shepherd. Does this statement appear somewhat ridiculous to you? Do you wonder how David ever could have learned principles of leadership that would aid him in becoming Israel's greatest king while tending a bunch of sheep? Then consider this fact: Throughout the Bible God makes an interesting and revealing linkage between the terms *shepherd* and *leader*.

One of the earliest Scripture names for God is found in Genesis 49:24 where He is described as "the Shepherd, the Stone of Israel." Numerous other Bible passages refer to the Lord as "Shepherd."[19] God calls the irresponsible and sinful religious leaders of Israel and Judah by the term "shepherds," as seen in Isaiah 56:11, Jeremiah 50:6, Ezekiel 34:2 and other verses. He even said the great Persian king Cyrus was His shepherd (see Isaiah 44:28).

A significant juxtaposition of almighty God as shepherd of His people and David as God's chosen shepherd for the nation of Israel is found in Psalm 78. Verse 52 pictures the Lord's relationship with the children of Israel in the Sinai wilderness as follows: "But He made His own people go forth like sheep, And guided them in the wilderness like a flock." Then in verses 70–72, the Lord describes David as the shepherd king of Israel.

So a leader is, in God's eyes, a shepherd. As a shepherd's task is to lead and care for his sheep, a leader is responsible for those over whom he has been given charge. Sheep may appear to be docile and phlegmatic animals, creatures who can be easily cared for and led. In truth sheep have some very complex and peculiar behavior patterns, as Phillip Keller, a former sheep owner and rancher, points out. For instance, he notes that sheep cannot be made to lie down and rest until four requirements are present: freedom from all fear; freedom from tension in the flock; freedom from flies and parasites; and freedom from hunger.[20] As a result good shepherds must possess a variety of skills and abilities if their flocks are to remain healthy and productive.

David was such a shepherd. Psalm 78:72 indicates that he was faithful to his responsibility in the daily care for all their needs. And sheep have a lot of daily needs, since they are unable to fend for themselves! The shepherd is required to find suitable pasture for them as well as pure, still water (and sheep must be watered several times daily). He must also provide safe shelter at night, bring back straying animals, minister medication and aid to the sick and lame, assist in lambing time and keep careful count morning and evening of all his flock (which could number up to a hundred animals).[21] Without the shepherd, sheep are virtually helpless.

The Value of Integrity

Maxwell calls integrity "the most important ingredient of leadership . . . [and] when I have integrity, my words and my deeds match up."[22] David developed and exhibited this quality. A few paragraphs earlier, we saw God's approval of David in His statement that he shepherded his sheep "according to the integrity of his heart." The Hebrew word for integrity is *tamam*, and its fundamental idea is "what is complete, entirely in accord with truth and fact . . . [and] that which is ethically sound, upright."[23]

At one point in my business career, I spent several years trading securities in what was called the "over-the-counter-market." This involved buying and selling various investments—often in the millions of dollars—by telephone with other traders, many of whom I never met in person. After making a trade, the other person and I would each write up a confirmation ticket including all the details of the transaction (name of the security, amount, price, etc.) and mail a copy to the other's firm. It frequently happened that within a moment or two of having made the trade, one side or the other dearly wanted to cancel it, because the market had suddenly moved against him. Yet each party stood firmly behind the trade even though the only record of the transaction at that moment was the word of each trader. In all these years, I can only recall one or two occasions where a disagreement over a trade required it to be taken before an arbitration board of the securities industry. Amazing? Not really. This facet of the securities business was built on the foundation of one simple statement: "Your word is your bond!" Try to "weasel out" of a bad trade, and the word would quickly flash throughout the trading community. The traders knew how critically important it was for them to maintain their integrity.

Many of us would sadly agree with John Maxwell that integrity, good character and trustworthiness are vanishing commodities today. It is particularly regrettable to see the growing lack of integrity in the Body of Christ. Integrity—or its absence—exposes who we really are for all the world to see.

The Requirement of Sacrifice

Psalm 78:70–72 reveals another aspect of leadership David learned as a shepherd—sacrifice. To quote Maxwell again:

> Sacrifice is a constant in leadership. It is an ongoing process, not a one-time payment. Talk to any leader, and you will find that he has made repeated sacrifices. Usually, the higher the leader has climbed, the greater the sacrifices he has made.[24]

David was willing to make the sacrifices, to pay his dues. Shepherding is most certainly not a 9-to-5 kind of employment; it is a 24/7 job. It is days and nights, seemingly without end, marked by the absence of human companionship and filled with menial tasks. In short, the shepherd is asked to make sacrifices again and again in order to maintain the well-being of the flock.

Sacrifice, however, is another commodity in short supply today. A lead article in *The Charlotte Observer* entitled "Salvation Without Sacrifice" hit the proverbial nail on the head:

> Americans (have) a growing fascination with "cheap grace" salvation, or balm for the spirit, that requires little work and absolutely no sacrifice. It is a religion without sweat, and in the land of consumer capitalism, it sells. . . . Traditional religion usually involves a measure of sacrifice. Cheap grace, by contrast, is financially profitable and materialistic. . . . It promises empowerment without work—like bigger muscles with no gym, or gym fee.[25]

Patience and More Patience

Finally, a servant leader must have great patience. People in leadership know that plans sometimes fail to go in ways they want or hope. They must "stay the course" with much patience and perseverance. David discovered this lesson very early in life. When Samuel anointed him, the startling event could have turned the teenager's head and caused him to fill up with pride. Instead he obediently and humbly returned to shepherding his father's sheep.

Shortly thereafter Saul heard of David's skill as a musician. The king was suffering from periodic bouts of mental illness, a condition resulting from his disobedience and rebellion against God. Music apparently was recognized as a form of therapy even in these early times. Since the Lord was with David, his music had the power to temporarily drive away the demonic spirits oppressing the king. David not only became the court musician, he conducted himself so well that Saul gave him the additional responsibility of serving as his armor-bearer. And David still had to serve his family by occasionally returning home to help care for Jesse's flocks.

Was David disappointed to be given only a servant's role in Saul's court as well as being required to continue serving at home from time to time? A lesser person probably would have started to become impatient or even angry with God over the failure of Samuel's anointing and prophecy to be quickly fulfilled. He or she would at least have wondered and questioned whether it really had been a true word from God. But David did not falter or waver in his trust. Nor did he give any indication of unhappiness or discouragement over the menial tasks assigned to him. He was in the early stage of learning to "wait on the Lord," a vital truth he would come to understand and refer to in his psalms.[26]

This time of patient waiting produced an additional benefit for the young shepherd. As he served the king, he was able to observe Saul's actions and decisions, listen to the conversations among the various members of the king's staff, watch the manner in which foreign envoys and ambassadors conducted diplomacy with Saul and become familiar with the ways of court life. The fact that Saul was slipping into mental disorder was of little consequence to David's introduction into political leadership. In my three decades in the world of business, I learned as much about right and wrong methods of leadership from poor and incompetent bosses as I did from the outstanding ones.

The Priority of Relationship

These few leadership traits were not the only ones the Lord worked into David. Jesse's youngest son would receive future classes from God in "How to Be a Leader," lessons that eventually would produce the person whom Charles Swindoll noted is mentioned in the New Testament more than any other Old Testament individual. Nor are these "hallmarks" meant to be an all-inclusive list of the ways God can work in our lives during the Foundation Season. We may experience some but not all of these five, and He may add a couple of new ones for our individual instruction. This should not surprise us. Each of us is a completely unique creation of His hand, so our Creator will fashion the people, settings and events of our lives in a similarly personal way.

One thing will remain constant, though—God's desire to draw us into a place of intimate fellowship with Him. So often our goal is to do things for God to the neglect of spending time in His presence. We want to "do for" rather than "be with" Him. Leadership, position and prestige in the Church are sought after by many, while the prayer meeting is the least attended function in nearly every Christian congregation. As a consequence, the Lord is constantly trying to get us to see this:

Principle #4: **Relationship precedes leadership in the Kingdom of God.**

Even a cursory look at the lives of the great men and women of God recorded in the Bible reveals a clear pattern. In almost every instance, Scripture relates how they were brought into an incredibly intimate relationship with the Lord *before* they attained the leadership positions God intended for them. There were very few exceptions to this.

The End of the Season of Beginnings

We sometimes read newspaper accounts of gifted young people who graduate from a four-year college curriculum while still teenagers. Young David was such a person, except his graduation was from God's Foundation School, the Season of Beginnings. This intense program often requires several years to complete and is one in which many older Christians become dropouts. As 1 Samuel 16 ends, David has just graduated with highest honors, and God has determined that it is now time for this teenager to put into practice the lessons he has learned.

Years ago in one of my classes at seminary, a student asked our professor to give us some guidance as to what might be on the final exam. The professor smilingly replied that our real final exam would take place only after we graduated from the seminary and went out into the ministry. David was about to get his real final exam, and it is recorded in chapter 17 of 1 Samuel.

FIGHTING

The Season of Battle
(1 Samuel 17:1–18:7)

"Only those who risk going too far will ever know just how far they can go."

—ANONYMOUS

6

DREAMS AND
REMEMBRANCES

*avid was filled with excitement and anticipation as he led his
donkey along the road toward the Valley of Elah. He had made some
attempts to get the little animal to go faster, but the donkey, carrying
several sacks containing a large quantity of food, seemed determined to set its
own pace.* Well, at least it is not much farther now, *David thought.*

*Just yesterday he had been given an unexpected but very welcome surprise.
His father, Jesse, had summoned him from his shepherding duties and told him
to take some food to his three oldest brothers who were with King Saul's army,
fighting the Philistines. What an opportunity! Ever since his early boyhood,
David had dreamed about someday becoming a mighty warrior and doing
battle against Israel's enemies. At least this trip would allow him to get a
first-hand view of real warfare. Right now all he knew about the military
and battles were the stories and reports he had heard from his three brothers
and from some of Saul's servants.*

*This trip had one added benefit: He would be away from home and its un-
pleasant atmosphere for a few days. David never complained openly or harbored
any lasting resentment about the treatment he received from the other family
members. Yet being the youngest in the household was difficult—continually*

being mocked and ordered around, being given all the unwelcome chores and never having any say in the family decisions.

The last couple of years had been especially difficult. Ever since the memorable day when Samuel had anointed him and spoken those strange and almost unbelievable words over him, David sensed the family's attitude toward him becoming increasingly cold and even hostile. He knew their animosity had been triggered by this event, but he was as confused as his parents and siblings by the old prophet's actions and words. Why did God choose him, and how could He possibly elevate the least important member of an ordinary household to the kingship of Israel?

Maybe Samuel had erred and given a false prophecy. This seemed highly unlikely, though. The entire nation recognized how mightily the Lord had used Samuel over the past decades to reveal His words to them. Surely this great prophet and judge would never have dared to perform this ceremony unless he knew for certain it was God's will. Still David could not help wondering how God could fulfill Samuel's prophecy.

His situation at home was the main reason he preferred to be out in the fields caring for his family's flocks. Shepherding was a lonely and monotonous job, and at times it could be a dangerous one as well. But it not only got him away from the family tensions, it allowed him plenty of time to practice playing his harp and singing. As a result he now was becoming recognized as an accomplished musician. His shepherd duties also provided him with many opportunities to improve his skills with the shepherd's sling, so he had become extremely proficient in throwing stones accurately with this weapon.

The day was beautiful and provided a perfect setting for his journey, but David was not looking around at the scenery. Instead he found himself getting lost in thought, recalling the time when he had first taken over the shepherding duties from his next older brother. He had felt so solitary and scared, especially the first time he had to keep the sheep out in the fields overnight. That was the moment he began putting aside his little "bless me" kinds of prayers and had begun to seek the Lord earnestly and often during the day and night.

David thought of how simple and stumbling his prayers must have sounded back then, but he remembered, too, the desperate need he had felt for protection, comfort and guidance. These things caused him to cry out to God with all the fervency and sincerity his young heart could muster. He smiled inwardly as he recalled how God had responded to his prayers back then, delighting once more in memories of the ways He had imparted divine peace, love and assurance. Their relationship had begun then to grow and mature, an almost unexplainable bonding that would develop over the ensuing months and years into an intimate communion in which the Lord became David's ever-present companion and friend.

The memories came flooding back, of dreams he fabricated in those early years, imagining himself as a mighty soldier leading his troops into battle! David chuckled as he thought of the long hours spent out in the shepherds' fields slinging stones and pretending his targets were enemy warriors. A little shepherd boy dreaming and playing make-believe. Then the memories brought back to him the day when those dreams and imaginary play suddenly became all too real and dangerous.

He had not noticed the lion stalking the flock. Dusk was falling and he was hard at work building a small pen in the open field to keep the sheep during the night. He had gathered some large stones and thorny brush in order to make a circular enclosure with a single opening. As soon as it was finished, he would lead his sheep into this makeshift pen and then station himself in the opening as a human door to keep the sheep from getting out during the night.

The fading daylight enabled the lion's tawny coat to blend in almost perfectly with the landscape. David was concentrating so intently on building the pen that he allowed the beast to creep carefully around the rock outcroppings and maneuver through the low brush until it was within easy striking distance of the sheep. Then the predator charged. In his memory David could almost experience again the surprise and shock he felt to suddenly catch sight of a brownish blur leaping from cover. With a couple of bounds it was in among the frightened flock and quickly seized a lamb with its powerful jaws.

David recalled how in this moment of sudden and unexpected crisis, his body seemed to react instinctively while his mind was still in the process of digesting the messages from his senses. The shepherd's sling, loaded with a heavy stone, was suddenly in his hand. With a couple of rapid whirls of the sling above his head, the stone flew true and hard into the lion's head. Grabbing the heavy club at his side, David had leaped at the animal, oblivious to danger.

The lion was momentarily stunned by the stone and slackened its hold on the lamb. Almost instinctively David pulled the small animal out of the lion's mouth with one hand, and in the next second brought the club he was holding in his other hand down upon the predator's head with all the strength his young body could muster. Again and again he swung this weapon crashing into the lion's head. With each blow he heard the cracking of the animal's skull, and he kept striking furiously until his target was a mangled mass of fur, flesh, bone, blood and brains.

Finally he arose slowly and stood for what seemed like many minutes. His chest was heaving as he gulped the cool evening air. He felt his entire body covered with perspiration, and he began to shake almost uncontrollably. The enormous wave of physical and emotional energy that had surged through him gradually began to dissipate. Soon he was able at least to partially calm his nerves, gather his thoughts and start calling soothingly to the sheep who had scattered in fear.

They came haltingly toward him, still fearful but wanting to get near to the shepherd whom they knew and trusted. He slowly walked among the flock, gently touching some of them as he continued speaking in a soft, comforting tone. Darkness had nearly fallen before he was able to get them all together and lead them into their temporary pen for the night. As he stood at the entrance of the small enclosure, he started to reflect upon what had happened in those few seconds of deadly conflict.

He knew himself to be an excellent shot with a sling. But to be called upon to hurl a stone instantly, in the dim light of evening, with enough accuracy and strength to temporarily disable a fierce predator was beyond his natural ability. And then there was the matter of the club. He seemed to have been able to wield this heavy weapon as if it were a light stick, pummeling the lion's head with a power and ferocity even his oldest brother, tall and strong Eliab, would not have been able to match.

He looked upward at the night sky as he often did, especially while praying. As his eyes swept across the panorama of stars covering the heavens, an uncountable number of celestial candles winking and shimmering against their dark background, the realization suddenly struck him: He had not been alone during the fight! In an instant of revelation, David understood that he never could have confronted and conquered such a mighty beast on his own. The One who had created this vast universe and who held it together had been there protecting and empowering him in the midst of his life-and-death struggle. David had grown to know this God in a personal and wonderful way, and now his God had shown Himself to be David's shepherd. Just as he had instantly rushed to defend his little flock of sheep, so his heavenly Shepherd had come to his aid. This divine shaft of truth caused an immeasurable sense of joy and gratitude to well up inside him. As David started to express his thanks to his almighty Protector, words came to him, words he would pen many years later in a psalm the Bible compilers would number as 27: "When my father and mother forsake me, then the LORD will take care of me."

Just at this moment of reminiscence, David's mind was brought back abruptly to the present. As he and the little donkey rounded a curve in the road, he was able to see some of the Israelite encampment in the far distance.

Hallelujah, thank You, Lord, for my swift and safe journey, *he said inwardly. Then he found his thoughts returning once more to the confrontation with the lion.* Isn't it curious, *he mused,* that my first battle with a wild animal came back so unexpectedly into my mind on this particular day? I had not thought about it for quite a while. *He had faced and killed more predators in the following months and years—bears, jackals and other lions—because his Lord was always with him through every danger. Why then had this particular memory returned to his consciousness today? As he pondered the question, he remembered again the way this initial battle had marked a watershed in his life. In killing the lion he had experienced God's miraculous intervention on his behalf for the first time, and it had changed him forever after.*

Sounds from the camp of Israel's army began to reach David's ears, and thoughts of those early battles were put aside. He was now close enough to see clearly the troops and tents of Saul's army. The sight thrilled the teenager, and his sense of expectancy and adventure grew by the moment. Ever since his brothers had left home to join Israel's army, he had listened anxiously, day after day, for any news about this war against the Philistines. Just recently he heard that the two opposing armies were preparing to confront one another at the Valley of Elah. Saul's forces were camping on the near side of the valley while the Philistine army was said to be assembling on the opposite side. David had tried to picture the scene. Now he was going to see it for himself! He made another attempt to hurry his donkey along the road. If there was going to be a battle today, he did not want to miss it.

The Dreams of a Child

Kids are not afraid to dream big dreams—to imagine themselves as top professional athletes or as world-famous musicians or movie stars. Maybe this is the reason they can so easily identify with the story of David and Goliath. As they read about this event, it reinforces in them the hope that someday they, too, may be able to accomplish some great victory or achieve popular acclaim. These childhood dreams begin to fade and die as we grow older. Life settles into a routine—trying to raise a family, working long hours on a job and paying a never-ending stream of bills.

No matter how humdrum our lives, however, most of us will encounter a giant sooner or later and find ourselves in a time involving a hard, significant battle. Sadly, many Christians will be unprepared for such events. Some will behave like the soldiers in Saul's army when they encountered Goliath, as recorded in 1 Samuel 17:24: "And all the men of Israel, when they saw the man [Goliath], fled from him and were dreadfully afraid."

The reaction of the soldiers is revealing. First, they "saw" Goliath and were intimidated by his enormous size and obvious strength. Then they "fled" from him as intimidation turned to fear. Finally fear led to their being "dreadfully afraid." The Hebrew words rendered "dreadfully afraid" are translated in several other Scripture passages as "be afraid . . . be discouraged."[1]

This progression from "seeing" to "being discouraged" is a revealing one. Why? Because discouragement is one of the major weapons Satan uses to weaken and disable God's people. He does not necessarily have to cause us to fall into some gross, sinful lifestyle such as drug addiction or flagrant adultery in order to divert us from living faithfully for God. Just a good dose of discouragement dropped into our spiritual lives is often enough to overcome our faith. The path of discouragement begins when we start to rely on what our natural senses tell us while ignoring God's Word and the prompting of the Holy Spirit. When we permit discouragement to overwhelm us, we, like Saul's army, will then shrink back from taking our rightful places as soldiers in the Body of Christ.

The Weapon of Experience

We have seen the many and varied ways the Lord prepared David, enabling him to build a spiritual foundation. While it is difficult to summarize this process in a single word, I believe the term *experience* comes closest to capturing the sense of what is imparted to us during the Foundation Season. It is absolutely essential that we have experience as we step into the Season of Battle. Paul counseled Timothy not to appoint either inexperienced Christians to positions of leadership (see 1 Timothy 3:6), or even to hastily select someone for service before they had proven themselves in small things (see 1 Timothy 5:22).

During my nearly thirty years in commercial and investment banking, I was able to observe the triumphs and tragedies of numerous organizations, public and private, large and small. I became convinced that experience, or lack of it, was the main determinant of success. The following quotation by Doug Hood makes the case for experience in the business world; I believe that this principle can apply equally well in other areas, including our spiritual lives:

> In business, the learning curve is steep—don't take a leap. The most common reason for business failure I've encountered is lack of experience. [All] other reasons for failure I've seen—such as insufficient capital, lack of proper planning, heavy competition, inappropriate location—pale in comparison to lack of experience. As a good rule of thumb in business, don't do what you don't know.[2]

This is an even better rule of thumb in the Body of Christ, where significant damage is sometimes done by well-meaning and zealous believers who are almost totally inexperienced and lack an understanding of the basic Christian doctrines and truths. David gained all the experience he needed while out in the fields, in God's 101 Foundation Season course. He graduated at the head of the class and was now ready to enter the Season of Battle.

What a season it would be! Although short in duration, it would involve the most famous battle in the Old Testament. This conflict would cause David's name to be remembered down through history as the epitome of a person who emerges victorious against overwhelming odds. I recently watched an exciting basketball game on television in which the eventual winner was the team that had been a heavy underdog. As the television cameras panned their happy crowd of supporters, one fan held up a sign proclaiming in bold letters, "David versus Goliath." In a day when so many Americans are Bible illiterates, when the names of Abraham, Joshua and Isaiah go unrecognized by the average person, David and his Season of Battle remain in the consciousness of our people.

7

God's Instructions

T he Season of Beginnings, the time of foundation building, had several aspects that seem common to many Christians today, as well as certain applications to our own lives. The same is true with the Season of Battle, and so we ought to be aware of its main characteristic.

Sudden and Unexpected

The day finally arrived for which the Lord had been training David during those long, lonely years on the bleak hillsides of Judea. The events began in a simple, unobtrusive way. God planted a thought in Jesse's mind—that he should send David to take food to his older brothers who were with King Saul. David would be able to report on how they were doing and could bring back any messages from the brothers to Jesse.

David must have arisen very early on this morning, perhaps much earlier than he had for countless dawns in the past. Although this was a special day because he was going to the Israelite army encampment, the boy was totally unaware of the life-changing event the Lord had in store for him. In a relatively few hours[1] David would be changed by God from a simple shepherd lad with some recognized musical skills into a mighty hero. He would have the starring role in a battle that would be told and retold down through three thousand years. Such is the unfathomable power and plan of our almighty God!

The "Suddenly" of God

This sudden and dramatic change in life circumstances was not unique to David's case. God seems to use this kind of method whenever He has prepared His servants to confront and overcome apparently impossible situations. Consider Joseph, forgotten and confined in a dungeon at daybreak, then promoted before nightfall to the second most powerful position in the most powerful nation in the world. Or look at Moses, an aging and humble shepherd living out his life in a bleak, inhospitable land. He suddenly meets God in a burning bush and then is sent to miraculously overcome the mighty ruler of Egypt and lead three million Hebrews from captivity through a trackless wilderness to God's Promised Land.

Since this season can arrive so suddenly and unexpectedly, the corollary is not to wait until it arrives before starting to make the needed preparations. When you see a large tornado advancing toward your house, it is a bit late to begin checking your homeowners' insurance policy to see if it covers this kind of catastrophe.

Two synonyms for *preparation* are "foresight" and "anticipation." Without proper preparation we will find ourselves hastily reacting to sudden events, allowing them to force our hand. But God does not want His people to be unprepared for battle. We would not want to push our children into important situations until we felt they were ready to handle them spiritually, mentally, emotionally and physically. Neither does the Lord want to see us fall into the deep end of the pool before we are able to swim. For this reason He is careful and compassionate enough to provide us with the spiritual revelation (knowledge and foresight) and training we will need to successfully confront the events awaiting us on our spiritual journey.

Perhaps you find yourself in the midst of a seemingly endless Foundation Season. You have a true hunger and thirst for more of God in your life and have been faithful in spending quality time in His presence, permitting Him as the Master Potter to mold and shape you into the vessel He desires. Yet you have watched other Christians, who appear far less dedicated and faithful than you, being promoted and prospered while your own life appears void of spiritual opportunities and victories.

Be encouraged! The Lord does not waste anything or anybody, and He will not neglect or forget you either. Be alert and watchful! God does not always give us an obvious warning when the seasons are about to change. But He will prepare and alert us. The longer a particular spiritual season goes, the greater the likelihood that its end is nearing and the time is approaching for a change of season. As you go through a particular season, faithfully learning and applying what God is teaching you, be alert to the increasing probability that the Lord is preparing you for a coming change.

Before the era of radio communication, sailors at sea relied upon the ship's barometer to warn them about a coming change in the weather. The sea and sky around their vessels may have appeared calm and fair, but if the barometer began to fall, they knew a storm was approaching. The Holy Spirit is our spiritual barometer. Just as the sailors of old checked the barometer throughout the day and night, we need to spend daily quality time in His presence. As we do we will find His gentle guidance directing us into position for our entry into a new season.

Keys to David's Victory

Absolute Trust

David's battle with Goliath is one of Scripture's finest examples of a believer's trust in the unlimited power of God. Consider how David lacked the material things considered necessary for combat in those days: He went into battle with no sword or shield, wore no armor and had not received any training in hand-to-hand fighting. He faced the giant while wearing the same clothes and carrying the same equipment as would any shepherd who was going out to care for a flock of sheep.

The sling and a club (usually referred to as a rod in the Bible) were the shepherd's only two weapons. The rod could be a fairly effective weapon, particularly if it had a large, heavy end with pieces of flint embedded in it. A Hebrew sling consisted of a leather pouch that held a stone two inches or more in diameter, attached to a pair of leather or sinew cords about two feet long. The shepherd would place a stone in the pouch and then begin to whirl the sling around so that the stone was held in place by centrifugal force. When one of the cords was released, the stone would be shot out of the pouch with tremendous force.[2] A sling could be a deadly weapon in the hands of a strong and skillful person. Judges 20:16 records the fighting ability of seven hundred warriors from the tribe of Benjamin who "could sling a stone at a hair's breadth and not miss."

David must have been extremely skillful with his sling; just as kids today spend untold hours working on their baseball or basketball skills, the shepherds in David's era spent considerable time during their lonely hours perfecting the accuracy and strength of their throws with the sling. But no matter how skilled David had become in the use of this deadly weapon, he could never have overcome Goliath with his own abilities, and David himself knew it! 1 Samuel 17 records him telling Saul, "The LORD . . . will deliver me from the hand of this Philistine" (verse 37). He spoke similar words to Goliath: "The battle is the LORD's, and He will give you into our hands" (verse 47).

Faith in God is the linchpin of Christianity, as Hebrews 11:6 reminds us: "But without faith it is impossible to please [God]." The world counsels us to trust in ourselves—in our own wisdom, learning, experience and strength. The gurus of our modern age (science, the media and the New Age movement) have caused people to believe that they are little gods. The Bible gives us a far different message. I find it interesting that its middle verse is Psalm 118:8, which reads as follows: "It is better to trust in the LORD than to put confidence in man."

Trust is a key component of the Greek word for faith (*pistis*). In his book *Ruthless Trust*, Brennan Manning strongly underscores our need for radical, life-changing trust, calling it "the essence of biblical faith." He bluntly acknowledges the difficulty involved in wholly trusting God. "Unwavering trust is a rare and precious thing because it often demands a degree of courage that borders on the heroic."[3]

David exhibited this kind of heroic trust when he faced Goliath, and that one battle changed his life forever. Your battle with your own Goliath can and will change your life, too, perhaps in a way you could never have thought possible. The greater the battle, the greater must be our trust in our miracle-working God.

Recognizing the True Enemy

Dissension, division and strife in a family, organization or church can weaken the strength and vitality of these smaller units just as they do the larger affairs of a nation. Satan is well aware of this truth, and uses it as one of his main weapons against the Church. By enticing Christians to waste their spiritual strength disputing with those who ought to be their allies, he is able to divert them from their spiritual responsibility—working under the guidance of the Holy Spirit to bring the Kingdom of God to all the people and areas of their lives. Regrettably, Christian churches and organizations often split or dissolve, not because of irreconcilable differences concerning fundamental Bible truth or doctrine but over certain small (and frequently silly) administrative and financial matters, or personality disagreements between the clergy and the lay leaders. Satan attempted to sow this same kind of discord into David's situation, but the teenager, young in years but well schooled and guided by the Lord, was not about to be distracted from his mission.

When David arrived at the camp of the Israelite army and delivered his supplies, he went to look for his brothers (see 1 Samuel 17:22). It was then that he saw Goliath and heard his defiant and mocking challenge to the Israelite army. David began to speak with his brothers and some of the soldiers about Goliath.

As David and the men were speaking, his eldest brother, Eliab, suddenly broke into the discussion and began to viciously criticize David (see verse 28). First he impugned David's motives and integrity by demanding, "Why did you really come here?" Then he sought to demean and humiliate David with the snide question, "Who did you leave those few sheep of yours with?" Finally he attempted to lay guilt and condemnation on him by declaring, "I know your prideful and insolent heart!"

Talk about sibling rivalry! Whatever the underlying cause of Eliab's verbal attack—whether jealousy and envy over Samuel's anointing this little brother instead of him, or offense, assuming that David was questioning the bravery and dedication of Saul's army—David did not give in to the very human temptation to argue or fight back. Rather than react in the flesh, he responded by simply but firmly saying he had done nothing wrong and was only asking some questions. Then he turned back and continued his conversation with the other soldiers.

By his actions David illustrated an important spiritual truth: *Our enemy is Goliath; do not get sidetracked into battling with Eliab.*

Sadly, the attacks we face can sometimes come from those closest to us. Eliabs can be found in many Christian churches and organizations. Marshall Shelley calls these types of people "well-intentioned dragons" and characterizes them in this manner:

Within the church, they are often sincere, well-meaning saints, but they leave ulcers, strained relationships, and hard feelings in their wake. They don't consider themselves difficult people . . . but for some reason they undermine the ministry of the church. They are loyal church members, convinced they're serving God, but they wind up doing more harm than good.[4]

In general, Eliabs are the people who will find fault, criticize and attack any proposal or program, no matter who is involved. Their opposition may be due to some offense they feel was given them in the past, a desire for control and an unwillingness to submit to godly leadership, a desire to keep things as they have always been or nothing more than plain, naked jealousy. Shelley believes that the two most common tactics used by these people are "personal attacks and plays for power."[5]

Do not misunderstand this spiritual truth: We must never suppress the honest and open discussions that a church or family needs in order to reach the best decisions about specific matters. This is a caution against the all-too-prevalent tendency among Christians to fall into the spirit of judgment that Jesus warned about in Matthew 7:1–2.

This type of spirit—an Eliab spirit—presumes to understand the motivations of other people's hearts and is willing to attack their inner selves and worth. Be alert for this spirit in others, but watch that you do not become an Eliab yourself! It is easy to slip into this role. Brennan Manning writes, "When I am most unhappy with myself, I am most critical of others. When I am most into self-condemnation, I am most judgmental of others."[6]

Spiritual Insight

David continued talking to Saul's soldiers, and I think we should note the striking contrast between the way they viewed Goliath and David's viewpoint:

The soldiers saw "the man." 1 Samuel 17:4 records his enormous height as six cubits and a span. Now a cubit in Old Testament times was about eighteen inches, or the length from a man's elbow to the tip of his middle finger. A span measured approximately nine inches, the distance from the thumb to the little finger on an outstretched hand.[7] So Goliath was nine feet nine inches tall! Clad in his great armor, Goliath was a walking tank. In the eyes of Saul's troops he looked absolutely invincible, a warrior who would prove impossible for any normal soldier to defeat.

Remember that warfare at that time was strictly hand-to-hand combat, man against man, with each combatant depending upon his individual strength and skill with his sword, shield and spear to give him victory over his opponent. Under these circumstances victory against Goliath was inconceivable. He would have seemed indestructible and unbeatable from a strictly human viewpoint.

But David's viewpoint was different! David viewed Goliath as "this uncircumcised Philistine" (verse 36)—a heathen follower of pagan gods. He measured the size and strength of Goliath by the size and strength of God, because he had developed the ability to see things as God sees. His comments about Goliath in verses 26 and 45–47 are particularly revealing. He told Goliath what he was going to do to him before he did it, including the cutting off of Goliath's head and the defeat of the entire Philistine army.

Here again we see the reason for, and importance of, David's triumphs over the lions and bears during his shepherd days. Having faith in God and acting upon it in a crisis situation, as David did against these wild animals, will always lead to a greater trust and confidence in the Lord.

The soldiers said that Goliath had come "to defy Israel." David said that he was "defying the armies of the living God" and, hence, really defying God Himself. (In many ancient cultures, including Israel's, a person's representative was regarded as the person himself.)[8]

Some questions arise as to the method chosen by the Philistines when they faced Saul's army. You see, most ancient battles consisted of two armies of foot soldiers who simply charged against one another in a massive melee until one side finally prevailed. It was on rare occasions that the opposing sides might agree to decide the outcome of the battle by having the best warrior in each army fight to the death in single combat, with the survivor gaining the victory for his army.[9] Earlier passages in 1 Samuel indicate that the Philistine troops were much better armed than the Israelites (see 13:19–22). (This advantage was due largely to their skills in metallurgy, in particular the smelting and fashioning of iron.[10] Iron weapons were superior to those made of bronze, and bronze weapons were probably the only kind available to the Israelites.) Through this control they were able to hold a decided military advantage over Israel.

But despite this superiority, the Philistines chose to have their champion challenge the best soldier in Saul's army to decide the battle's outcome. Why did they adopt this plan? It seems that God directed the counsels of the Philistines in some divine manner. When they decided on this particular course of action, they fulfilled God's desire for this battle to be decided by representative warfare. David was His representative and symbolized Christ. Goliath represented the forces of evil and symbolized Satan.

Here is an Old Testament foreshadowing of what the Lord Jesus Christ would do to Satan in the spiritual realm a thousand years later, as recorded in Colossians 2:15: "In this way, God disarmed the evil rulers and authorities. He shamed them publicly by His victory over them on the Cross of Christ" (NLT).

Saul's soldiers reported that the man who could kill the giant would be rewarded by King Saul with great riches, the hand of his daughter in marriage and exemption from taxes. David saw Goliath's conqueror as the person who would take "away the reproach [disgrace] from Israel" (verse 26).

The army was thoroughly intimidated, and became "dreadfully afraid" (verse 24), but David ignored Goliath's words just as he did his size. Dr. Gary Collins reports that anxiety and fear often arise because people have irrational beliefs. "To help these people, these irrational beliefs need to be challenged."[11] David certainly challenged the wrong thinking and irrational beliefs of Israel's soldiers. Where they were filled with fear, he was filled with God's presence, because he had spent so much time fellowshiping with Him. He had learned about and experienced God's love, protection and power.

The Lord's sovereignty over the lives of individuals and nations is well documented by Scripture passages such as Jeremiah 10:23: "O LORD, I know the way of man is not in himself; it is not in man who walks to direct his own steps." How much different might our lives be if we exercised our God-given spiritual insight and knowledge instead of reacting with our fleshly senses and emotions!

Do Not Follow the Formula

David's words about Goliath spread through the camp. They soon reached the ears of Saul, who sent for the boy. The young shepherd told Saul that he would fight Goliath, and Saul attempted to dissuade him (see 1 Samuel 17:33). He clearly thought that it was impossible for David to defeat the Philistine giant, and he told him so.

But David refused to listen to human reasoning, even though Saul was the leader of his nation. David knew his God, and so he recounted to Saul how he had been able on several occasions to rescue his sheep from predatory animals because the Lord delivered him from the paw of the lion and bear. The literal meaning of the Hebrew word for *paw* is "hand," and the hand in Scripture symbolizes power and strength.[12] David was certain, therefore, that his God would deliver him from the hand of this human predator, Goliath, who was attacking God's sheep, the people of Israel (see verses 34–37).

When David testified and argued with such conviction, the king relented and offered David his armor. David at first tried on the armor but quickly realized it was a mistake. He intuitively knew that if he was to overcome Goliath it would have to be in God's strength and in His way.

And what a way it was! A teenage shepherd armed with only a sling, confronting the mightiest warrior in any army at the time. But a short while later, when Goliath crashed to the ground, none of the thousands watching that day would have any doubt that it was God and God alone who gave David the victory. David did not need Saul's armor or advice to win the battle. He needed only to hear from God, to trust Him and to obey.

Putting on someone else's armor is an expedient used frequently by Christians. It is copying a technique or procedure or way of ministering that someone else (usually a well-known minister) has used successfully. It is trying to find a formula, a short-cut to spiritual success and victory. But it is almost always the wrong thing to do. For one thing, what works for one person may not work for you, since no two churches, settings or ministry needs are exactly alike.

Even worse, it removes you from the intimate personal relationship that the Lord desires to have with each of His children. When you depend on some formula or procedure to deal with decisions or problems in your life, you no longer feel the need to spend time in God's presence, seeking His face in order to find His will and way for the situations you are facing.

David never resorted to formulas when he went into battle. As we will see later in this book, the Bible recounts instances all throughout his life where he sought the Lord's will before entering into engagements with the enemy. No matter how many battles he won, David never felt himself so knowledgeable and experienced that he no longer needed God's counsel and guidance. Nor did he resort to using formulas, blindly following past practices or relying merely on the opinions of other people. He never took the Lord for granted, and neither should we.

God set His appointed moment for this battle. The stage was prepared to bring the young shepherd to the attention of his nation and begin the process that would culminate years later in David's rise to the kingship over all Israel. And He knew that it was time to curb the Philistines' growing military might.

God furthermore selected the place for this battle. The Valley of Elah was the perfect setting. At the time of this battle Elah was approximately on the border between Israel and Philistia, and no modern sports stadium could have provided a better venue. Elah is a smallish valley and lies several miles west and slightly south of Jerusalem. The Philistine army was encamped on the hills on the valley's southwestern side, while Saul's troops ranged along the northeastern ridge. A *wadi* (a stream that runs only during periods of rain) winds through the valley close to the northern side. This is where David collected his "five smooth stones" before crossing over to confront Goliath on the valley floor.[13]

Scripture tells us that the battle is the LORD's (see 1 Samuel 17:47; see also 2 Chronicles 20:15). This statement means that He has the right and the power to select the combatants, the time and the place. He made the correct selection of these things for David, and He will do the same for us—if we will let Him! Too often we allow our adversary Satan to do some of the selecting. Remember the military adage, "Never let your opponent choose the battlefield" (or the battle).

To God Be the Glory

Finally everything was in readiness as God intended. We Christians today will do well to remember that the Lord desires to prepare all the aspects of the battles we face. Let's also allow Him to give us His plan concerning our part and conduct—because our conduct involves a critically important spiritual principle, a principle too often overlooked or ignored:

Principle #5: **Be extremely careful never to take any of the glory that belongs to God nor to misrepresent it.**

The Hebrew word for God's glory is *kabod*, a word that conveys a rich range of meanings. The literal meaning is "to be heavy, weighty." The more common figurative usage conveys the idea of something that is noteworthy or impressive. Scripture uses this word to describe the concept that the Lord is honorable, impressive, glorious, worthy of respect and that His reputation is of central importance.[14] He is the Supreme Sovereign of the universe, awesome in power and greatness as well as in purity and perfection.

Readiness to act with pure motives is a key trait of servant leadership. As a shepherd, David sometimes had to confront and kill wild predators, but such actions were only to protect the sheep. He never used these exploits to promote himself or gain the applause of others. Likewise his reason for confronting Goliath was not to gain great fame. Nor was he foolishly tempting God. He was not motivated by the substantial rewards Saul had offered. David's twofold purpose was to kill the heathen who had dared to openly and continuously blaspheme almighty God and to deliver His people from Goliath's reproach.

David was careful to give the glory and credit to God from the time he testified to Saul of God's protection and deliverance all the way to the end of his days. A number of the psalms he wrote are filled with thanksgiving to God, acknowledging that it was His power and might that permitted David to triumph over his enemies. David understood that he was merely the instrument in the Lord's hand, the sword God wielded to defeat Israel's enemies. Here may be another of the major reasons why the Lord referred to David as "a man after My own heart" (Acts 13:22).

Could it be that one of the major reasons we fail to reach the promises God has for us is our tendency to misrepresent His glory? Scripture attests to the fact that God takes His reputation seriously.[15] Too many believers do not, however. Their focus appears to be on furthering their own ministries or place in the Church. These Christians will tell you quickly and often that "God told me to do (such and such)." Often a short time later, "God" tells them to do just the opposite. God seems to change His mind quite often!

Listening to some television preachers or reading the latest pop-theology best-seller, one almost gets the idea that God is like a slot machine, and if we just put enough money into this ministry or that church, we will hit the jackpot. In some Christian circles, Jesus is represented as our buddy, our errand boy whose job it is to help us achieve our life goals of self-fulfillment, health and prosperity. John Bevere writes, "There are people who are quick to acknowledge Jesus as Savior, Healer and Deliverer . . . yet they reduce His glory to the level of corruptible men by their actions and heart attitudes."[16] Given this kind of casual and flippant attitude toward almighty God, I was not surprised recently to see a bumper sticker that read, *God, please protect me from Your followers!*

David's heart was strikingly different from the attitudes and motives seen all too frequently among the leaders of today's businesses, governments or even religious organizations. Leadership involves a responsibility before God because all promotion ultimately comes from Him (see Psalm 75:6–7; Daniel 2:21). Just as Ezekiel condemned Israel's shepherds (the religious leaders) for failing to care for their people (see Ezekiel 34:2–10), James indicts the rich and powerful leaders who exploit those under them in their driving desire for personal gain (see James 5:1–6).

What Is in Your Hand?

As Goliath approached closer to David, he saw what weapons the boy had in his hands and began to sneer at these apparently puny things, calling them "sticks." But then the world has always ridiculed the small things of God. David was not the least bothered by Goliath's estimation of his weapons. He ignored the giant's words because he understood a truth the prophet Zechariah would write some five hundred years later: "'Not by might nor by power, but by My Spirit,' says the LORD of hosts" (Zechariah 4:6).

What has God placed in our hands? We may think it is too meager to be of much value in His work. Think again! "What is that in your hand?" God asked Moses at the burning bush (see Exodus 4). Moses replied, "It is only a rod." But backed by God's infinite and awesome power, Moses later raised that rod to bring the Lord's plagues of judgment upon Egypt, to part the waters of the Red Sea and to bring water from the rocks in the Sinai wilderness.

"What is that in your hands?" someone might have asked the priests as they and the children of Israel marched around the high, strong walls of Jericho. "It looks like you're only carrying trumpets and not weapons." But when they blew those trumpets on the seventh day and the Israelites all shouted, the supposedly impregnable walls of that fortress city collapsed.

So it goes throughout Bible history: Gideon and his 300 men held trumpets and pitchers with lighted torches in their hands as they put to flight an enemy army of over 125,000. Samson took the jawbone of a donkey in his hand and killed a thousand Philistine soldiers with it.

"What is that in your hands?" Jesus might have asked His disciples. "We have here only five loaves and two fish," they replied. But when Jesus touched and blessed this food as He had done with

- David's sling
- Moses' rod
- The priests' trumpets
- Gideon's trumpets and pitchers
- Samson's donkey jawbone
- The flour bin and oil jar of the widow of Zarephath (see 1 Kings 17:8–16)
- Elijah's fallen mantle that Elisha picked up (see 2 Kings 2:12–14)
- The widow's empty jars and vessels (see 2 Kings 4:1–7)
- Peter's hand (see Acts 3:7) and
- Paul's handkerchiefs and aprons (see Acts 19:12)

miraculous things happened!

Isn't it time for all born-again Christians to

- Stop being embarrassed and worried about the world's mocking and criticizing of Christianity's message?
- Cease complaining to God about the lack we see in our lives and begin using the things He has given us in an obedient and faithful manner?
- Recognize that the "sticks" God has placed in our hands are "mighty in God for pulling down strongholds" (2 Corinthians 10:4)?

Perhaps we just need to begin doing two things in our everyday lives: First, like David, let's ignore the enemy's attempts to intimidate us with his loud, humanistic words and arguments. Second, let's rejoice because we serve "the God of the Impossible," as we are told in Genesis 18:14; Jeremiah 32:17–27; Matthew 19:26; Mark 10:27; and Luke 18:27. That is something well worth remembering since, as Rick Howard writes, "To receive a miracle, you must begin with an impossibility!"[17]

Christians today like to talk about faith, and many of us can quote several Bible verses on the subject. Far fewer of us, however, live out our faith through corresponding actions. David did not merely speak words of faith to the Israelite soldiers, to Saul and finally to Goliath. Real faith *acts*, and David had that kind of faith. He did not wait for Goliath to come to him. He went to meet the enemy head on, fully trusting in the Lord. David knew that he was the instrument God would use to utterly defeat his evil opponent. In a few short moments, both armies would also know this truth.

8

THE BATTLE

Imagine the scene: The battle is short, lasting only a moment, but it is a moment forever frozen in time. The two armies, the Israelites and the Philistines, are clustered on the opposite hillsides of the small valley, their tents and equipment covering the upper part of the slopes.

Toward late morning an enormous metal-clad figure emerges from the front line of the Philistine encampment. This colossus appears to be nearly twice the size of any ordinary warrior. He is the famous Goliath, coming to shout another challenge to the Israelite army.

The giant has been doing this same thing morning and evening for forty days, daring any of their soldiers to face him in single combat to decide the outcome of the conflict between Philistia and Israel. He feels certain that no one will be foolhardy enough to accept his challenge. Very few men ever have. Those who did were quickly and brutally slain, for nobody could even begin to approach him in stature, strength and fierceness. So Goliath feels confident that he and the Philistines will shortly win this conflict by default. Saul and his troops must soon recognize the impossibility of their situation, accept the inevitable, admit defeat and become the Philistines' vassals.

He waits a while after issuing his challenge and then starts to move down the hill to the valley floor, to see if the Israelites might finally send out a champion to face him. *The sunlight reflecting off his massive armor emphasizes his already obvious power and strength. He wears a bronze helmet and his body is protected from shoulders to knees by a coat of mail reputed to weigh 125 pounds.[1] His lower legs are also shielded by greaves, bronze plates form-fitted to his calves and held in place by leather straps. He carries three weapons—a javelin, spear and sword—each one much larger than those used by a typical soldier.[2] The shaft on his spear resembles a weaver's beam, with an enormous iron point weighing fifteen or sixteen pounds.*

An ordinary warrior wearing such heavy armor and carrying these outsized weapons would be so encumbered that he would have difficulty in marching to battle, much less fighting. Great Goliath, though, wears this armor as easily as if it were a cloak, and carries his weapons with no more effort than a normal person would tote a couple of loaves of bread. He is accompanied by an armor-bearer, a soldier who is laboring to lug the giant's huge shield, a standing shield. Its size dwarfs the ordinary round shields of common foot-soldiers.[3]

Suddenly a teenage boy steps out of the ranks of Saul's army. He is wearing no armor and is clad only in the homespun clothing of a shepherd. He carries a wooden staff, a pouch and a sling. He walks down the hillside to the little stream on the valley floor and begins picking some stones out of the stream bed and putting them into his pouch.

The giant sees the figure, but at first does not notice that it is just a boy. He simply sees that someone has at last come to accept his challenge. So he continues striding down the hill, accompanied by his armor-bearer. As he walks across the valley floor, however, he recognizes that this figure is merely a youth—a stripling with no armor and only a stick and a sling as his weapons. The giant is insulted! Are these miserable Israelites trying to mock him by sending this insignificant creature to do battle with him? His anger turns to rage! He stops and starts to curse this puny lad.

But the boy does not flinch or draw back. Instead, the onlookers hear him shout back his own challenge to the giant. The huge man becomes even more incensed. The audacity of this insolent, worthless worm of a child, to dare to cast words at him! He starts moving toward the boy with great, long strides, his movements accentuating his size, ferocity and an invincibility that is obvious next to the youth's stature and lack of protection.

The soldiers on both sides hold their collective breath, amazed at the reckless and inexplicable actions of this boy. Most probably they wonder what could have possessed the lad to attempt such an impossible feat, to try confronting this mighty military champion. Both armies believe Goliath to be unbeatable in hand-to-hand combat, and this foolish youth is not even dressed and equipped for combat! In a few seconds they expect to see the giant hurl either his spear or his javelin and skewer the boy like a quail to be roasted. But Goliath disdains to throw either of these weapons, as is normally done at the beginning of a battle.[4] Nor does he take the shield from his armor-bearer. Why should he bother with these usual battle tactics? His "opponent" is only some half-witted, young upstart. One powerful stroke with his great iron sword will either decapitate the fool or practically cut him in two.

Unbelievably the boy displays no signs of fear! As the monstrous figure lumbers forward, David never hesitates. He knows that Goliath has one vulnerable spot in his otherwise invincible appearance. The Philistine's helmet protects his temples, ears and the nape of his neck, but not the lower part of his forehead. It is only one very small target on a very large and well-protected adversary, but it is enough of an opening for young David.

He puts one of the stones in his sling as he runs toward the Philistine. Still running, he begins whirling his sling around faster and faster above his head. The distance between the two figures closes rapidly. The giant starts to raise his sword to deliver the one mighty killing stroke that the onlookers expect. He never makes it. With only a few paces separating them, the boy unleashes the stone from his sling in one smooth, incredibly swift and deadly motion.

He has practiced countless hours with his sling during his shepherd days, slinging thousands of stones at hundreds of targets. Sometimes he would aim the stone just in front of a wandering sheep to bring it back to the flock. Sometimes he launched a stone with much greater force at a wild animal that was approaching the sheep. Most often, though, he practiced throwing at a variety of inanimate objects—perhaps a small plant or wildflower, a particular spot on a rock outcropping or at anything that caught his eye. He practiced at all times of the day, from the bright glare of noonday to the half-light of dawn or evening, in all kinds of weather and in every season of the year. He practiced until he literally could hit the bulls-eye every time, even at distances of many paces.

The distance between David and his target is very short this time, and his stone does not miss. It is a special stone, thrown with absolute faith in the power, might and judgment of David's awesome God. The deadly missile strikes the one vital part of the giant's body not protected by his great armor, with such power that 1 Samuel 17:49 reports, "The stone sank into his forehead."

The enormous figure is brought to a sudden standstill for a fraction of a second. Then he pitches face forward, hitting the ground with such force that even the distant onlookers can hear the crash of metal armor striking the rocky ground.[5] Every soldier in both armies is stunned and amazed by this swift and unbelievable event. For the briefest of moments, a collective gasp is the only sound heard from the mass of troops on the two hillsides. Their minds cannot immediately grasp the truth of what their eyes have just told them. The impossible has happened!

A few of the onlookers wonder: Has the giant actually been killed or has the stone only momentarily stunned him? David does not stop to debate the matter, however. As soon as the giant's face smashes into the ground, David runs to him. And just as quickly, Goliath's armor-bearer drops the heavy shield and runs in panic from David, back toward the Philistine encampment.

David takes Goliath's own enormous sword and cuts off his head (see verse 51) and then triumphantly lifts it up in the air for all to see. In this instant, the role of the two armies is dramatically reversed. It had been Saul's troops that, moments before, were "dreadfully afraid" as Goliath hurled his challenges at them. Now it is the Philistines who are overcome with fear, a far greater fear than the Israelites had experienced over the previous forty days. Cries of dismay and screams of panic rise from their ranks as they turn and begin to run wildly from the battlefield, almost trampling one another in their frantic efforts to get away. Now it is the army of Israel that is filled with boldness and strength. The valley reverberates with the blast of their shofars as they sound the call to battle. Saul's troops respond as one man, charging down the hillside, across the valley and up the opposite hill in angry and vengeful pursuit of the frightened, fleeing enemy.

Not only was David's victory over Goliath complete, but he put an exclamation point on it by two actions that completely humiliated the Philistines. Killing your enemy with his own weapon, as David used Goliath's sword to decapitate him, was the first such action. The second was when he took Goliath's head to Jerusalem, where it was displayed as a trophy of war (see verse 54). (This practice was a common occurrence in ancient Near East warfare).[6]

This Old Testament battle provides a foreshadowing of what the Lord Jesus Christ would do a thousand years later to Satan and his forces. In Colossians 2:15 the celebration of Christ's triumph over our spiritual enemy is described in terms of a homecoming parade for a victorious Roman general: "Having disarmed principalities and powers, He made a public spectacle of them, triumphing over them in it."

Ignoring Goliath Will Not Make Him Go Away

The biblical Goliath confronted Saul's army for forty days until David arrived on the scene and immediately challenged and destroyed him. The Goliath in our lives will continue to mock us for forty weeks or months or even years if we will allow him. One thing is certain: He will not leave of his own accord. The reason? Satan's Goliath wants to keep you in bondage as long as possible.

Goliath's (read "Satan's") promises are not to be believed. He is only out to "kill, steal and destroy," as Jesus warned us in John 10:10. In his challenge, Goliath promised that the victor of the fight between the Israelite champion and himself would determine whether Philistia or Israel would be the ruling nation over the other. This statement turned out to be a lie. Goliath's words were disregarded by the Philistine army as soon as they witnessed his death.

The Honor of Homage and the Peril of Pride

We know that David's story does not end with "And he lived happily ever after." The aftermath of the battle did begin quite well for him, however. He did not attempt to promote himself and become great and famous. His sole desire was to faithfully and humbly serve his God, and God blessed David as He had promised in 1 Samuel 2:30: "Those who honor Me I will honor, and those who despise Me shall be lightly esteemed."

God honored David immediately in three ways (see 1 Samuel 17:55–18:7). There was the *honor of position* as King Saul promoted him to a senior leadership post in his army.[7] David was transformed overnight from a lowly shepherd to one of the most important people in Saul's retinue.

Next came the *honor of friendship*. David met Saul's son Jonathan, the crown prince, and a deep, enduring friendship began that lasted for the remainder of David's life. Consider how many people today would be delighted to have even a very casual relationship with a well-known public figure. Many of us do know someone who is a "name-dropper"—a person who tries to impress others with the fact that he or she supposedly knows some important person. David's relationship with Jonathan went far beyond the level of mere acquaintanceship. They entered into a friendship sealed by a covenant.[8]

Lastly David received the *honor of public acclaim* from the entire nation. Fame and praise of this sort could be heady and dangerous stuff for anyone, much less a teenaged boy.

But despite these high honors David continued to maintain a humble and submissive spirit both before God and all the people of Israel. He knew how to live with fame and success; he had it, but it did not have him. What a rare quality! What a stark contrast to the public demeanor of many of today's sports heroes, movie or musical stars and politicians! And, sad to say, what an indictment to some in the Body of Christ today, clergy and laypeople alike, who lust after the spotlight and the opportunity to parade their gifts and talents before others in an attempt to gain recognition and rewards.

Further Blessings

Much more resulted from David's triumph than just the death of a Philistine champion. As wonderful as this event was, God used it to produce many more victories and blessings for David and the Jewish nation. These added results simply illustrate the law of sowing and reaping (or "planting and harvesting," in modern language), found in Galatians 6:7–8. It says that if you plant seeds in the ground and cultivate them properly, three things will happen: You will harvest *what* you planted, you will harvest *more* than what you planted and you will harvest *after* you have planted.

David planted seeds of faith and trust in God when he fought this battle, and the harvest of both temporal and spiritual blessings began at once. First it gave a tremendous national victory to Israel. Saul's army pursued the retreating Philistines and slaughtered them all the way to the very gates of their major cities, including Goliath's hometown of Gath. Then the Israelite soldiers returned to the battlefield and plundered the camp of the Philistine army. Much equipment and wealth had been left behind due to the sudden and chaotic retreat of the Philistine soldiers. So Israel not only enjoyed a great military triumph but gained considerable material wealth as well.

In addition, all Israel began to recognize the Lord's divine anointing upon David. It was probably only David's immediate family and the elders of Bethlehem who knew that God had selected him as Israel's next king. After this battle, however, the entire nation became aware of the Lord's special anointing on Jesse's youngest boy. Little wonder then that the Bible reports, "He was accepted in the sight of all the people and also in the sight of Saul's servants"(1 Samuel 18:5). God had begun to launch David, probably a seventeen-year-old boy at this time, into the position of prominence and leadership he would occupy for the remaining 53 years of his life.

David's slaying of the giant started a process of building faith and boldness in Israel's warriors. The culmination of this process would lead to great national military accomplishments as well as numerous and remarkable individual exploits of valor. David's reign as king saw Israel conquer or bring into subjection nearly all of the land the Lord had promised Abraham in Genesis 15:18, and David never again had to fight a giant, even though there were several still in the land. His mighty men disposed of them (see 2 Samuel 21:15–22).

The Road Ahead

We know that David's battle with Goliath was only one of many battles he would face. His future years held an almost unending stream of struggles, so calling this section "The Season of Battle" may seem illogical. And yet David's life-and-death conflict with the Philistine champion was a pivotal point in his life. Had he not been both willing and able to confront Goliath, we may never have read about David the king.

Our willingness and God-given ability to confront the Goliaths we may be facing are, like David's, crucial to our futures. God promises to meet His people at the level of their commitment, and David proved his total commitment to the Lord by this battle.

It Cannot Be Done

History is full of stories about societies who said for years and years that a certain thing could not be done . . . until somebody actually did it, after which others suddenly discovered that they, too, could do it. Such was the case with the most sought-after goal in running during the first half of the twentieth century: the four-minute mile. Many outstanding athletes attempted to run a mile in under four minutes. Several came close, but no one was able to do it. Some medical experts of the time believed that such an extraordinary physical feat was too hard for the human body to withstand.

They were dead wrong. On May 6, 1954, Roger Bannister, a British medical student, broke this barrier many thought impossible. Just a few weeks later an Australian runner, John Landy, duplicated Bannister's feat. And then the rush was on, as more and more runners over the next few years were able to conquer the once unbeatable four-minute mile, including three high-school runners. If man, with his own limited human abilities, can accomplish such great feats, how much more will God's people be able to accomplish if they walk in obedience and trust with their almighty God?

Why David's Battle Is Remembered

So the nation celebrated David's valor and the army's triumph as the news spread throughout the land, "from Dan to Beersheba," and the telling and retelling of this battle has never stopped capturing the imaginations and touching the hearts of myriads of people in every culture throughout the world over the following centuries.

When you consider all of the battles fought down through recorded history—the great and the small, the earth-shaking ones and the insignificant ones, those involving millions and those consisting only of a handful, battles pitting famous leaders and generals against one another and battles composed of non-entities—the question arises, "What makes this particular conflict so unique, so capable of maintaining a freshness and imparting a blessing no matter how many times one has encountered it, and so able to exert a magnetic pull on readers and listeners of all ages?"

All it took was one thing. It took an unknown, insignificantly regarded teenage boy, a boy who had been schooled by his Creator on the lonely hills outside of Bethlehem, a boy who knew beyond any doubt that "the Lord was his Shepherd," a boy who was willing to step out in faith and obedience carrying only some small, weak-looking weapons into a seemingly impossible situation.

And when he did, the God of the Impossible showed up!

FUTILITY

The Season of Barrenness
(1 Samuel 18:8–30:6)

"You can either complain that the rose bush has thorns, or rejoice that the thorn bush has roses."

—IVERNA TOMPKINS

9

Our Thoughts versus God's Thoughts

*I*f Hollywood wrote the script . . .
I am sure you can picture how this movie of David vs. Goliath would come to its thrilling and satisfying conclusion. David is shown in the final scenes, standing over Goliath's slain body and raising his arms in triumph while the exuberant Israelite troops cheer wildly in the background. The camera zooms in on King Saul who stands in amazement upon seeing the death of the Philistine monster, the terrible opponent of his army. Then Saul's enormous exhilaration and joy burst forth as he rushes down the hillside with all of his troops running close behind him to congratulate this young shepherd hero. He embraces David as tears of joy cascade down his face. Then the king acknowledges to David what he now realizes—that David is indeed the Lord's choice to be the nation's new ruler. In roles likely to win Oscar nominations for the actors playing the parts of Saul and David, the king tells the victorious young champion that he will immediately hand the kingship to David and allow him to marry his favorite daughter, Michal.

Michal—breathtakingly beautiful Michal. The camera has shown this alluring and captivating young woman standing at her father's side during the battle, her lovely face creased with concern and fear for David. She has secretly loved this brave teenage warrior ever since he first came as a musician to the palace. Suddenly David senses her presence. He turns from Saul and looks up at the hillside to see Michal running down toward him. (Now it is quite true this part of the story is not in the Bible, but after all, this is Hollywood and some amount of poetic license is allowed, is it not?) As the soundtrack music builds to a crescendo, David sweeps her up into his arms and begins covering her face with kisses as the final scene fades and the ending credits start to roll.

Expectations

Let's be honest! We would probably want to give David's story the same happy ending that the movies would, and this reaction is a perfectly human one. After a movie or novel has taken us through almost every conceivable emotion with the hero and heroine, we want the plot brought to a hoped-for conclusion, with every question answered and every character getting his or her just reward.

Life does not follow a movie script, however, and neither does the Lord. How much disappointment and frustration we could avoid in our lives if we stopped

- trying to write our own life's scripts
- telling God how He should write them
- becoming bitter at Him when we do not like the scripts He has written for us!

Our attempts to chart our own course through life, relying upon those human expectations of what we think is best for us, will usually lead us down the wrong roads. Such expectations need to be put aside. They represent one of the greatest barriers there is to our union and fellowship with the Lord. Our spiritual vision is so blurred and limited, while He knows perfectly the end from the beginning of our existence. How much more satisfying our lives would be if we truly took to heart God's words in Isaiah 55:8–9 and trusted that His thoughts and ways are always best.

A Pair of Paradoxes

An interesting paradox exists in the attitudes of many Christians. On one hand the Lord's people often appear to be *afraid* of His will being done in their lives. On the other hand, they eagerly look forward to spending eternity in heaven! Yet heaven is the place of infinite peace and joy *because* God's will is perfectly fulfilled there, as the Lord's Prayer says: "Thy kingdom come, Thy will be done on earth as it is in heaven."

One of the most difficult things for Christians to do, however, is to give up control of their lives and trust the Lord to care for and lead them. Like the apostle Thomas, we want to be given a good look at the road ahead; only then will we trust and believe it. We want God to settle all of our doubts and questions before we are willing to go on. "Seeing is believing," we say, but the reverse of this statement is the essence of biblical faith. True faith is simply taking God at His word.

There is another drawback to this "Thomas attitude." Brennan Manning points out this danger: "Craving clarity, we attempt to eliminate the risk of trusting God. Fear of the unknown path stretching ahead of us destroys childlike trust in the Father's active goodness and unrestricted love."[1]

Our thoughts and actions about the future are oftentimes confused and contradictory. On the one hand we desire to have clear vision of the future with ample proof and reassurance from God. On the other hand we are experts at bringing worry and distress concerning the future into our lives. We do this by conjuring up in our minds a host of negative "what ifs." If we reflect on this matter carefully and honestly, we will probably conclude that about ninety percent of our "what ifs" never came to pass. No wonder Jesus told us in Matthew 6:34 not to worry about tomorrow!

Consider for a moment a further aspect concerning our desire for clarity: One of the ways God demonstrates His love and mercy toward us is by *not* showing us the future (and thankfully, by not answering all of our prayers). We truly are blessed by His keeping us from seeing what will happen in our lives even in the next moment. Spend a few minutes recalling some of the events and experiences you have been through over the past years, things you did not have to worry about beforehand because you never knew they were in your future. Then ask yourself a couple of questions. How much different would your actions and decisions have been if you had known the future? And how much worry and anxiety were you spared by not knowing beforehand all of the events that were about to enter your life?

Buckle Up

If we thought the Foundation Season had some unpleasant aspects to it, this Season of Barrenness and Futility can seem unpleasant and unwelcome to a multiplied degree. My dictionary defines the word *futility* as "the quality of being ineffective or useless, unimportance, triviality." The term *barrenness* means "unproductive, unfertile, unprofitable, sterile." Therefore, this season may appear on the surface to be a wasted period of life, a time to be gotten through as quickly as possible, and then forgotten even more quickly.

But *just the opposite is true*, as paradoxical as this may seem. The Lord uses these times of apparent futility and barrenness to eventually lead us into some of the greatest experiences of fulfillment and blessing we have ever known. Unfortunately Christians too often become discouraged and despondent during this season. They focus so intently on the physical world around them that they become almost blind spiritually to the deep and vital work God is trying to undertake in them.

The antidote to this wrong viewpoint is to develop our spiritual sensitivity by learning to see things through the eyes of faith. We must seek to gain God's perspective on all aspects of life. The giants of faith listed in Hebrews 11 all walked by this principle, and while this kind of spiritual sight is important to have throughout our lives, it is never more needed than in the Season of Barrenness and Futility.

10

The Start
of God's Lessons

We, like David, will face numerous and varied tests and trials when we find ourselves in the Season of Futility and Barrenness. David's season is covered in chapters 18–30 of 1 Samuel, but these chapters are so filled with people and events that a reader might miss the broader sweep of God's divine plan and purpose as He continues His molding and shaping of David into the person who was to be Israel's most godly and famous ruler.

I am going to use the remainder of this section to peel back the layers of people and events, so that we can focus on the lessons God was teaching David through the experiences of this season. Together we will see how indispensable the Season of Barrenness was in preparing David for the authority God would give him, and how the Lord uses similar experiences to help us grow and mature spiritually.

The Reason for the Season

This season, the one called Futility or Barrenness, is the period when God desires to impart something very powerful and magnificent into our beings. It may involve preparation for a significant change in life situation or ministry, or an experience to prove our faithfulness and perseverance in the face of great trials or a test to correct some key attitudes or habits we have acquired. Whatever God's reason, however, His ultimate desire remains constant: a far greater degree of Christlikeness in all aspects of our lives, and a much deeper and more intimate personal relationship with the Lord Jesus Christ, the Holy Spirit and Abba Father.

Rick Howard refers to this period in a believer's life as "the finding times of God" in his excellent book of the same title. He says that these "finding times are specific *kairos* moments in which God desires to bring forth a full expression of Jesus Christ in our lives."[1] (*Kairos* is a Greek word meaning a special period of time, a decisive point, thereby stressing the fact that it is divinely ordained.[2] The other Greek word for "time" is *chronos*; it means a period or extent of time, while *kairos* denotes the kind or quality of time.)

Beware of Complacency

Having gone through the Foundation Season, and perhaps having achieved some spiritual victories, we are tempted to relax. David certainly could have felt this way after defeating Goliath and receiving the applause and acclamation of the nation. Scripture, however, gives us a far different message. The writer of Hebrews, for instance, exhorts believers who have learned the foundational principles of spiritual living, "Let us go on to perfection [maturity]" (Hebrews 6:1).

Peter closes his second epistle with a command to Christians to "grow in grace and knowledge of our Lord and Savior Jesus Christ" (2 Peter 3:18). The Greek tense of the verb *grow* is a present imperative, meaning that this command is to be applied continuously and repeatedly in our own lives. In short, we are being told never to cease growing spiritually.

Christians are prone to the temptation of thinking that they have arrived and are mature once they have achieved some leadership position in their churches or Christian organizations. We should desire and pray for opportunities to serve the Body of Christ. But we frequently overlook the truth that the Lord is not so much interested in what we do but in who we are. *Being* should precede *doing*. As John Wesley remarked, "Commitment to the truth comes before commitment to the task."

Let's not ever suppose that we will someday graduate from the Lord's "College of Discipleship." Our graduation day will only occur when Christ takes us home to heaven. Our responsibility until then is to obey Jesus' exhortation in the parable of Luke 19:13—"Do business till I come." His words negate the erroneous belief that Christians get a kind of spiritual Social Security retirement package once they have reached a certain age.

A Good Beginning

The young shepherd entered his new season on a high note, as we are told in 1 Samuel 18. Jonathan, the crown prince, struck up a deep friendship with him (see verses 1, 3, 4). King Saul took David into the palace (see verse 2) and made him leader of his army (see verse 5). David did not let his newfound fame go to his head, moreover, but demonstrated his godly character by wise and prudent behavior. Therefore, it is not surprising that both the general populace and Saul's own retinue regarded David very favorably (see verse 5).

Yes, everything appeared to be going extremely well for David. As we see him in these days immediately after his victory over Goliath, we might be inclined to say that he seemed ready to assume the kingship of the nation. His only possible drawback would appear to have been his relatively young age, and students of history know that it was not uncommon in those ancient times for young men of David's age to be elevated to the position of king or pharaoh.

But the Lord knew David still needed a much longer and more intense period of training and learning before he would be fit for the role of king. It is certainly true that God had laid a remarkably strong foundation in David's life. Now, however, was the season to begin building upon that foundation. Little did this teenager realize how long the Lord's construction project in his life would take. Nor could he foresee that it would bring him into one of the deepest and darkest valleys of his life. Though the sky over him was blue and the sun bright at the moment, a massive storm was fast approaching.

As I write these words, I am reminded of the weather in Chicago on January 26, 1967. The day was unseasonably warm, with temperatures reaching into the 60s on the Fahrenheit scale. People shed their winter clothing and walked around as if it were springtime. Unnoticed by many, however, an unusual set of atmospheric conditions was already developing and moving toward the city. This weather pattern arrived the next day and Chicago experienced the heaviest one-day snowfall in its history. Nearly two feet of white blanket fell, and it virtually shut down the metropolitan area for the next few days.

David was about to discover not merely one storm but a whole season of storms. The change in the spiritual weather of his life began slowly, and it began with Saul. This stormy season would build and build until it reached a crescendo of trials such as few people in the Bible had ever experienced.

The Most Difficult Season of All

Before we follow David through this very difficult and trying season, let's first analyze David's spiritual growth and maturity to this point in time. This assessment will help us to better understand God's purpose when He takes us into this kind of season. Consider everything the Bible has revealed to us about David up to this moment when he is entering this new season:

- He was always obedient to his parents.
- He spent much time alone with God.
- He avoided sibling rivalry and arguments.
- He demonstrated his great faith and trust in God through his battles with wild beasts and Goliath.
- He behaved modestly and wisely, both when anointed by Samuel and after vanquishing Goliath.

In short, Scripture does not mention any significant flaw in David's character during these years. Talk about the model child! What parents would not be pleased if their children displayed the same behavior and virtues as young David? Notwithstanding these accomplishments and his many admirable qualities, David was still under construction by the Lord.

It is important to understand that the onset of this season in our lives is *not* caused, in most instances, because we have some sin problem in our lives. Quite the contrary. The Lord will usually take us into this period *because* we have been faithful to Him! Follette emphasizes this truth:

> Proving and testing may befall us without our being any personal or direct cause of it. Many times it is quite beyond our control. If it were otherwise we would probably avoid all such testing and keep an easy path. Let us remember it is all part of the divine arrangement and has a place in our program as well as the hours of sunshine and music. Trouble or severe testing is not necessarily a sign of sin, failure, or lack of spirituality. It is often a sign of spiritual life and growth which God must test and prove. We are His workmanship.[3]

God may take us through trials because He wants to bring us out of a time of spiritual complacency, or even stagnation. Like the church at Ephesus in Revelation 2, we may subconsciously begin to "lose our first love" with Him (see verse 4). Or God may simply want to prepare us for some unique and significant position or purpose He desires to give us in the future! You may be tempted to downplay this possibility, believing that your age, lack of education or other limitations will preclude the Lord from ever choosing you. How often we limit God by focusing on our lack of ability while ignoring "the God for whom nothing is too hard!"[4] The well-worn phrase used in so many Sunday school classes and sermons is still worth repeating here: "God is not so much interested in your ability as in your availability."

A number of years ago my wife and I attended a couple of Bill Gothard's seminars, at which he passed out buttons carrying the acronym *PBPGIFWMY*. This strange grouping of letters stood for the slogan "Please be patient, God isn't finished with me yet." God was far from finished with David at this point in time, and if you are still breathing as you read these lines, He is not done with you either.

The goal of a Christian's life should be to find and follow God's will for his or her life, even though that path may take the person through great difficulties and worldly misfortunes. The reason? Because only in God's perfect will can any of us find true success.

How easily and often Christians get sidetracked! Instead of finding our fulfillment in God and His plans for our lives, we search for satisfaction by adopting the world's outlook and methods. Spending great chunks of our precious earthly existence striving for the four Ps (prosperity, pleasure, power and popularity), we realize only too late these goals are like mirages in the desert. One unknown writer summed up the futility of this worldly search by observing, "I've never heard anyone on his deathbed saying, 'I wish I had spent more time at the office.'"

Long and Longer

The second reason this season can prove to be such a difficult one is the time factor. This period of futility and barrenness can be a very lengthy one. It is never measured in days, very seldom in weeks, sometimes in months but usually in years. If you have experienced this particular season, you know that it seemed as if it would never end, and possibly would continue until Jesus came.

David may well have felt this way. Scholars estimate that he probably was seventeen or eighteen years old at the time his troubles with Saul began. If this is true his Season of Futility and Barrenness lasted some twelve to thirteen years, until the time when he was anointed king over Judah at the age of thirty (see 2 Samuel 5:4).

Countless men and women of faith have been called by God to persevere through times of seeming futility and barrenness. Consider Noah, Abraham and Sarah, Joseph, Joshua and Caleb, Ruth, Hannah. The list goes on and on.

A Final Word

Near the beginning of this section we discussed the danger of having wrong expectations, so let's conclude by visiting this significant topic once more. Because the Season of Barrenness and Futility usually proves to be the most difficult one in our spiritual lives, it carries a hidden danger. Believers are prone to allow their relationships with God to weaken and sour when they find themselves undergoing the tests and trials of this period. We must consciously avoid any tendency either to criticize God or become bitter toward Him when we are in this season.

Perhaps the most important thing we can do when we are in this Season of Barrenness is to let go of our expectations. We frequently want the Lord to change our circumstances, while His desire is to change us first.

So if we find ourselves in the midst of this particular season, remember His promises in Isaiah 43:2:

> When you pass through the waters, I will be with you; and through the rivers, they shall not overflow you. When you walk through the fire, you shall not be burned, nor shall the flame scorch you.

This verse says God is for us, not against us—and the key to this whole passage is the word "through." The floods and the fires are not our final destination! God may take us, like David, through the valley of the shadow of death, but He will be with us all the way and eventually lead us out into a time of glorious blessing and victory.

11

WHEN THE GOING GETS TOUGH

Amerian football coaches are notorious for using slogans to spur their teams to practice and play harder, to strive with greater effort for victory. One popular slogan of years ago was the phrase "When the going gets tough, the tough get going." Christians would be well advised to remember these words, because the Bible's heroes of faith were willing to persevere through tough times, against great odds and in the midst of fiery trials.

As we look at David's life during this season, the unjust persecution, the constant dangers, the loss of friends and family, rejection and betrayal by those he helped and the lonely fugitive existence he was forced to live may lead some to question the mercy and love of God. "David was innocent! Why did God allow him to go through such terrible times?" Rick Howard offers a succinct proposition as an answer to these kinds of questions:

> God's activity upon us—the trials, the circumstances, the leadings, even the judgments of God—is the guarantee, the evidence of the value He places in us and the ultimate intention He has for us.[1]

110

Let me pose a question to those readers who are parents or grand-parents: In the process of raising your children, are you now or were you then willing to allow them to continue in immaturity, to retain childish habits and outlooks and to avoid the necessity of taking on more responsibilities and duties as they grew older? Did you shelter them from every possible disappointment, trouble or hurt? No? Well, neither does God with His children!

God's ultimate intention was nothing less than to make David into Israel's greatest king. This process required two elements. First, much time and many trials were needed. As shown throughout this book, spiritual maturity cannot be developed quickly or easily. Second, the ways David responded to God's dealings with him were crucial to his spiritual growth.

This last point is vitally important for us to understand. People often say, "Difficulties, problems and struggles will make you a stronger Christian." That is wrong; they will not by themselves make you stronger. The key is our willingness to walk daily in faith toward God, trusting Him to guide and sustain us through every one of life's situations. Only this kind of scriptural attitude and outlook will enable us to reap the spiritual benefits such events and circumstances can bring us.

Principle #6: **Our response to God's dealings with us will determine our degree of spiritual growth and maturity.**

The children of Israel faced numerous trials and difficulties in the wilderness, and they failed nearly every test. They never proved willing to act in obedience to God's word and His appointed leadership. Instead they fell into unbelief and fear, constantly grumbling and complaining and giving themselves over to despair and hopelessness. As a result they all died before reaching the Promised Land, except for faithful Joshua and Caleb.

As we face the vicissitudes of life it is important for us to always respond in a Christlike manner as David did, rather than reacting out of fleshly emotion as the Israelites were prone to do. We have already seen how David responded both to fame and honor. The question before us today is, Are we responding correctly to the experiences, both good and bad, of our lives?

The Troubles Start

David was entering into a long series of harder times and more battles than he had ever known or could ever have anticipated. This period lasted for a considerable time, a dozen years or so, and it often must have seemed as long as a lifetime to this young man.

When we read the accounts of the Bible's great men and women we are sometimes handicapped by the fact that we already know the ending of their stories. Noah and his family are vindicated because the flood really does occur and they are brought safely through it. Joseph is miraculously freed from thirteen years of slavery and overnight becomes the prime minister of the world's most powerful nation. Abraham and Sarah produce the child of promise in their old age. Joshua and Caleb survive the long years of wilderness wandering to reach their inheritance in the Promised Land.

But consider how you would have felt if you had been in their places *before* God completed His plans for them. Imagine your uncertainties and fears as you debated whether or not you had really heard from God. Think of the discouraging thoughts trying to invade your soul and spirit as the months and years passed and God's promises and answers failed to be fulfilled in your life.

One of the most difficult places to be is in the middle of a miracle, and that is exactly where David found himself! God had promised him the kingship of the nation of Israel through the anointing and prophecy of Samuel. Yet as the weeks following this event turned into months and the months into years, the fulfillment of this promise may have seemed to slip further into the distance and grow fainter with time.

David's Season of Barrenness began when King Saul heard the women extolling David's great accomplishments while seemingly giving much less honor to his own victories in battle (see 1 Samuel 18:7). Such praise would have caused only a bit of envy and jealousy in most people. In Saul's case, however, this event triggered a vicious anger. He started to become insanely jealous and fearful of David.

Saul's reaction should not be surprising in light of several earlier happenings in his kingship:

- His disobedience to God's specific commands
- Samuel's pronouncement that none of Saul's descendants would succeed him as king and that the Lord had rejected him as king and had selected another man to replace him
- Saul's loss of God's anointing on his kingship and the influence of evil spirits on his life[2]
- His signs of mental instability

Saul's swift and awful plunge from being selected and anointed as Israel's first king (see 1 Samuel 10:1, 6, 9) to the tormented, dangerous and demonized man pictured in chapters 18–31 is a vivid and awesome reminder of the terrible power sin and rebellion can have on a person's life.

His secret envy and jealousy soon boiled to the surface and he set out on a course to destroy David. First Samuel 18:10–11 describe the first of several attempts he made to kill David; two times it involved Saul's hurling a spear at him. But with God's obvious divine protection, David escaped unhurt.

David's reaction to these two attacks is, in fact, remarkable. He continued to serve the king and, as we shall see, continued to suffer many future ordeals at Saul's hand. Yet he never struck back, even when he had the opportunity.

What enabled David to respond in such a self-controlled and composed manner? The answer is provided by an often-repeated phrase running through the Bible's account of David's life. It states (with some variations), "The Lord was with him."[3] We could expand this phrase to say, "The Lord was with him because he was with the Lord."

Demotion

When Saul's two direct attempts on David's life failed, he began to use more subtle means to attack him. First he demoted David from leadership of all the king's men of war to the rank of captain over only a part of his army (see verse 13). The king clearly intended this to humiliate David and demean him in the eyes of the army and the general population. But notice what happened. David "behaved wisely in all his ways" (verse 14). The word *wisely* means he acted in a prudent and circumspect manner, using good common sense and, most importantly, demonstrating by his behavior "a life conformed to the character of God."[4] Saul's plan backfired as a result. Verse 16 tells us that the entire nation expressed their love for this young man in spite of the king's actions.

Have you ever been demoted from a job to a lesser position in the same company because of "office politics"? Have you ever been fired from a job, either fairly or unfairly? I have been demoted once and fired twice. Such experiences can be confidence-destroying and humiliating, with emphasis on the word *can*. But they can also be an opportunity to trust the truth of God's promise in Romans 8:28: "And we know that in all things God works for the good of those who love him, who have been called according to his purpose" (NIV).

Defrauding

Next King Saul defrauded David by promising him the right to marry Saul's oldest daughter, but then giving her to another man (see verses 17–19). To defraud someone simply means to cheat him. This trait almost seems, sadly, to be the *modus operandi* of many people and companies. In years past Americans may have snickered at the corruption and bribery so prevalent in some third world countries. Now it is we who are beginning to experience this sickness, as we find more and more individuals and organizations whose words, services or products cannot be trusted. Why should anyone then be surprised to see our legal profession becoming such a growth industry?

By contrast, David did not call for a lawyer when his rights had been violated by Saul. Everyone in the Israelite army knew that the king had promised his eldest daughter in marriage to whoever could kill Goliath. This pledge was considered a great prize in the ancient world, since marrying the eldest daughter of the reigning monarch would place that person in line to be a potential heir to the throne. But David displayed no embarrassment or rancor at Saul's treachery.

Deception

When Saul discovered that his younger daughter Michal was in love with David, he next offered to make *her* David's wife. But behind his gesture lay an evil purpose. David was poor and could not give the king a suitable bride-price or dowry. Saul said David could satisfy this requirement by killing one hundred Philistines and bringing the proof to him.

The offer was a calculated suicide mission. By this subterfuge the king obviously hoped that David's love for Michal and his reckless bravery in combat would result in the young man's death (see verse 25).

God thwarted Saul's plans once again. David brought back evidence that he had killed double the number of enemy troops Saul had requested. The king was trapped. He had no choice but to take the person he hated most and make him his son-in-law, a member of his own family! One almost has to chuckle over the way God continually frustrates the plots of evildoers.

David's Vanishing Support System

All of us have some degree of companionship and support from others—family members, friends, the ministers at church, co-workers, neighbors, teachers and so on. David, too, had his own support system, but God was about to allow circumstances to remove these supports from his life.

David's wife Michal was the first support to go. Saul's subtle plans had failed, so he now turned to attacking David directly. In fact, Saul sent soldiers to David's house with orders to kill him![5] Michal helped David to escape, but then lied to her father about the assistance she had given him, claiming that David would have killed her if she had not helped him (see 1 Samuel 19:11–17). Michal's lying may have saved her from Saul's murderous anger, but it produced serious consequences. If her lie was told to others, as it most likely was, it would have stained David's exemplary character. Furthermore Michal's false story probably increased the king's rage against David. Most importantly of all, Michal betrayed her relationship with her husband. It is probable David eventually heard of Michal's words; if so, it may help explain why the two never again came back together in sincere and honest love, even though David did have her brought back as one of his wives years later. So one major support in David's life vanished.

Next the young warrior escaped to the home of Samuel. Together they went to a place called Naioth, where Samuel had assembled a "school of the prophets," a group of young men who were being discipled by this great old man of God. David undoubtedly found a momentary time of peace and encouragement in Samuel's presence. This marked the last time he would see Samuel, as the Lord allowed another support in David's life to be taken away (see 1 Samuel 19:18–20:1).

The friendship between David and Jonathan is one of the most outstanding and noble found anywhere in the Bible. It began immediately after David slew Goliath and lasted their entire lives. The modern term *friendship* is wholly inadequate to describe the relationship between these two young men. They were not just friends; we are told in 1 Samuel 18:3 that they made a covenant. The Hebrew word for *covenant* carries the meaning of a treaty, pledge or compact in a deeper sense than these words imply in our modern world. David and Jonathan "placed under legal guarantee a spontaneous love which [demanded] self-commitment . . . thus supporting the deep friendship. It also makes it a legal fellowship with sacred guarantees [and] is contracted in the presence of God."[6] This was no casual or spur-of-the-moment pact but a profound, committed and caring relationship involving complete trust and unwavering willingness to sacrifice for the benefit of the other. Their individual, wholehearted commitment to the Lord provided the foundation for their unbreakable commitment to each other.

Some proponents and apologists for the gay lifestyle, citing 1 Samuel 18:1–3 where the text says Jonathan "loved" David, have argued that these verses prove their relationship was a homosexual one. Here is a prime example of how people can twist Scripture to make it appear to support their own humanistic desires.[7] Schultz and Youngblood are two highly recognized Old Testament scholars who decisively refute such arguments. A brief summary of their analyses can be found in this endnote.[8]

David and Jonathan were open, honest and vulnerable with each other. Neither one wore a mask; both were willing to share their deepest feelings. One writer in discussing David's leadership says, "All men, and especially leaders, hide behind masks. . . . It takes an even greater leader to set the mask aside. The Psalms show that David knew how to take off his mask."[9]

Now each young man found himself caught on the horns of a dilemma, yet neither acted in a self-seeking or ungodly manner. While David was sorely grieved and greatly perplexed by Saul's mad behavior, he never displayed anger or hatred toward the king, nor did he allow it to negatively affect his deep friendship and feeling for Jonathan. Jonathan found himself pulled between his commitment to and love for his father and his new covenant with David. Despite Saul's rage against his son and his mad, precipitous attempts to kill David, Jonathan never abandoned his father or rebelled against him, and eventually died with him battling the Philistines. His life demonstrated his true obedience to God's command to "honor thy father."

When Jonathan and David parted, they reaffirmed their covenant, not merely to each other but to their descendants as well. But Jonathan's companionship now was becoming a thing of the past. They would meet only one more time. So another human support was being pulled away from David.

Away from Home

Throughout these days of running from Saul, Scripture never mentions David going back even momentarily to his home and family in Bethlehem. Perhaps he knew that Saul would expect him to do just that, and so he would place his family in danger if he attempted to return to them. Whatever the reason, David was separated from his family and his boyhood surroundings. And even though his family's treatment of him may have been lacking in love and acceptance, Bethlehem still represented his home territory.

What happens to people when the things that have helped sustain them are suddenly pulled away, when they find themselves almost alone facing the major problems of life? They can begin to react irrationally. David's life up to this point had been the biblical model of "how to live wholly for God." Now as chapter 21 opens, he changes character almost overnight and starts to behave like an unbelieving, fear-ridden fugitive.

The Bible makes no mention that David sought the Lord for help at this critical juncture. David seems rather to have forgotten the vital lesson he had been taught during his lonely shepherding years: that he was to put his trust in the Lord and not in man for his ultimate safety and success. The Lord may give us spouses, children and fellow Christians to help support and assist us. But we are not to exclude God from our lives by depending solely on them or our own efforts.

David is suddenly shown allowing his carnal self to dominate his thoughts and actions. He begins by resorting to human means and trickery to save himself. First he goes to the town of Nob where a large company of priests lived. He lies about the true nature of his being there in order to get food and weapons. The priests innocently believe his story and assist him (see 21:1–9). Saul is told later what they did and, in his demented mental state, accuses them of being in league with David and has them all executed, including their families—wives, children and livestock (see 22:9–19). David's lies led to the deaths of many people, while he himself escaped unharmed.

Then David becomes even more irrational and he flees into Philistine territory, to the town of Gath. Gath was the hometown of Goliath! What could have possessed David to put himself in the very midst of the enemy's camp? Not surprisingly he soon hears some of the people talking about him as the next king of Israel and the person who has killed many Philistine warriors. David then comes to his senses all at once and recognizes the dangerous situation he has gotten himself into.

At this point he once again turns to the Lord for deliverance and safety, as shown in the two psalms (34 and 56) he wrote about this incident. David testifies throughout these psalms of God's swift response to his cries for mercy and help. The Lord enabled David to devise and carry out a cunning plan of escape. He pretended insanity by his behavior; he "scratched on the doors of the gate, and let saliva fall down on his beard" (21:13). People in Old Testament times pitied and were in awe of mental illness and insanity, attributing it to the work of gods and evil spirits.[10] Consequently the king and people of Gath refused to harm David, believing he really had become mad. By this subterfuge, he was able to leave the Philistines' territory.

David's journey led him to find a hideout in a cave near Adullam, a town located some ten miles southeast of Gath (see 22:1). A cave does not provide the most pleasant living conditions. Caves are dark, often damp, have rocky and uneven interiors and usually harbor undesirable wildlife.

But caves were God's provision for David and his entourage, not only at this time but also later when he moved to the wilderness of En Gedi (see 1 Samuel 23:29). Caves offer shelter from the elements and can be cooler in summer (and warmer in winter) than the surrounding landscape. The caves in this region, with their usually small entrances and interlocking passageways, would also have been both easy to defend and easy to escape from if necessary.[11]

While the Lord promised David protection from harm and deliverance from enemies, He did not guarantee him five-star living accommodations and *haute cuisine*. Similarly, Christians today do not have an inalienable right to first-class treatment in this world, despite the claims of certain hyper-prosperity proponents.

Here then is David, running for his life from Saul, having lost nearly all of his earthly support, and forced to live in a harsh wilderness area.

The Bible presents us with a window into David's spirit at this time, since we know that he probably wrote Psalms 57 and 142 during these trying experiences. In these two Scripture passages David desperately pleads for God's mercy and rescue from the dangers surrounding him. Along with his cries for divine intervention, though, David expresses his hope and trust in the Lord's eventual answer.

An Unexpected Answer

Have you ever noticed how God sometimes responds to our prayers by sending the answer in a way we do not expect or like? Well, David had a similar experience at this time. God did answer his prayer, but probably not in the manner the young fugitive had hoped for. Shortly after David had settled into his new hiding place, his father's household left Bethlehem and joined him in hiding. Perhaps this move was dictated by the family's fear concerning Saul's hatred of David. Since the king had been frustrated in his attempts to reach David, conceivably he could have turned his rage upon Jesse and his clan. So David now had a number of new people demanding shelter, food and protection.[12]

David's relations were not the only ones who came to his hideout. According to 1 Samuel 22:2, four hundred men and their families also arrived at Adullum to join forces with David. And what a group they were! The Bible describes them as being either in "distress" (under great external pressure, in serious straits),[13] or in "debt" (had harsh creditors like our modern "loan sharks")[14] or "discontented" (bitter, discontented with Israel's leadership).[15]

The Bible presents us with the picture of a young man almost overwhelmed by the stress of numerous adversities. Yet we see the Lord suddenly send him his family plus four hundred more problems! Was God being unkind and unjust to poor David? If you and I were in David's sandals at that moment, we might have been tempted to say to God, "Lord, why did you bring me this bunch of dissatisfied, debt-ridden, bitter malcontents? Haven't I got enough difficulties as it is?"

A Right Response

David showed great wisdom in not becoming angry or depressed. He was about to learn one of his most valuable lessons from the Lord: the importance of people to your success. In one of his books on leadership, John Maxwell urges leaders to "develop your most appreciable asset: people," and says one of the key principles to developing people is our attitudes and assumptions toward them—in essence, how we value them. "People tend to become what the most important people in their lives think they will become."[16]

David learned and applied this lesson incredibly well. How do we know this? Look at the results. It was from this unpromising and unlikely group that David developed perhaps the finest military force of all time—the ones Scripture calls his "mighty men." Their individual deeds and exploits were almost beyond belief.[17] And as leaders in the Israelite armies, they helped David to extend the territory and power of the nation to the greatest geographical extent in its history.[18]

This transformation did not happen overnight, however. Much time and effort were required on David's part, but through this long and laborious process David gained more than the magnificent army he would need to carry out God's future plans for Israel. This ragtag band of misfits forced David to learn the leadership skills he would never have acquired had he been the general over a group of fully trained professional soldiers.

A true leader must develop and employ a variety of attributes if his leadership is to be really effective. At various times a leader may have to be a teacher, trainer, exhorter, encourager, problem-solver, delegator and visionary. He should be a person with self-discipline, integrity and the ability to set right priorities. David learned thoroughly these lessons of leadership as his troops developed both their proficiency as warriors and their traits of courage, commitment to David and Israel, and dedication to God.

Leadership principles and character cannot be learned and developed merely by reading a book. Nor can they be acquired in isolation. Marshal Shelley concludes:

> Developing Christian virtues demands other people—ordinary, ornery people. True love isn't even learned among friends we have chosen. God's kind of love is best learned where we can't be selective about our associates.[19]

Although David came from a common, ordinary background, these people helped him to see and hear the problems, complaints and aspirations of Israelite citizens in a way his boyhood experiences on the isolated hillsides of Judea never allowed. He gained a broad and deep understanding of the people he would one day serve as king, and this knowledge would prove invaluable in the future seasons of his life.

A Very Important Trait

As noted several times in this book, one of David's most consistent and outstanding traits was his willingness to be teachable. David was able to learn from his mistakes throughout his life, to listen carefully to friends and critics alike and to pay special attention to the prophets God sent his way. So when the prophet Gad advised him to leave Adullum (see 1 Samuel 22:5), David immediately obeyed, even though the move was a difficult one, considering the number of people involved. He understood that God can and does use other people to bring us spiritual direction and insight, even to a person like himself who enjoyed such intimate fellowship with the Lord.

Sadly, some long-time Christians allow themselves to become the "Frozen Chosen." Having spent a lifetime in regular church attendance, Sunday school, Bible reading and study, these veteran saints can too often project an attitude of "I've heard it all and learned it all, so don't try to teach me." Not only can these people make life miserable for pastors, particularly younger ones, their rigid spiritual mind-sets can lock a church into the deadly rut of unbreakable tradition, especially if they are in positions of lay leadership.

More Betrayals

The Philistines, ever the opportunists, took advantage of the division between Saul and David, and of Saul's increasingly apparent irrational behavior, to attack an Israelite border town called Keilah and rob them of their harvest (see 1 Samuel 23:1). David heard the news and asked the Lord if he should go to their rescue (see verse 2). God said, "Go." David's four-hundred-man army, however, was afraid of such an expedition (see verse 3), so David once again asked counsel of the Lord, and once again received God's assurance that he would be victorious (see verse 4). This double assurance from the Lord must finally have convinced the men. David was able to lead them into battle where they achieved complete victory, including capturing much spoil from the Philistines. This victory was noteworthy because it marked the opening stage in the long, steady development of David's untrained, unruly band into the famous, formidable fighting force we still marvel at today.

When news reached Saul concerning David's whereabouts, he determined to go to Keilah and capture him. David discovered the king's plans and once more sought God's counsel. In response to David's prayers, God told him Saul would come against Keilah and the inhabitants of the town would hand him over to the king (see verses 10–12). So David and his men left the city, and when Saul heard that he had gone, he and his army returned to their headquarters.

What a tragic situation! Here was a community whose people and property had been saved from destruction by a brave man. Yet they callously turned on this man in order to help their own self-interests with a mad king. Before condemning the residents of Keilah, though, recognition should be given to a similar kind of action that many Christians perform against other members of the Body of Christ. How is this done? By gossiping. Gossip can and does have a corrosive effect on the spiritual health of any Christian group. The numerous verses in Scripture condemning this practice and warning believers against it testify to this fact.[20]

This short Bible passage shows David's growth in more than one area. First of all, David sought the Lord at least three times during this episode. He had come out of the swamp of self-pity and depression in which he had wallowed during his Nob and Gath experiences. He once again realized the necessity for him to remain in continual, close fellowship with the Lord, even when his problem might appear small or the answer seem obvious.

Second, David exhibited no anger or rancor against the inhabitants of Keilah for their willingness to betray him. His response was due partly to his awareness that Saul would have wreaked devastation on that city if its citizens had helped him, just as the king had annihilated the priests and families at Nob (see 1 Samuel 22:18–19). But I believe that David's action also speaks of his attitude of forgiveness, forbearance and longsuffering. He was learning to place his hope and trust in God instead of people. This is a truth that many of us in the Church would do well to learn and remember. All too often Christian brothers and sisters will disappoint us or, like the people at Keilah, turn on us. Do not let the wrong behavior of other believers cause you to react in an angry and vengeful manner.

It is with good reason that the Lord counsels us in Jeremiah 17:5, 7: "Cursed is the man who trusts in man and makes flesh his strength, whose heart departs from the LORD. . . . Blessed is the man who trusts in the LORD, and whose hope is in the LORD."

After David left Keilah he moved his troops to the wilderness of Ziph, an area west of the Dead Sea. But the local inhabitants informed Saul of David's whereabouts, so the king gathered his forces and went after him. Just as Saul's army was positioned to encircle and capture him, an urgent message for help came to Saul: the Philistines had launched another invasion of Israel. The king was forced to break off his assault on David's camp and return to repel the Philistine attack.

David wrote Psalm 54 about this episode. These verses, along with 1 Samuel 23:25–28, bring out several wonderful truths. They reveal once again that David understood his ultimate safety and deliverance from Saul depended upon God's divine protection and not merely on his own strategy to escape capture. He furthermore did not seek revenge against these betrayers, fellow Israelites, but left them to God. As we saw in the previous section, David knew who his real enemies were. They were the Philistines and the other foreign foes of Israel, not the people of God. God's people were God's problem; He, and not David, had the responsibility of judging and dealing with them.

The Lord's timing in rescuing David was obviously miraculous. It clearly demonstrated that our God's answer always arrives at the right time, never too early or too late, and that He is able to use anyone, including His enemies, to achieve His purposes and plans.

Hunted by Authority

Having failed to capture David at Keilah, Saul launched a manhunt. During this time, however, 1 Samuel 24–26 records two instances where David had a perfect opportunity to *kill* Saul but refused to do so—much to the bewilderment of his troops!

Here is one of the major keys to David's spiritual growth and worldly success. He learned (by some means the Bible does not fully reveal) the importance God places on our attitudes toward authority. Since all earthly authorities are appointed by Him, they are to be honored and respected. John Bevere summarizes this scriptural instruction quite bluntly: "We must learn to honor—to revere, respect: to treat with deference and submission, and perform relative duties to—all who are in authority."[21] For David, this requirement included mad King Saul, the man who was attempting to kill him!

David's long and intimate relationship with his God and the presence of the Holy Spirit in his life undoubtedly caused him to understand with certainty the spiritual truth in this situation. Saul was still the Lord's anointed authority, despite his disobedience of God's commands and his murderous mind-set toward David. Since God had appointed Saul to be the ruler over Israel, only God could remove him from that position. David acknowledged these facts, knowing the Lord would do it in His way and in His time, when he said, "The LORD shall strike him, or his day shall come to die, or he shall go out to battle and perish" (1 Samuel 26:10). David's constant willingness to trust God in difficult circumstances like these was a dominant element in his life.

Other Christians may counsel us, or even urge us, to ignore or disobey the authority figures God has placed over us, just as David's troops did to him. But God holds us responsible for our attitudes toward His appointed people. Who are these authorities? The Bible clearly lists those we will be under at various stages of our lives:

- *Parents*—Exodus 20:12; Deuteronomy 27:16; Ephesians 6:1–3; Colossians 3:20
- *Family order*—Ephesians 5:21–24
- *Work*— Ephesians 6:5–8; Colossians 3:22–24; Titus 2:9–10; 1 Peter 2:18
- *Government*—Romans 13:1–7; 1 Peter 2:13–14
- *Church leaders*—Ephesians 4:11–12; 1 Timothy 5:17; Hebrews 13:17; 1 Peter 5:5

Christians in general are sadly ignorant of the basics of biblical authority. God is the ultimate source of all authority throughout the universe. In giving the Great Commission Jesus said, "All authority has been given to Me in heaven and on earth" (Matthew 28:18). So all earthly authority flows from the throne of God, and the Lord has delegated His authority to those men and women whom He has appointed to positions of leadership, whether those positions are great or small (see Romans 13:1). God calls those people He has appointed to positions of authority His "servants." This term includes all secular authorities.

Failure to honor and respect God's authority is a form of rebellion. When Saul flagrantly disobeyed God's command to him, Samuel boldly confronted the king and told him, "Rebellion is as the sin of witchcraft." Saul's rebellious spirit ultimately cost him the kingship for himself and his descendants, and eventually led to his death. The sin of rebellion is no small matter. Witchcraft is a doorway into the demonic realm. By rebelling against God's delegated authorities—not to mention His direct authority—Christians *can* open themselves to the influences of the devil.

It is particularly important for God's people to respect and honor church leadership. Jesus said in John 13:20, "Most assuredly, I say to you, he who receives whomever I send receives Me; and he who receives Me receives Him who sent Me." In fact, Scripture commands us to give twice the honor ("double honor") to those who serve in ministry leadership that we give to secular authorities (see 1 Timothy 5:17). Paul goes on to say this is to be done especially for those who labor in the word and doctrine (pastors).

These scriptural commands seem, sadly, to be ignored in large numbers of American churches. If that seems incredible, one has only to look at some of the recent statistics on our local churches, such as the data compiled by George Barna and his research group. Barna reports the average pastor is well-educated (sixty percent are seminary graduates), works more than sixty hours per week and has been in full-time ministry for seventeen years. Yet the "average compensation package is barely above that of a newly-degreed college student starting his/her first [entry level] job." Moreover, this pastor "has served at his current church for just five years."[22]

This last statistic tells me that the typical congregation is constantly searching for the "perfect" pastor (meaning one who will tell them exactly what they want to hear, regardless of whether or not it is God's will for themselves and their church). In discussing the overall condition of the U.S. Church, Barna cites "the spread of spiritual anarchy" as the cause for the diminished role and weakened impact of today's local churches.[23] This type of anarchy certainly exists where churches are continually changing pastors because some influential members claim they are not being fed or do not like the pastor's personality, method of leading the church services, his staff or his failure to wholeheartedly support their pet projects.

America is rapidly turning into a nation of rebels. People find it convenient to ignore God's Word concerning authority because it interferes with the modern mantras we hold so dear. "I demand my rights!" "Nobody's going to tell *me* what to do!" A bumper sticker I have seen on several recent occasions simply said, "Question authority!"

This mind-set is increasingly infecting the Church, but often in subtle ways. One example is our tendency to ignore Christ's spiritual authority structure. In the Kingdom of God, authority flows down through the spiritual offices He has provided and appointed for His Church—apostles, prophets, evangelists, pastors and teachers (see Ephesians 4:11–12). One or more members of a local church may be more gifted and anointed in certain areas than the pastor, but this does not give them authority over the pastor!

It would be irresponsible of me to end this discussion without advising caution in our approach to the issue of how a Christian should properly relate to authority. This subject is complex and difficult! David respected Saul's position of authority but could not continue to function under his leadership. In the same way some Christians may find themselves forced to leave a church because of a pastor who is not shepherding the flock but is hurting the sheep.

On the question of *obedience* John Bevere rightly notes:

> The Bible teaches unconditional submission to authorities, but does not teach unconditional obedience. Submission deals with attitude and obedience deals with what we are told. . . . The only exception in which we are not to obey authorities is when they tell us to do something that directly contradicts what God has stated in His Word. We are released from obedience only when leaders tell us to sin.[24]

An excellent scriptural illustration of this truth is found in Acts 5:17–32. In the same way, David refused to obey Saul's sinful wishes—to give up his life, family and calling to the throne—but he also refused to harm or speak evil of the king. David was learning that he could trust God to deal with Saul and to care for David's own "flock."

HIS PRICELESS
PROVIDENCE AND
PROTECTION

When we are in the midst of great struggles and trials, with one crisis following another, we have a tendency to think that God has abandoned us or is punishing us for some unknown reason. We think that perhaps these difficulties are due to some sin in our lives or that maybe we have missed God and gone down the wrong road or that maybe we just do not have enough faith. The truth is that God's providential presence and protection are always available.

God's Providential Protection—Part 1

First Samuel 25 presents the first of two stories demonstrating how God kept David from getting himself ensnared in a situation that could have compromised his integrity and reputation.

This episode started because David had a problem familiar to military leaders before the modern era: Where could he find adequate provisions for his troops? This problem is a particularly difficult one for guerilla forces, and David now had six hundred men and their families under his command. They could not stay in one place long enough to farm, so David was almost entirely dependent upon the generosity and good will of the local inhabitants.

David learned of a man named Nabal whom he had quietly helped in the past. He was a very rich man and a resident of the area where David and his army were hiding. David's troops had not only refrained from taking any of Nabal's flock over the past months, they had shown their goodness by protecting both his sheep and shepherds from the bands of robbers who roamed those wilderness regions. Nabal was in the process of shearing his large flock of sheep. This was a festive time, "when the profits were distributed and several days of celebration followed . . . [for] all those who had been involved in the care of the sheep."[1]

So David sent ten of his men to Nabal, giving them explicit instructions as to how to ask for food. They were to come in peace, politeness and humility, mentioning the protection David had provided his flocks, and encouraging Nabal to verify the truth of their statements from his servants. They left it up to Nabal as to what and how much should be given them. All in all, their approach and speech were the epitome of courtesy. Nabal, however, lived up to his name, which meant "fool." He flatly refused to provide David's men with any provisions, and then compounded his selfish and churlish answer with insulting comments about David.

David's response was immediate and ferocious. He armed four hundred of his troops and rode toward Nabal's home with the stated intention of killing Nabal and all the males in his household (see verse 22). Talk about an overreaction! Here is David who, despite being pursued for several long years by Saul, staunchly refused to retaliate against the mad king, even when presented with two unbelievable opportunities. But because he received a few thoughtless and offensive words from an oafish man, he set out at once to annihilate both this man and a number of innocent servants! His reaction was infinitely more foolish than Nabal's because David was "God's man."[2]

An Admirable Woman

At this highly dangerous and explosive time, God had prepared a woman to save David from the consequences of his precipitous and vengeful actions. Abigail appears only in this chapter (although her name is mentioned in five other scattered verses, which are genealogical). But even this brief report pictures her as one of the outstanding women in all of Scripture. As we read her story in this passage her godly wisdom and understanding in combination with her great beauty (see verse 3),[3] her creative and careful planning (see verses 18–20) and her faith, courage, tact and humility (see verses 23–31) all show her to be an extraordinary person.

Abigail hurried to intercept David before he reached her home. Upon seeing David, she prostrated herself on the ground and began to voice her urgent appeal. "Abigail's speech is a masterpiece of rhetoric, appealing not only to reason and the emotions, but also to her credibility."[4] She accomplished two remarkable things by her anointed speech. First she saved her household from almost certain disaster. Second and equally important, she was able to dissuade David from carrying out his hasty and needless plan of bloodshed. This intemperate act would have seriously stained both his conscience and reputation. Abigail helped him look into the future and evaluate the longer-term consequences of his proposed revenge. David's immediate response to her entreaties is another evidence of his sensitive heart toward the things of God. He recognized and acknowledged that Abigail was a messenger sent by the Lord to stop him from fulfilling his violent plan (see verse 32). David once more proved he had a teachable spirit by a demonstrated willingness to admit his faulty or sinful actions, repent when necessary and make the needed changes. This trait is sorely lacking in today's world. Perhaps it is one of the chief reasons we see so few "David types" in our churches.

This brief episode in David's life contains a significant lesson for each of us. Everyone will encounter several Nabals along the road of life. We need to be on guard spiritually and not allow their mean-spirited words and actions to cause us to react in like manner toward them.

This chapter shows vividly how quickly and easily even the most spiritual of us can slide into carnal and sinful behavior. Bob Mumford tells about one time he and his wife were driving to church for a prayer meeting. Suddenly another car cut in front of the Mumford's vehicle, dangerously close and without warning. Bob began at once to berate the other driver, and wished out loud that he could confront him personally and give him a piece of his mind. Mrs. Mumford rebuked him gently, "While you're doing that, why don't you invite him to the prayer meeting?"

Be sensitive to God's frequent use of other people to bring us His counsel and guidance. Christians are too often looking for some major event, miraculous occurrence, powerful public prophecy or dramatic dreams and visions for insight and direction. So do not be surprised if He sends the answer to your prayers in the person of a humble Abigail!

Was David's hasty and intemperate action caused by a lack of faith in God's ability to provide for his needs? If so, his attitude may appear surprising, considering all the miracles the Lord already had performed for David. Be mindful, however, that we, too, can fall into unbelief and fear when faced with a serious material need. Jesus' disciples reacted to their material lack when faced with feeding four thousand people in the wilderness. They asked, "Where could we get enough bread in the wilderness to fill such a great multitude?" (Matthew 15:33; Mark 8:4). Of course, the answer is, "We can't," but our Lord has maintained a well-stocked restaurant in the wilderness from the time of Moses until the present.

God's Providential Protection—Part 2

As chapter 27 of 1 Samuel opens, David has been a fugitive for almost a decade. These years of hiding have taken their toll on his faith and trust in God's promises. Verse 1 shows him giving himself over to hopelessness and despair, voicing the belief he never will attain the kingship prophesied by Samuel. As we look at David's sudden and surprising spiritual collapse, it should be a sharp reminder: "Therefore let him who thinks he stands take heed lest he fall" (1 Corinthians 10:12).

David exhibits two significant changes in attitude in the passage from 27:1 to 28:2. These two things help to explain his new behavior pattern. Verse 1 of this chapter reveals David's inner thoughts to us. He entered into failure by starting to focus on his situation from a strictly human standpoint. This perspective led him to invent his own reality, just as Saul had done years earlier. David had overcome Goliath because he measured that human giant against the omnipotence of his almighty God. Now, however, he permits his human reasoning and perspective to dictate his actions. He even avoids consulting the Lord because the idol of the human intellect has become his oracle.

David starts to concoct what he considers a clever and cunning scheme. He seeks to align himself with Achish, son of the king of Gath, a chief ruler of the Philistines. This is not a foolhardy move, politically speaking, despite the narrow escape he made from Gath a few years earlier. David knows that the present situation is quite different from his previous stay in this enemy stronghold. By this time the Philistines know about Saul's hatred of David and the king's attempts to kill him. So the Philistines no longer see David as the great Israelite warrior but as an experienced, independent fighter they might use to their advantage. In addition David brings with him a sizeable military force that the Philistines can employ as mercenaries (a common practice among the ancient Near Eastern nations).

David begins a series of deceptions, a chain of clever arrangements that he thinks will allow him to live free from real control by the Philistines. He persuades Achish that he can be trusted, calling himself Achish's "servant." Amazingly Achish believes David and gives him Ziklag, a country town on the southern border of Philistia. Thus, David and his troops and their families will be far away from the watchful eyes of the rulers in the royal city of Gath.

From Ziklag David and his men support themselves by raiding and pillaging the settlements of the Geshurites, Girzites and Amalekites, all of whom are enemies of Israel. By this stratagem, David enjoys the security of the Philistine territory but is able to assist the nation of Israel. Whenever he has to give a report of his activities to Achish, however, he tells him he was raiding the areas of southern Israel. Achish is extremely pleased by this news, thinking David's actions will cause him to be so hated by the Israelites that he will be his servant forever. In order to hide the truth, however, David is forced to kill every man, woman and child in the places he raids, so no survivors will be left to tell the Philistines what actually happened. In the meantime David's army acquires a considerable amount of plunder from these bloody expeditions.

His successes during these months may have led David to congratulate himself on his skill in "playing both ends against the middle" as the old saying goes. His maneuvers did allow David to be free from Saul's unrelenting pursuits, but the strategy was man's solution and not God's. Unknown to him, his human schemes and deceptions were bringing him closer and closer to the brink of disaster.

Consider how far David had backslidden at this moment:

- He had walked away from God's incredible promise of a kingship by allowing his carnal thoughts and reasoning to dominate him with feelings of hopelessness and despair.

- He deluded himself into believing he had successfully outwitted his enemies and was now secure and prosperous as the leader of a mercenary army. After all, hadn't he escaped once and for all from Saul, and hadn't he outfoxed the Philistines while fighting against Israel's enemies and acquiring large amounts of plunder?

- Scripture makes no mention of any attempt by David to seek the Lord throughout the sixteen months he spent with the Philistines. In view of the frequency with which he called upon God at other points in his life, this omission is striking. Scholars have, moreover, not attributed any of David's psalms to this period of time.

- His decision to ignore God's promise and do his own thing had a profound effect on the many hundreds of people who loyally followed him—his two wives plus his six hundred fighting men and their households (see verses 2–3). The world tries to tell us that our private, self-centered actions will not have an effect on anyone else. They are dead wrong! Charles Swindoll sets the record straight:

> You do not live independently of everyone else. When you make a decision that is wrong, when you choose a course that is not God's plan, it affects those who trust you and depend on you, those who look up to you and believe in you. Though innocent, they become contaminated by your sinful choices.[5]

David's deception proves so convincing that he eventually finds himself between a rock and a hard place. This dilemma arises when the Philistines decide to mobilize their forces for a new and powerful attack on Israel. Achish has been so pleased with David's seemingly loyal and effective service, he wants him and his six hundred men to be a part of the Philistine army as Achish's personal bodyguards (see 28:1–2)!

David cannot refuse Achish's order. To do so would reveal that his loyalties still remain with Israel and would undoubtedly cause the Philistines to turn on David and his entire retinue. But to fight on the side of the Philistines against his own people would irreparably wipe out David's right to the throne.

David's human cunning and cleverness are of no avail to him in this perilous predicament. He is completely trapped and helpless. Only one person can deliver him from this impossible situation. In his present situation, he seems alienated from God's presence and counsel. Still, the Lord, in His incredible and infinite mercy, comes to David's aid. In a situation filled with irony, He uses the enemies of Israel, the Philistines, to unwittingly intervene and provide David with a way of escape.

As the entire Philistine army assembles for battle against Saul's forces, their five kings become alarmed at Achish's plan of allowing David and his men to fight alongside their troops. They fear that David might betray them in the heat of battle and fight on the side of Israel (29:5–11). So Achish is forced to send David back to Ziklag.

We can only surmise about David's true intentions had he gone into this battle with the Philistines. Scripture is silent as to whether or not he had a plan to betray them and actually fight for Israel. So David found himself once more the outcast. He had used the Philistines for support at a critical juncture in his life, and now they had rejected him. But this latest rejection may have served as a wake-up call, causing David to realize that God had not forgotten him but was once again working behind the scenes on his behalf. Certainly only divine intervention could have extricated David from the perilous predicament he had so foolishly fallen into. As he pondered his truly miraculous deliverance, he may also have begun to realize how far he had walked from God's plan. David had experienced the sad results of trying to serve two masters, as Jesus taught a thousand years later (see Matthew 6:24; Luke 16:13).

David's failure is the same one responsible for causing many present-day Christians to get stuck in their own Seasons of Barrenness. Their failure certainly does not mean the loss of salvation or even the loss of God's love. Having been endued with a free will by their Creator, Christians can choose to quit in the midst of this or any other season the Lord brings into their lives. If they do, however, the point at which this occurs marks the stopping point in their spiritual growth.

Principle #7: **There is no such thing as standing still spiritually. Either you are growing in Christ or you are backsliding.**

Hitting the Bottom

The Lord had one final episode to confront David with, one last hard lesson to purify his heart and turn him completely back to trusting Him.

This episode is recounted in chapter 30 of 1 Samuel. As David and his six-hundred-man army approached Ziklag, they were horrified to discover the town burned to the ground and all their families and possessions taken captive (see verses 1–5). The Amalekites, repeating what they had done previously, took advantage of the absence of David's army as well as those of Israel and the Philistines and boldly raided the unprotected towns. David's troops were so distraught and grief-stricken that they actually spoke of stoning him to death—David, the man who had provided for them and their households ever since they came to him at the caves of Adullum, the man who had trained and molded them into a disciplined fighting unit! Such can be the price of leadership.

This event contains several lessons in spiritual warfare. The Amalekites represent our adversary, Satan. Like them he is always ready to attack us whenever he sees an opportunity. And like David's troops, Christians can become so emotional and irrational over Satan's attacks that they begin unjustly blaming their fellow Christians for being the cause of their troubles. The question is, At such times, how will we respond?

David's response marks a major watershed in his life and is a good example of how we should respond in the midst of a truly critical situation. David was indeed confronting his greatest crisis, his lowest point, the absolute nadir of his life. What was left to him? Just one thing, but it was the most precious and powerful thing David or any believer could have in a moment of crisis.

At this point of extremity Scripture tells us, "David strengthened [or encouraged] himself in the LORD his God (verse 6)."[6] Please notice that David did not gain this strength or encouragement through some kind of worldly "positive thinking" method. He found precisely what he needed "in the LORD his God [Yahweh]." The Hebrew name translated *Yahweh* is the Old Testament's *covenant* name for God, the God who will fulfill all His promises to His people, the One who "will never leave you nor forsake you" (Hebrews 13:5).

When Christians fall into sin or drift away from regular church attendance, prayer or Bible reading, they tend to become embarrassed or fearful of returning to the Lord when a crisis strikes. And Satan is, of course, quick to try to reinforce their feelings of shame and unworthiness. How foolish of us to become disconcerted or nervous over God's imagined response to our needs or to permit ourselves to buy into Satan's lies! David did not hesitate to go before the Lord, even though the absence of God's name throughout the Scripture passages covering his sojourn in

Philistine territory strongly suggests his fellowship with Yahweh during this period was haphazard at best.

The few moments David spent in precious, personal communion with his God in the midst of a horrible and hopeless situation marked a monumental and pivotal point in his life. David was about to enter a new season. The Season of Futility and Barrenness was ending, and the Season of Blessing was about to begin. It would encompass approximately two decades filled with some of the most glorious blessings any of the Bible's heroes of faith had ever enjoyed. This new season was to be so filled with miracles, honors and prosperity as to seem impossible to David's mind as he prayed to God at this moment, in the midst of the wreckage of his life.

The bottom line: Hold fast and stay faithful to the calling God has given you.

The Season of Barrenness Is a Season of Perseverance

Do you know what is one of the saddest and most serious mistakes a Christian can make in his walk with the Lord? It is giving up on—or never recognizing—the calling God has given to every one of us. It is allowing wrong thinking, or feelings, or people, or events or anything else to divert us from the wonderful plan God wants to work in our lives. One can only wonder how many believers have thrown away potentially life-changing blessings and opportunities from God because of one or more of these diversions. Only too late will many realize how much of God's true treasures they missed because they spent their time, energy and resources chasing after the mirages of the world. The well-known line from a poem by John Greenleaf Whittier speaks to this point:

> Of all sad words of tongue and pen,
> The saddest are these: "It might have been!"

Wrong thinking comes in many guises. One of the more prevalent involves the mistaken belief that God does not really have a specific divine plan for each of His people. Scripture refutes this notion in passages almost too numerous to quote. Rick Howard writes, "We were all put here for a purpose. The world should know that you lived. Something should be left of meaningful involvement in something that matters."[7]

You may never be called to be an ordained minister, but the Lord still wants to give you some vital ministry.

Wrong feelings can be even more dangerous than wrong thinking. Feelings of inferiority, worthlessness, unworthiness and low self-esteem are some of the most insidious dangers Christians ever face. One of the most frustrating problems facing many churches is the ongoing struggle to find, motivate and sustain the active participation of lay members for the many needed ministry jobs, whether serving in the infant nursery or teaching a Sunday school class. A reason churches frequently have difficulty in getting volunteers to serve is that people feel inadequate and inferior. The Bible, in contrast, from Genesis to Revelation consistently declares the value and worth of every human being. All of us were created in His image! Henri Nouwen observed, "Self-rejection is the greatest enemy of the spiritual life because it contradicts the sacred voice that calls us the 'Beloved.' Being the Beloved constitutes the core truth of our existence."[8]

Other people can add yet another wrinkle to the difficulties facing us. We should all be aware of how other people's wrong expectations can be an obstacle to living a committed Christian lifestyle. Jesus warned in Matthew 10:34–36 of the division and rejection His followers might expect even in their own households.

We are inclined to think of peer pressure as a matter largely confined to teenagers, and psychologists agree that teen culture exerts a strong group pressure. "In seeking popularity and acceptance, conformity to peer group ideologies, loyalties and standards is paramount."[9] But the social pressures adults face are no less real. A fast-growing attitude in our society demands that Christians confine their religious activities to Sunday mornings and not attempt to bring their ideas and philosophy of life into the public arena.

A popularly voiced criticism of Christians who give public testimony of their faith in Jesus Christ is "You're trying to impose your religious views on other people." The mix of politics and Christianity is particularly explosive. "Overt expressions of faith by elected officials can make some Americans uncomfortable . . . some worry frequent prayers [by public officials] mix with policy."[10] Of course, proponents (including public officials) of other lifestyles—radical feminists, homosexuals and so on—would never think of trying to inject their personal agendas into the public sphere!

The influence of events is perhaps the one diversion, more than any other, which keeps Christians from reaching the fulfillment of their divine callings. I am not talking about merely a single event but about a long series of events, and the events can be either good or bad. The thing that caused David the greatest problem and almost led him to abandon his call from God was the very long series of difficulties, dangers, distresses and disappointments he had to endure during the years chronicled in this section. I find it interesting that David and Joseph's Seasons of Barrenness each lasted approximately thirteen years. For Joseph this was the period from when he received a dream from God until the day he was called to interpret Pharaoh's dream. For David this period spanned the time between his battle with Goliath until his victory over the Amalekite raiders and the death of Saul.

David's Season of Barrenness meant more than thirteen years of running for his life, more than losing the companionship and support of loved ones and friends, more than rejection and betrayal and living as a fugitive. It meant thirteen years of perplexity and questioning about why he was being so persecuted; of waiting for God to fulfill His promise of a kingship; of crying out to God for help and deliverance.

The temptation to give up can be especially strong in the midst of a long period of what we consider to be futility and barrenness. When it appears God has temporarily forgotten you, when one test/trial/crisis follows another in almost faith-destroying succession, when the "heavens which are over your head [are] bronze, and the earth which is under you [is] iron" (Deuteronomy 28:23)—then each week in this season can seem like a month, every month like a year and a single year like an eternity.

Hang In There

At such times Christians can begin to ask the question "Lord, did You really call me to this place/ministry/church/job [take your pick]? Because as soon as I started into it, all hell broke loose!" This type of query comes from a faulty understanding of God's ways and of the spiritual realm in which we live. A good antidote to the questioning-and-quitting temptation is the realization that God's calling will *eventually* result in His blessing since

Principle #8: God's blessing does not automatically and immediately follow God's calling.

The time of victory, success and prosperity—all we hoped for—will come. Here is a spiritual lesson from a secular activity. Years ago I took up jogging for health and weight control reasons. Being a Type-A personality, though, I soon began to enter local 5K and 10K races, and eventually decided to try running a marathon. Consequently I discovered a couple of interesting things about this event. When you tell people you ran in a marathon (which is 26 and a fraction miles), invariably their first question is "Did you finish?" Seldom does anyone ask how long it took you to complete the race. Everyone I know who has run a marathon tried his hardest to complete it and avoid the embarrassing "DNF" designation.

What is "DNF"?

When newspapers print the results of everyone's position and time who ran in the marathon, those shown at the end of the listing have these three letters after their names. They mean, "Did not finish."

In viewing the condition of the Body of Christ today, it sadly appears that numbers of believers will eventually face the Lord with these letters summing up their Christian experience because they were unwilling to complete the spiritual seasons God planned for them. Our life in Christ is not meant to be a 100-meter dash, and too many of us become discouraged when we discover that we are in a spiritual marathon.

As this section has shown, David wavered in his faith and spiritual endurance on more than one occasion, including a moment when he came perilously close to giving up on God's promise of the kingship (see 1 Samuel 27:1–4). At times he demonstrated only too starkly his humanness by permitting his emotions to gain the upper hand and behaving as any carnal person would. Through God's mercy and grace, however, he never truly and completely walked away from His call. Most significantly, he proved able to put his hope and trust in the Lord at the very lowest point in his life (see 1 Samuel 30:1–6).

Many Christians know the Hebrew word *shalom* signifies "peace." While it does mean "absence of strife," the word actually carries a much fuller meaning. "The root meaning of the verb, *shalem*, better expresses the true concept of *shalom*: completeness, wholeness, harmony and fulfillment; implicit in the word is the idea of . . . fulfillment of one's undertakings."[11]

We are also too unfamiliar with the beautiful Song of Solomon. This short book is an unparalleled masterpiece picturing God's covenant love for His people. Solomon (the beloved) is a type of Christ, and his bride (the Shulamite) represents the Body of Christ. The passage 2:10–13 is spoken by the Shulamite, yet it could also mirror some of the thoughts David must have felt as God finally called him out of his winter of Barrenness into a spring of *shalom*.

> My beloved spoke, and said to me:
> "Rise up, my love, my fair one,
> And come away.
> For lo, the winter is past,
> The rain is over and gone.
> The flowers appear on the earth;
> The time of singing has come. . . .
> . . . Rise up, my love, my fair one,
> And come away!"

David would rise up and come away with his Beloved, the King of kings, into a Season of Blessing where he would begin his reign as Israel's greatest king.

FAVOR

The Season of Blessing
(1 Samuel 30:6; 2 Samuel 10:19; 1 Chronicles 10:1–19:19)

"Because there is no character development without suffering, suffering is a necessary preparation for rulership."

—PAUL E. BILLHEIMER

13

A MOMENT OF CRISIS

David's heart sank like a heavy stone inside him as his eyes surveyed the destruction of his home base of Ziklag. Everything was gone—wives, children, livestock, tents and household goods—everything. An acrid pall of smoke hung over the ravaged and deserted landscape; fires still smoldered among the piles of rejected items the raiders had burned rather than carry away.

The somber stillness began to be broken by the moans and cries of grief from his troops. Fierce warriors hardened by years of fighting, men who had been resolute in the face of uncounted dangers, who had ridden with death as their constant companion and witnessed the gruesome reality of warfare, started to sob uncontrollably, overwhelmed by a distress far deeper than any of them was able to bear. David, too, cried with them, stricken with an overpowering sorrow at the loss of his wives and family, all that was so precious to him. Never had Jesse's youngest son felt so despondent or so helpless in the face of unexpected tragedy. None of the many trials he had endured at the hands of Saul or the Philistines could begin to compare with this black moment.

Many minutes passed. The onlookers stood frozen like statues, letting their tears and moans gush from them, a dark river of utter and uncontrolled helplessness. Then slowly the tortured cries and unrestrained laments of hundreds of men began to subside. They had poured out their grief until they had no more

143

tears to weep. A strange silence came over the scene and a new mood started to arise among the hundreds of distraught men.

David noticed it first in the looks they directed toward him and in the snatches he was able to hear of their murmured conversations. He sensed a bitter undertone of vengeance gradually welling up among them. For a moment he could scarcely believe what was happening. Then the brutal truth struck home. They were actually blaming him for this disaster! And their bitterness did not stop there; they were even speaking of killing him! His own loyal troops—the outcasts whom he had taken in when they had nowhere else to go, the men he had trained and provided for and led to numerous victories over Israel's enemies—were now considering stoning him to death!

David had never experienced such a depth of despair. A fear unlike any he had ever known began to coil its tentacles around his mind and heart. At the same instant another unseen host moved into David's inner being. The Holy Spirit, who had come into his life fifteen years earlier when Samuel anointed him, gently but firmly nudged him to turn away from the scene before his natural eyes and look with faith toward the One who had always been his Shepherd. And so the distraught young leader began in silent prayer to earnestly and fervently petition his God:

> *Save me, O God!*
> *For the waters have come up to my neck.*
> *I sink in deep mire,*
> *Where there is no standing;*
> *I have come into deep waters,*
> *Where the floods overflow me.*
> *I am weary with my crying;*
> *My throat is dry;*
> *My eyes fail while I wait for my God.*
> *Those who hate me without a cause*
> *Are more than the hairs of my head;*
> *They are mighty who would destroy me,*
> *Being my enemies wrongfully.*[1]

David did not know how many minutes he spent praying to the Lord. But upon finishing he realized exactly what must be done next. He called for Abiathar the priest to bring him the ephod with the Urim and Thummin,[2] *a method of divine guidance he used only infrequently. Now was a time when the Spirit seemed to direct this means to know God's will.*[3] *David asked for very specific answers as he cast the sacred stones. Should he go after these marauders? Would he be able to find and defeat them if he did? The Lord answered clearly, unequivocally: "Pursue, for you shall surely overtake them and without fail recover all" (1 Samuel 30:8).*

Even as he gave thanks for the answers, he added one final plea: "A miracle, Lord; I need nothing less than Your miraculous hand upon me and this tragic situation." God did not fail His distressed servant, for He was about to perform not merely one but a series of miracles. The events that would transpire over the next few days would make this time one of the most remarkable of David's noteworthy life. They would mark his entryway into a phenomenal Season of Blessing.

David arose and called his troops together. They stood before him tight-lipped and sullen, their bitterness and anger clearly visible and close to bursting forth into violent action. The young leader began to speak slowly and firmly, his eyes traveling from one man to another, seeking to draw them bit by bit out of their pit of despair and wrath. David was aware that the words and phrases he was speaking were not coming from his own human intellect. They seemed to flow from a wellspring deep within him—words of hope and promise, phrases of faith and encouragement, statements guaranteeing certainty and success.

The angry countenances of his audience began to soften; glimmers of hope started to appear in some of their eyes. The Lord was intervening in a way David's son would report many years later when he wrote that God can sovereignly direct the heart of a king or any person just as a farmer directs and regulates the flow of water in an irrigation channel (see Proverbs 21:1).⁴ The rage, frustration and hopelessness of earlier moments were slipping quietly away. By the time David had finished speaking the six hundred–man army was persuaded to pursue the Amalekite raiders, determined that they would recover every member of their families and all of the stolen property. The first miracle had been accomplished.

"The spirit indeed is willing, but the flesh is weak," says Mark 14:38. David's warriors were already weakened by their three-day journey from the Philistine encampment at Aphek, a distance of some sixty miles from Ziklag. Because their home base had been destroyed, they had to begin their pursuit of the Amalekites with few supplies and no rest. As a result even the start of their pursuit proved too hard for many of the men. After they had traveled only ten or fifteen miles, one-third of them had to be left behind at the brook Besor. The remaining four hundred troops were then faced with a daunting journey of many additional miles through a harsh, trackless and unpopulated desert environment.

Traveling through a desert is not only taxing physically for both men and their animals, the lack of roads and absence of people makes it difficult to find the place for which you are searching. David had no way of knowing where the Amalekites had gone, and could have spent days in a fruitless hunt for their encampment, so God provided miracle number two. David's troops came suddenly upon a sick, half-dead Egyptian. The man had been without water and food for three days, and likely would have died in a few more hours had David's men not "happened" to find him when they did. They gave him water and nourishing food, and so were able to revive him. Then came the remarkable discovery: He had been a servant of one of the Amalekites and knew the direction this enemy host had taken and the probable location of their camp. When David wisely promised him safety, the Egyptian was able to lead the Israelites right to their campsite.

The third miracle occurred when David and his reduced army of four hundred reached the Amalekite encampment. As they looked down upon a vast sea of people, tents and animals, neither he nor his men voiced any anxiety or fear over the size and strength of the enemy compared to their own small, tired band of soldiers! Instead David and his men were able to carefully observe their enemies without being detected, because all of them were "eating and drinking and dancing" (verse 16), having a wild celebration over the plunder they had acquired not just from Ziklag but in raids on other settlements along the southern borders of Philistia and Judea. The Amalekites must have considered themselves safe from any counterattack by either Saul or the Philistines or David, since all of these armies were thought by now to be engaged in a great battle many miles distant.

David knew that his weary army would have to engage in a pitched battle with a large force of fierce warriors and, in the natural, such a prospect might have seemed insurmountable. But God fulfilled His promise to David and enabled the Israelites to experience a truth Isaiah would pen nearly four hundred years later: "They that wait upon the LORD shall renew their strength." The Lord had set the stage wonderfully for David, and he, in turn, exercised godly wisdom, resting his men and waiting until early dawn to launch a surprise attack.[5] This was the opportune time because the Amalekites were just starting to awaken and recover from their drinking and feasting, and so were from a military standpoint at their most vulnerable.

The Israelites attacked with a terrible fury and vengeance just as dawn was breaking. So great was the size of the Amalekite camp that the battle continued throughout the entire day (see verse 17).[6] Despite overwhelming odds, however, the army of David completely routed their foes until only four hundred of the enemy warriors remained alive and were able to escape—the same number as the total of the Israelite force. God's fourth miracle was to provide David with one of most phenomenal military victories in all of Scripture.

David miraculously recovered all the people and goods taken from Ziklag as the Lord had promised (see verses 18–19). Not a person or any of their goods was missing. But this was not all! He also acquired a great amount of additional plunder that the Amalekites had gotten from their raids on other areas ("David's spoil," verse 20).

Lessons from David's Example

Both during and after these events this "man after God's own heart" demonstrated several key spiritual qualities, traits important for today's Christians to emulate. David was faced with a critical choice when everything seemed lost. He could have given over to the temptation to wallow in despair and hopelessness. Instead he turned his attention away from his earthly problems and looked to the One he knew was able and willing to rescue him. David realized that faith is the catalyst that releases God's divine power. We, like David, will experience only as much of God's manifest presence in our lives as our faith permits. I have occasionally pondered how often Christians have given up just short of some great blessing God had been preparing for them. Thankfully David persevered and gained the glorious future that was just over his horizon.

Next he was willing to let the Lord lead him one step at a time. David had no idea where the Amalekites had gone, but trusted his Shepherd to guide him. How many people miss God's best because they are unwilling to fully trust Him, and instead demand that He show them the whole of their journey (or at least most of it) before they will agree to start?

Moreover, David displayed no fear or anxiety when he finally found the enemy encampment and saw how their size and strength greatly exceeded that of his own small group of tired soldiers. He simply stood on God's promise of both victory and a recovery of all the enemy had stolen. What was the reason behind his great confidence? He had learned many years earlier, as a young boy confronting the lion and the bear, that "the battle is the Lord's." It was a lesson he never forgot, but one we often do.

An Enduring Principle

David's lifelong spirit of generosity is shown by his actions after this battle. When the two hundred men who had remained behind at the brook Besor came out to welcome the returning four hundred warriors, some of the victors did not want to share the plunder with those who had stayed behind. David immediately exercised his stern and wise leadership, making a decision (which became a precedent) to allow everyone to share equally in the rewards of victory whether they had fought in the battle or remained behind with the supplies (see verses 23–25).

By this decision David established a principle that carries a vital spiritual truth. Just as this truth guided the attitudes and actions of the Israelite warriors throughout David's later battles, they should guide God's people (and especially His leaders) today. This truth involves the true cause of the victory. David realized that his triumph over the Amalekites had been the Lord's doing, so neither David nor any of his troops could claim the credit and honor for themselves alone. The spoils had, furthermore, been given to them by God (see verse 23) and they were merely His stewards; they could not claim that they owned these riches and could do with them as they pleased. David's decree is an Old Testament foreshadowing of a truth the apostle Paul set forth in 1 Corinthians 12: Each one of God's people is an important and necessary part of His Body, and this spiritual interrelationship demands that no one exalt himself at the expense of others. One member of the Body may stand behind the pulpit while another changes diapers in the infant nursery, but the Pulpit cannot say to the Nursery, "I have no need of you."

David was a "people person" over the entire course of his recorded life. He fulfilled many roles from his youth to old age. Yet in all of these life stages he remained first and foremost what he became while still a youth—a godly person with a shepherd's heart. He acknowledged the Lord as the Chief Shepherd, seeing himself called by God to eventually have the task of serving as His under-shepherd to the nation of Israel.

Dean Smith, the long-time coach of the men's basketball team at the University of North Carolina, was one of the greatest coaches of any athletic team in any era. In discussing the leadership style of this famous sports figure, David Chadwick made this observation:

> Why is Coach Smith such a successful leader? I believe it is because he cares first about people. They are his most important products. He knows

everything meaningful in life flows out of relationships, and he steadily refuses to manage people as things.[7]

The same and much more can be said about David! How different might the businesses, governments and churches of our country be today if their leaders were motivated more by concern for those under them than by personal aggrandizement? Mike Royko, a well-known columnist for a Chicago newspaper a number of years ago, often took shots at the less-than-honorable antics of that city's politicians. On some of these occasions, he wrote (tongue in cheek) that the Latin motto on the city seal should be changed to read "*Ubi est meum,*" which he said meant, "Where's mine?" All too often the actions of our leaders in government and business, and (sadly) even some in the Church, would lead us to believe these words really do express their personal agendas.

14

PUTTING GOD FIRST

D avid's Season of Blessing lasted approximately two decades. During these years lay a life filled with such a wide-ranging array of people, activities, decisions and battles that it would take many chapters to adequately review them all.

Consequently the remainder of Section 5 will focus only on what I see as the main themes of David's career during these years. I chose to include the events I did because each one illustrates an important aspect of David's walk with the Lord and provides some key spiritual insights and applications for present-day Christians.

These events have been sorted topically into the three main themes of David's life, and we will not always discuss them in chronological order. You will, therefore, find it helpful to read chapters 1–10 of 2 Samuel and chapters 10–19 of 1 Chronicles before continuing through the rest of this present chapter.

An Extraordinary Era

Three great themes characterize David's life during this Season: his constant effort to put God first, his godly kindness and his willingness to work hard and fight for what God had promised him. At the forefront of David's life was a sincere and wholehearted devotion to his Lord. Certain of his attitudes and actions during this period are truly noteworthy, especially in contrast to the normal "Christian" way of doing things. In each of these events he demonstrated his love for, and obedience to, the Lord in a manner that emphasizes that he put God first in his life.

> The great characteristic of David, brought out especially in his Psalms, is the reality and nearness of his fellowship with God. We may find other men who equaled him in every other feature of character—who were as full of human sympathy, as reverential, as self-denying, as earnest in their efforts to please God and to benefit men. But we shall find no one who lived so closely under God's shadow, whose heart and life were so influenced by regard to God, to whom God was so much of a personal Friend, so blended we may say, with his very existence.[1]

Just three days after returning to Ziklag, David learned of the Philistines' triumph over the Israelite army and of the deaths of Saul and Jonathan (see 2 Samuel 1:1–12). Scripture shows David to be deeply grief-stricken, as are his troops, because all of them know only too well what this defeat means for their nation—a great loss of both life and territory, as well as the shame and humiliation it will enable the Philistines to heap upon Israel. David and his men have lived for years as outcasts, but they still see themselves as an integral part of "the house of Israel" (see 2 Samuel 1:12).

Just as God's heart must have been grieved over Saul's tragic end and Israel's defeat, David's heart is likewise saturated with sorrow. In response he writes one of the most moving laments found anywhere in the world's literature: the Song of the Bow, eulogizing the greatness in both his soulmate, Jonathan, and in Saul, the man who sought to kill him. David's attitude stands in vivid contrast to the sorry behavior of some believers today, who almost seem glad when a minister or ministry they dislike fails. How easily we forget Paul's admonition concerning the Body of Christ: "And if one member suffers, all the members suffer with it" (1 Corinthians 12:26).

Putting God First—Making Plans and Decisions

When David's time of mourning over the deaths of Saul and Jonathan ends, he begins to consider what his next course of action should be. It seems that the most reasonable step would be to establish himself in a major Judean town. There are a couple of reasons why this move looks to be the obvious and logical one: David is from the tribe of Judah and tribal loyalties are very strong during these years; moreover, he and his army had helped to protect some of Judea's southern territory during his fugitive years. So such a plan *seems* to be the right choice, the one that could provide David with the greatest advantage on his road to the kingship.

This man after God's own heart does not, however, place his reliance upon human reasoning and start marching to Judea the next morning. He understands a divine truth his son Solomon will pen many years later, a truth he has lived by since his shepherding times and will continue to follow for the rest of his life: "There is a way which seems right to a man, but its end is the way of death" (Proverbs 14:12).[2]

David demonstrated throughout nearly all the years of his life a fervent desire to be led by God, and this moment is no different. Before anything else he begins with prayer and petition, seeking divine counsel and direction. What a contrast to the way we sometimes try to make decisions and solve problems! Prayer and seeking God's will often seem to be the Method of Last Resort. Only after trying everything else without getting the desired results do we finally begin to think, "Maybe we ought to pray about it." One Bible commentator makes this observation concerning our willingness to honestly seek and obey the Lord's guidance.

> Most of us say we want to be led but we don't want God to show us His will; we simply want Him to confirm our will. When God sees that we really want to be led, then He will lead.[3]

Notice also how David *first* seeks God's will before attempting to make any decision. Only then does he feel the freedom to go up to Hebron. This is the scriptural type of approach to divine direction.

> When a goal, plan, or idea begins to form, that's when to consult with God. We should pray over our plans before our minds are made up. A made-up mind is almost impossible to change.[4]

Another illustration of David's willingness to seek divine guidance is found in 2 Samuel 5:17–25. The Philistines have attacked Israel and David goes to confront them in the Valley of Rephaim. Before going into battle, however, he consults the Lord. David is an experienced, battle-hardened warrior, but he is not willing to rely upon his own human wisdom even in an area where the world considers him to be an expert. Encouraged by God's words and obeying His instructions, he engages the enemy and achieves an overwhelming victory.

Some time later the Philistines return to challenge the Israelites in the same location, and David does not assume that he can merely follow God's previous direction and all will be well. Once again he questions God for needed insight, and it proves to be important. This time the Lord instructs him to use a different strategy—a flanking maneuver. God also tells David to strike quickly the moment he hears a sign God will give. David obeys and is once again victorious.[5]

Putting God First—Waiting for His Timing

After inquiring of the Lord, David and all his army and their households travel to Hebron, an ancient and important city in the territory of Judah. When David arrives, the elders of the tribe of Judah, David's tribe, anoint him king over Judah (see 2 Samuel 2:2–4). Samuel had anointed him in a private ceremony thirteen years earlier. Now he is anointed again to be king, only this time the ceremony is public.

But wait a minute! God promised David he would be king over the entire nation, over all twelve tribes, and here he is being given a limited reign involving just one tribe in Israel. Furthermore, he will remain in this same position for the next seven and a half years (see verse 11).

Where is the fulfillment of God's original promise? David has already waited a long time, suffering through extended times of great danger and hardship. Yet the consummation of Samuel's prophecy has not come. What has gone wrong?

The answer is, of course, that nothing has gone wrong. The Lord remains in full control of David's situation. The confusion is due to our own misunderstanding concerning God's perfect timing. Have you noticed how we always seem to be in a hurry but God never is? Has it occurred to you how many times His priorities turn out to be different from our own?

David is not upset or anxious about this further wait. He has learned a valuable lesson about the way God has been directing his life; a lesson he records when the Lord finally establishes him as ruler over all Israel: "As for God, His way is perfect" (Psalm 18:30). Here we can see again Principle #8—*God's blessing does not automatically and immediately follow God's calling*—at work. Chafin puts it this way: "The distance is often great between the time God puts a dream in our hearts about our life and the fulfillment of that dream."[6]

The deaths of Saul and Jonathan create a political power vacuum in Israel and give another strong leader the opportunity to attempt usurping the throne. This man is Abner, Saul's cousin and the commander of his army. He takes Ishbosheth, Saul's youngest and only surviving son, and makes him king over the remaining areas of Israel that are not under the control of the Philistines (see verses 8–9). Ishbosheth is a weak person and functions merely as a puppet king. Abner is the real power behind the throne. Unfortunately Abner's ambitious power grab leads the nation into civil war.

The contrast between David and Abner in their attitudes toward the kingship is instructive. David knows he is God's choice; Ishbosheth is man's choice. David relies solely upon the will of God; Abner follows his own self-seeking will. David is content to wait for God's perfect timing; Abner determines to set the time himself. God's plan will always be completed despite the attempts of men to overturn it. A good question to ask when we are working to advance ourselves in life is, Are we behaving like David or more like Abner in the pursuit of our goals?

The waiting and the warfare last several years, but God is at work throughout this time. David's military and political influence grow stronger every day, while the forces of Abner and Ishbosheth decline (see 3:1). The young king of Judah exhibits an amazing amount of godly patience during this tumultuous period. He fully trusts the Lord to elevate him to the rule of all Israel. When this event finally does come, God confirms David's faith and patience by telling him: "And I have been with you wherever you have gone, and have cut off all your enemies from before you, and have made you a name like the name of the great men who are on the earth" (1 Chronicles 17:8).

Twenty-two years elapsed from the day when Samuel anointed David in the privacy of Jesse's home until the day when he was finally recognized as king over the entire nation. Twenty-two years seem almost a lifetime in our modern society, where "I want it, and I want it NOW!" is a popular maxim. The phrase "waiting on God" sounds old-fashioned, an anachronism from another century. We have become so obsessed with trying to reach our goals and objectives as quickly as possible that we run the risk of short-circuiting God's plans for developing and maturing us. Like young children sitting in the back seat of the family auto on a trip, we are constantly asking God, "Are we there yet?" Then we have the temerity to wonder why we see so much shallowness and superficiality in 21st-century Christianity.

Yes, 22 years is a long time. When it was over, though, God had fashioned the king who would lead His people to their greatest heights. David also received a promise that the Lord would "establish the throne of his kingdom forever" (2 Samuel 7:13). David's direct descendants only sat on the throne for four centuries. But Jesus Christ, who came to earth in the lineage of David, will be given "the throne of His father David" by God the Father. It pays to wait on God.

Putting God First—Building a Nation

When David is finally anointed as king over both Judah and Israel, he and his army conquer the Jebusites and take control over all of Jerusalem. He then sets about the task of making this city into the nation's political and spiritual capital. The political goal is greatly aided by Jerusalem's location. It is situated on the border between the tribes of Judah and Benjamin. Located on the high mountain ridge running from north to south almost the length of the land and near the axis of the east and west borders, the city is the nation's geographical linchpin.

A different situation exists in the spiritual realm, however. Israel has no central place of worship at this time. So as the major step to create such a place, David determines to bring Israel's most holy and sacred object, the Ark of the Covenant, to Jerusalem.

Shortly after the children of Israel entered the Promised Land, the Tabernacle and the Ark of the Covenant had been set up at Shiloh, a place located some twenty miles north of Jerusalem. By the time of David the Tabernacle had been moved nearer to Jerusalem, at Gibeon,[7] but the Ark had made a journey of its own. It had, in fact, been captured years earlier by the Philistines, but God had punished the Philistines by sending plagues into whatever city the Ark entered. As a result the Philistine leaders sent the Ark back into Israel and it was eventually placed in the house of a man named Abinadab, where it apparently remained until David came to claim it.[8]

David's desire is to make the city where Israel's king rules also be the place where the Lord is honored, worshiped and glorified as King of kings. His intention is laudable, but zealous motives without corresponding knowledge and wisdom usually lead to problems. David's problem is his ignorance of God's instructions regarding the method for transporting the Ark. According to Exodus 25, the Ark had a ring located in each of its four corners. Long poles were to be put through these rings on either side so the Levites could carry it on their shoulders by its poles. No one was to touch the Ark under penalty of death (see Numbers 4:15).

Being ignorant of God's Word, David and his men load the Ark onto an ox-cart to transport it to Jerusalem. None of them thinks he is doing anything wrong or being irreverent to God by using this method. Quite the opposite! They accompany the cart with a joyful celebration, loudly praising the Lord on a variety of musical instruments, rejoicing that soon the Ark will reside in the capital city of their country. But their method of transport is the world's way and not God's. So when the oxen suddenly stumble, the Ark starts to fall. A man named Uzzah reaches out to steady it, and the Lord immediately strikes him dead (see 2 Samuel 6:3–7).

Is God being overly harsh and cruel? David believes so, for verses 9 and 10 tell us that he becomes both angry and frightened. He has attempted to honor and glorify his Lord and tragedy has resulted instead.[9] He feels himself humiliated in front of his subjects. Confused and uncertain, David leaves the Ark in the nearby house of a man named Obed-Edom where it remains for the next three months (see verse 11).

Two things happen during this time: God greatly blesses Obed-Edom's household, and David discovers from the Law of Moses how the Ark is to be correctly transported (see 1 Chronicles 15:11–15). David has now gained the necessary spiritual understanding. He recognizes that the blessing Obed-Edom has been experiencing from the presence of the Ark demonstrates God's desire to be gracious and loving toward His people, just as He has always been merciful to David. The problem has come entirely from David's error in trying to do things in his own way. He is now able to see that his initial fear and anger against God over Uzzah's death was a sinful response. David and his men return to Obed-Edom's house and begin to carry the Ark in the prescribed manner to Jerusalem, by putting poles through the rings on the Ark and having the Levites carry the poles on their shoulders.

This short episode may strike some readers as strange and difficult to comprehend. For God to strike Uzzah dead over a relatively minor sin seems overly severe and vindictive to our modern eyes. This kind of reaction, though, reflects the lack of importance and reverence many of us give to God's Word. We often tend to play "fast and loose" with the Bible's teachings. We pick and choose those Scriptures we agree with and are willing to follow, and we ignore the parts we believe impose restraints on us or seem too trivial to deserve our attention.

God thinks much differently about this matter and tells us so in numerous passages throughout the Old and New Testaments. For instance, 2 Timothy 3:16 says, "*All* Scripture is given by inspiration of God, and is *profitable* for doctrine, for reproof, for correction, for instruction in righteousness" (emphasis mine).[10] It does not matter whether we classify a particular Bible teaching as major or minor; it only matters that we obey. Swindoll makes an interesting observation about David's failure to carry the Ark in the proper manner:

> The world's system says, "Don't worry about those little details; God's bigger than little golden ringlets." No, He's not. Because He sees the whole scene, He puts our obedience to the test in little things, like a ringlet and a pole and a shoulder.[11]

The Value of Worship

The Ark is brought into Jerusalem with a great display of enthusiastic rejoicing and praise. At the head of this singing, shouting, celebrating throng of thousands is David. He is the king but at this moment he is also the worship leader, leading by example as he dances spontaneously, exuberantly, joyfully without reservation or inhibition. He has even set aside his royal robes and put on a linen ephod, the dress the priests wear as they minister before the Lord (see 2 Samuel 6:14–15).

The procession accompanies the Ark as it is brought to the tent David has prepared for it. From this day until the Temple is built by Solomon, the Ark will remain here as the physical reminder of God's presence in the center of Israel's capital, in the center of His people's lives. David then offers sacrifices to the Lord as an act of consecration and thanksgiving.

David had learned as a young boy the personal importance of regular and true worship to the Lord, and he recognized how vital worship must be on a national level for Israel's spiritual health and vitality. Cornwall believes, "It is unlikely that there was another period in Israel's history when worship was so commonly practiced as it was in the days of David."[12]

But one person is not entering into the spirit of this joyful celebration. David's wife Michal greets him with sarcastic criticism when he arrives back at the palace. "How glorious the king of Israel looked today. He exposed himself to the servant girls like any indecent person might do!" (2 Samuel 6:20, NLT). David does not allow her cold, caustic words to spoil his excitement and joy over the day's events. His reply to her is pointed and powerful. He reminds her that God chose him over her father to be king, and so he is not ashamed to show his love and joy for the Lord openly, even if he appears foolish to onlookers (see verses 20–22).

There are Michals in many of our churches today. These are the people who cannot tolerate enthusiastic worship. Several things seem to offend them during the praise and worship portion of the church service: raising of hands to the Lord, clapping, dancing, shouting, loud music and singing, the use of guitars or drums, modern choruses projected on a screen instead of hymns sung from a hymnal and a praise and worship time lasting longer than ten minutes.

Guard yourself from a Michal spirit. We need to give ourselves frequent attitude checks because our attitudes determine our actions. Proper worship requires a proper attitude of spirit and soul. A Christian's lack of honest and wholehearted praise and worship to God can be one of the major causes for unfruitfulness in his or her spiritual life.

In our culture, worship (like prayer and meditation) usually takes a back seat to service and activities for God. I believe this is because we tend to be people who are "bottom-line oriented," and we can see fairly quickly the results of our "doing things" in church. I am not depreciating the value of such service but merely trying to put it in the right perspective. Corporate and personal worship is a vital element to our spiritual health and growth. Consequently, I heartily agree with Foster, who uses Jesus' first commandment in Mark 12:30 to make the following point:

> If the Lord is to be Lord, worship must have priority in our lives. The divine priority is worship first, service second. Our lives are to be punctuated with praise, thanksgiving, and adoration. Service flows out of worship. Service as a substitute for worship is idolatry. Activity is the enemy of adoration.[13]

A House for God

The final way David seeks to bring the Lord into the life of the nation is recorded in 2 Samuel 7 and 1 Chronicles 17. By now he is living in his palace, a truly royal home of cedar which Hiram the king of Tyre has played a major role in building for him.[14] David and the prophet Nathan are conversing there when the king begins to share his concern about living in luxury while the Ark of God is kept in a simple tent. He wants to rectify this circumstance by building a temple, a permanent structure to house the Ark and glorify the God who has so blessed both him and his nation.

David's motive appears totally sincere and without any hint of seeking the personal fame and honor building such a temple could bring him. What a refreshing attitude he displayed! Compare David's heart desire with that of a 21st-century Christian whose spiritual focus is on how the Lord can be persuaded (manipulated, even!) to meet his or her wishes for wealth, happiness and self-fulfillment. Chafin remarks, "Not everyone is bothered by the contrast between their opulent lifestyle and the neglect of the church."[15] The Bible instructs us to give God our "firstfruits," but in many instances Christians behave as if the word was spelled "leftovers."

Scripture pictures Nathan to be a true prophet, a fully devoted servant to the Lord and a trusted friend and confidant of David. But at this moment, his first appearance in Scripture, Nathan makes a mistake. It is an understandable mistake, but a mistake nevertheless. He gives David his approval and encouragement without first seeking to discover God's will on the matter. Why does he do this? Because he sees David's desire as an honorable and unselfish one, knows the king's godly character and recognizes that the Lord is with David. The moral should be obvious. None of us will ever become so spiritual that we can ignore the Scriptures exhorting us to always ask for God's guidance before making our decisions. Remember the warning of Proverbs 3:5–6 to "lean not on your own understanding."

When Nathan leaves the royal palace after his meeting with David, the matter of building the Temple appears to be settled. The king has, more than likely, already begun to develop his initial plans for the construction process. God has His own plans, however, and He reveals them in detail to Nathan this same night (see 2 Samuel 7:4–17; 1 Chronicles 17:3–17).

(Although Nathan appears in Scripture on only three occasions,[16] he is one of the Bible's most interesting minor characters because each of these three appearances involves a major turnabout in David's life. On each of these occasions Scripture reveals Nathan's sensitivity to God's plans concerning David and the nation, his fearlessness in confronting David and the powerful impact his words had upon David's life and Israel's future course.)

Nathan obeys the Lord immediately, returning to the palace early in the morning. He explicitly delivers the divine response to David's plans, a message containing three major points. God begins by telling David He had never asked the Israelites to build Him a rich temple but was always fully satisfied to dwell among them in a movable tent. He moreover reminds the king of how He had taken him from humble beginnings and raised him to the heights he now enjoys, and He declares His intention to provide abundant future blessings for Israel. Lastly God makes an astounding promise. David's heart's desire was to build a temple for God, but God turns the tables on David and makes a dual declaration about the future: Not only will David's son be given the task of building this glorious Temple, but God promises that He will establish a dynasty from David's offspring that will never come to an end.

"You can't out-give God" may be a cliché, but it is eminently true. God's pledge to establish the throne of David forever must have seemed so awesome to the king as to be beyond comprehension. The Bible and secular history are replete with records of how short were the reigns and dynasties of the kings in the Near and Middle East. Most were ended by rebellion from within the kingdom—led by ambitious and unscrupulous usurpers—or by the conquest of another nation. It was a bloody thing when power changed hands; the king and every possible heir was put to death.[17] Little wonder that Shakespeare wrote the line in his play *Henry IV*, "Uneasy lies the head that wears a crown."

As Nathan delivers God's message to the king, two highly admirable qualities are revealed in David. They are qualities he possessed throughout most of his life, and they ought to help us understand why this man was so blessed by God. First we see again David's teachability. Many of us, as we grow in age, education and status in life, gradually take on the attitude of "My mind is made up; don't confuse me with facts." Yet here is David, the *king*, willing to receive correction from one of his subjects.

To use a modern phrase, Nathan's message pops David's balloon. But because he has a teachable spirit, David is able to perceive God's message not as rejection but as a redirection. The Lord, in essence, tells him that he has been called to rule a nation and subdue its enemies, not to build landmarks.

The second quality is revealed by David's prayer of response to the Lord (see 2 Samuel 7:18–29; 1 Chronicles 17:16–27). Consider the following aspects of David's feelings and reply to the Lord's message for him through Nathan:

- David gives no indication of any disappointment, nor is there any hint of bitterness against God.
- His first words are ones of humility and thankfulness, referring to himself as "Your servant," recalling how far God has already brought him in life and expressing an overwhelming sense of gratitude for all of the blessings He has brought to him and his nation.
- The entire reply rings with joy over the Lord's past goodness and His future promises for David and his descendants.

- David ends his response by taking the words of God's promise and turning them into a prayer.[18]

These verses convey an air of childlikeness in David. He begins by going and sitting before the Lord, probably in the tent he has erected for the Ark of God. (The picture comes to mind of how my small children would sometimes come to me as I sat in my easy chair to discuss a certain tiny matter that loomed very large in their little eyes.) David's whole demeanor expresses his humility and respect for God's awesomeness and ability. He does not presume upon the Lord's goodness or take His blessings for granted.

One of Paul's first indictments of unbelievers was their failure to glorify God and their lack of thankfulness to Him (see Romans 1:21). David's words are the exact opposite of this worldly behavior, and he concludes his prayer by saying, in effect, "Yes, do it, God!"

THE "GOD KIND" OF KINDNESS

Kindness is a word that carries a rich depth of blessing, because this quality flows from the heart of our Heavenly Father. Kindness is a fruit of the Holy Spirit and carries the meaning of God's goodness and gracious attitude toward mankind. Forgiveness, mercy and grace are all implied in this word.[1] Kindness of heart characterizes David's life during the Season of Blessing, yet it is also a quality that is becoming more and more rare in today's society, even in the Body of Christ. This is sad partly because acts of kindness often cost so little to give and can have such profound impact.

Godly Kindness—Not Bitterness

Finally the elders of all of the northern tribes come to Hebron to make David king over the entire nation of Israel (see 2 Samuel 5:1–3; 1 Chronicles 11:1–3). They support their decision with three revealing acknowledgments, and they begin with the obvious truth: David really

163

is one of them. He is a fellow Israelite and the blood bond of kinship is very powerful in this society. He has furthermore shown himself from the time of Saul to be the nation's outstanding warrior and military leader. Finally and most importantly, they recognize that David has been called by God to be Israel's ruler.

A lesser man than David might be tempted to say something of this sort: "If you have known these things for so long, then why did you wait seven years after Saul's death before coming to accept and anoint me as your king? Don't you realize all the lives our nation lost in the civil war during these years because you failed to do this when I first came to Hebron after Saul's death?"

David, however, evidences no animosity or bitterness toward them, nor does he demand any apology. Instead he graciously receives their invitation. Then he begins organizing his forces and sets about the work of strengthening the nation. He eliminates the enemy within Jerusalem by defeating the Jebusites who hold the stronghold of Zion, a strong fortress in the city.[2] He makes Jerusalem the nation's capital city, a decision showing his godly wisdom and his desire to heal Israel's wounds caused by the civil war. Jerusalem is the ideal choice because the city is not within the territory of any Israelite tribe; it lies on the border between Benjamin to the north and Judah to the south. So David establishes a capital that is not only neutral to the tribes but is entirely his by right of conquest.[3]

Godly Kindness—Instead of Vengeance

Many years earlier David and Jonathan had made a covenant (see 1 Samuel 20:12–17). Saul's son knew David would be Israel's ruler one day. He also must have known that when a new family or dynasty took over a country they often executed summarily all the members of the former king's family so that none could attempt to reclaim the throne.

Consequently one of the things Jonathan asked David to promise was to show God's kindness to himself and all his descendants. The Hebrew word translated "kindness" in these verses is *hesed*, one of the most beautiful words in all of Scripture. *Hesed* conveys the quality of God's nature often translated as "mercy" (Psalm 51:1) and "lovingkindness" (Psalm 63:3).[4] Haven't you often heard people characterize the God of the Old Testament as stern and judgmental, a deity who almost seems to delight in dispensing punishment to young and old alike? On the other hand, they picture the New Testament God as a sort of benign grandfatherly type who looks down with inexhaustible patience at mankind's wanton behavior and other sins, but simply smiles, shakes His head and says, "Well, kids will be kids."

Those who truly understand Scripture know this dichotomous view of God is faulty. One of the aspects of the Lord's nature is His *immutability*. In other words, *He never changes*. Numerous passages in both the Old and New Testaments affirm this truth.[5] In Psalm 136, the phrase "for His mercy endures forever" plainly means that His mercy is eternal—without beginning or end. This point is emphasized by the phrase being repeated in each of this psalm's 26 verses. God commanded His people in the Old Testament to show mercy (see Proverbs 3:3; Hosea 6:6; and Micah 6:8), and Jesus says He requires this trait in us (see Matthew 9:13; 23:23).[6] People who believe the New Testament God is nonjudgmental need to read chapters 6 through 21 of the last book in the New Testament, the book of Revelation!

When 2 Samuel 9 opens, the king is firmly established in Jerusalem and he now recalls the promise he had made to Jonathan. So he makes inquiries to determine if there are any remaining descendants of Jonathan. His search uncovers a former servant of Saul named Ziba, and David learns from him of Mephibosheth, Jonathan's son. David brings Mephibosheth to the palace as soon as he hears Ziba's report.

Mephibosheth's life up to this moment must have been an unhappy and fearful one. He was only five years old at the time his father and King Saul were killed by the Philistines. When his nurse heard of the Israelites' disastrous defeat, she took the child to flee to a safer location. In her agitation and haste she dropped the little boy, and this accident caused him to be permanently crippled.

Mephibosheth has spent many years living in obscurity because he was fearful of some revenge being exacted upon him. He is, more likely than not, apprehensive about David's motives, and must be remembering how his Uncle Ishbosheth had suffered assassination. So he falls prostrate as he enters the king's presence and refers to himself in humiliating terms as a "dead dog." It is obvious that he knows nothing of David's generous spirit or of the close friendship and covenant between the king and his father, Jonathan.

Ministers who frequently deal with those lost in gross sin—prostitutes, drug addicts and other hardened criminals—report how such persons often believe that God could never accept them and forgive their sins. Even born-again believers can be prone to avoid God when they fall into sin. They may become so ashamed and fearful over their wrong-doing that they cannot bring themselves to go to Him, repent and ask His forgiveness. How wrong they are! The Lord's *hesed*—His love, mercy, grace and forgiveness—is immeasurably greater than our greatest sins. J. I. Packer writes:

> The grace of God is love freely shown toward guilty sinners, contrary to their merit and indeed in defiance of their demerit. It is God showing goodness to persons who deserve only severity and had no reason to expect anything but severity.[7]

Mephibosheth is about to be amazed, because the king will manifest a beautiful picture of God's *hesed* channeled through a human being. "David never showed more of the true spirit of God than he did on this occasion."[8]

David begins by receiving Mephibosheth graciously. Next he restores to this frightened, lame young man all of the land formerly belonging to King Saul (which was David's by right of his position) and also provides him with a permanent place in the royal court for "Jonathan your father's sake." Then he orders Ziba and his large household to work and manage these estates for Mephibosheth's benefit. As a result Jonathan's son, who a few days earlier was a forgotten, physically impaired person living as a guest in the household of someone not a relative, is suddenly elevated to a place of wealth, honor and security.

All of this happens because David keeps a promise, even though it was made in a different time and situation. In our own time, the number of promise-keepers seems to be shrinking almost daily. "For many people in our day, any change in circumstances becomes a valid reason for breaking contracts and for forgetting our promises."[9] In other words ours is becoming a society willing to keep a promise only so long as it seems in our own best interests to do so.

The well-known poem by Robert Frost, "Stopping by Woods on a Snowy Evening," ends with the lines "But I have promises to keep and miles to go before I sleep. And miles to go before I sleep." How much greater would our Christian witness be if more believers were willing to adopt the mind-set expressed by Frost! Far too many people drift out of our lives or slip off into eternity leaving behind a string of unfulfilled or broken promises. Is this the way any of us want to be remembered?

Thankfully God is the ultimate promise-keeper, a fact we often tend to forget or overlook. As we read His promises in the Bible, our responsibility is to act in faith and obedience toward them. The Lord never asks us to exercise faith for anything He has not first promised to do for us.

BLESSING, WARFARE
AND WORK

The phrase "Season of Blessing" may convey the impression of a
period filled with peace and prosperity, one devoid of any difficulties or dangers. And herein lies a danger for many Christians,
particularly in today's society with its emphasis on personal satisfaction,
happiness and retirement years filled with wealth and ease. Life is hard,
and every season, including this one, will contain periods of struggles,
trials and tests. Why? Because God's purpose for you and me is to con-
form us to the image of Christ, and this process will last a lifetime; it will
continue uninterrupted through every one of our spiritual seasons.

David's Season of Blessing offers a good illustration of the types of
tests the Lord may bring us during this time. It is true that these years
were a golden age for the king and the nation he ruled. There is another
side to this period, however, and it deals with the third major theme
characterizing David's life in this season: warfare and work. Had God's
man not been victorious in these encounters, a significant portion of Old
Testament history could have been written quite differently.

Some believers might ask why the Lord required David to engage in more warfare at this time. He had, after all, already spent many years as a warrior since his fabled victory over Goliath. Nevertheless the lesson God had for David is the same one today's Church needs to learn. We the believers in the Lord Jesus Christ are in a never-ending battle against our adversary the devil, no matter what the spiritual season might be. Several New Testament passages give testimony to the ongoing struggle we face.[1]

The Internal Warfare

As we discussed earlier, warfare begins as soon as David is anointed king in Hebron, and it is the worst kind of war—a civil war with two large groups of God's people opposing one another. How difficult this time is for David! Knowing the Lord will eventually bring him to rule the whole nation, he has to watch the tribes confront one another in deadly combat because of people's unwillingness to submit to God's chosen leadership.

Once the civil war is ended and David is anointed the nation's king, he sets about the task of establishing Jerusalem as the center of the nation's political and spiritual life. There is a problem, though. A remnant of the Canaanite people called the Jebusites hold the fortress known as the stronghold of Zion, overlooking the city. This citadel seems impregnable with its strong walls and the steep slopes around the sides. Even Joshua had been unable to capture it when the children of Israel conquered most of the Promised Land four centuries earlier.

The Jebusites certainly believe that Zion can withstand all attacks. In their overconfidence they taunt David by saying that even a group of lame and blind people could successfully defend this stronghold against any assault. David is not deterred; he has faced greater odds in the past. So he proves able to take this fortress because "the LORD of hosts was with him" and he renames it "the city of David" (see 2 Samuel 5:6–10; 1 Chronicles 11:4–7). Once again the Bible attributes the victory not to David's wisdom, bravery and considerable military skills, but to "the God of the Impossible" who was his eternal resource.

Now the Philistines enter the scene once more (see 2 Samuel 5:17; 1 Chronicles 14:8). They have left Israel alone ever since they killed Saul and routed the Israelite army at the battle on Mount Gilboa. Why? Because during the ensuing years Israel was divided between two kingdoms, David's versus Abner/Ishbosheth's. God's people posed no real threat to Philistia so long as they were occupied with internal conflicts. There is another lesson here, and Chafin summarizes it well:

> As long as we use up our energy competing with one another, the world isn't going to worry about us. This is probably why the world tends to be so patronizing of the church. When God's children join their considerable resources to do God's work, they always get a reaction from the world that operates with different values and goals.[2]

The battle between David and the Philistines is critical to his future ability to govern, as well as for the stability and strength of the entire nation. If the Philistines are victorious, the newly crowned king will undoubtedly have difficulty in maintaining his leadership over all the tribes. Israel itself will moreover be in danger of falling into the role of a vassal province to Philistia.

A "type" in Scripture is a person, thing or event that God uses to teach a spiritual truth. The Philistines are a type of Satan, constantly opposing God's people. The text says, "All the Philistines went up to search for David" (2 Samuel 5:17). And like that spiritual foe, they attack at the opportune time. The chosen moment occurs when Israel is not very strong militarily, since David has not yet been able to build up the army that in a few years will be the dominant power throughout the Near East. In the situation facing David, we find still another spiritual lesson.

Have you ever received what you knew to be a calling from the Lord, but all hell seemed to break loose as soon as you began to follow the call? At times like this we need to recognize that the problem is almost always a spiritual one. Satan knows a stiff injection of doubt and discouragement into our minds can be most effective when we are beginning a new work for the Lord. His attack at this point will frequently cause a believer to either start questioning whether or not he or she really has heard from God or to begin thinking the assignment is too hard.

David's example is the one to follow. He does not allow himself to be dismayed or fearful over the sudden turn of events, even though the enemy forces probably outnumber the Israelites by a significant amount. David once again consults the Lord, trusts in His words, enters the battles with faith and achieves two great victories despite the odds against him.

(Remember, more than one battle may be involved in a given situation because our enemy does not give up easily.) These conflicts have a significant impact upon David's future. The Philistines are no longer a serious threat to Israel, and David's reputation for military prowess begins to spread among the surrounding nations (see 1 Chronicles 14:17).

The nation is now internally secure. All the tribes have come under the rule of David, the Ark is residing in Jerusalem and the new king has received the awesome promise that God will permanently establish his throne. As a result he is finally in a position to begin expanding his nation's territory into all the regions God had promised to Abraham and his descendants a millennium earlier.[3]

The External Warfare

David starts the next phase of his military campaigns by taking the battle into the Philistines' own territory and capturing one of their main cities—Gath, the home of Goliath (see 1 Samuel 17:4; 1 Chronicles 18:1)! Sometime during these various battles David's mighty men destroy the remaining four Philistine giants (see 2 Samuel 21:15–22; 1 Chronicles 20:4–8). Such cumulative defeats humiliate and subdue these long-time enemies of Israel, restricting them to a reduced strip of territory along the coastline of the Mediterranean.[4] "Despite their survival in later centuries, David effectively eliminated the Philistine threat. [And] they never figured again as a significant political or military force."[5]

Now he turns his attention to the surrounding nations, peoples who had taken advantage of Israel's disobedience to the Lord during the periods recorded in the book of Judges. These battles and military campaigns will consume much of David's time for the next decade or more. Reading their accounts can be a bit difficult for several reasons. First, Scripture may not always report events in a strict chronological sequence. Some scholars suggest that 2 Samuel 8 and 10 and 1 Chronicles 18–19, for example, report David's military operations topically rather than chronologically. This simply means events in a later chapter actually may have taken place before events in an earlier chapter.[6]

Second, the text does not offer much detail about most of these individual conflicts. Nor does it give insight into David's generalship and expertise in warfare. The reason is that the outcome of the battles really depended on one thing: the miraculous presence of the Lord on Israel's side. David always welcomed God's mighty help and continually relied upon it: "And the LORD preserved David wherever he went."

Few of the battles David fought during this time were minor skirmishes; most were fierce and deadly conflicts involving armies of thousands. Defeat in any of these encounters might have placed both David and his nation in jeopardy because it would have exposed their potential weakness and tempted the surrounding kingdoms to carry the warfare back into Israel itself. The battles were by no means mere "walkovers."

To gain a better perspective on the high risks and numerous dangers involved, read Psalm 60, which David wrote during this time. These verses indicate that victories were not always immediate. There could be an ebb and flow in such military engagements, and even some momentary setbacks. David knew he was fighting the warfare of the Lord, but he never presumed God would automatically deliver him easy victories.

For instance 2 Samuel 8 and 1 Chronicles 18 recount some of David's warfare against Hadadezer the ruler of Zobah, a powerful kingdom controlling the land northeast of Damascus all the way to the Euphrates River, a distance of hundreds of miles from the Promised Land.[7] Israel captures large numbers of chariots, horsemen and twenty thousand foot soldiers in this battle. When the kingdom of Damascus/Syria sends a large army to help Hadadezer, David kills 22,000 of their troops as well.

In another battle the Israelite army finds itself caught in a dangerous pincer movement by a huge combined force of Ammonites and Syrians. Once again, though, they call upon the Lord and achieve a great victory, slaying over forty thousand of the enemy (see 2 Samuel 10; 1 Chronicles 19).

The Work

David has to confront a second major matter during this season. It involves an area of leadership considered to be necessary for secular success, but one most of us would probably classify as "non-spiritual." This is the area of organization and administration. A common problem among ministers and laypeople alike is the tendency to think of only certain positions within the Church as being in the "spiritual" category.

It is not surprising, then, when Christians seem more willing to volunteer for assignments where they will be considered spiritual leaders than for positions of service.

This kind of thinking is non-biblical and may help to explain why numbers of Christian churches are poorly run. Whether you are serving the church as a secretary or janitor or volunteer in the infant nursery, you are a servant leader! A well-known writer on church management makes a statement about church leadership that I believe qualifies as a good principle for the Body of Christ:

Principle #9: **"The spiritual leader and the servant leader are synonymous. The Church is an organism, the Body of Christ; but it is also an organization, and organizations require proper servant leadership."**[8]

Up to this point the Bible has shown David to be an obedient son, caring shepherd, accomplished musician, anointed psalmist, fearless warrior and brilliant general. In addition to this list of outstanding traits, David must have been one of the greatest organizers and administrators in the entire Bible, because circumstances demanded him to be eminently skilled in these disciplines. Military power and success alone would not have enabled Israel to rise to such great heights of power and fame. One scholar claims that this small nation, under their new king's leadership, "for the moment probably was as strong as any power in the contemporary world."[9]

Both times David is crowned, first in Hebron and later in Jerusalem, he takes the throne of nations whose governmental structure is anarchic. Saul undoubtedly allowed the affairs of state to disintegrate during his later years of madness, while he became increasingly consumed with his frenzied pursuit of David. According to 1 Samuel 22:7, much of his staff in these later years came from his own tribe of Benjamin, thereby revealing a lack of involvement by the other tribes in his ruling circle. The deaths of Saul and Jonathan and the long civil war caused a further erosion of national unity, so the remaining authority resided with various tribal leaders.

Here we see David's wise and skillful leadership in organization and administration. While Scripture provides few details about the makeup and functioning of his government, he must have been able to select and place highly capable people in key positions, and to ensure the bureaucracy throughout his entire kingdom was staffed with efficient people. How can we know this? By considering the remarkable transformation in the fortunes of Israel in a relatively short span of time. David not only unified the nation, but he proceeded to subdue many of the nations in the Near East—Edom, Amalek, Ammon, Moab, Syria, Zobah and, of course, Philistia. He was able to absorb and rule over these conquered territories by placing military garrisons in them (see 2 Samuel 8:14; 1 Chronicles 18:13) and/or by putting his governing officials and other personnel over their local governments.[10]

In short, David was blessed with a good quota of servant leaders. He apparently organized these officials into a well-structured system so that they were answerable only to him. By this means he kept a firm control on the reins of government and limited the independence of Israel's twelve tribes.

The Final, Fruitful Results of This Season

Israel soon became extremely prosperous, not merely from the treasure and tribute David amassed from his conquests but from Israel's control of the lucrative trade routes between Egypt, Arabia, Phoenicia and the Euphrates region. This once-despised little nation enjoyed a period of security and material abundance that would have seemed unthinkable after Saul's disastrous defeat and death at the hands of the Philistines. Students of geography will recognize that David's empire at its zenith took in substantial portions of land now occupied by the modern nations of Jordan, Lebanon and Syria, as well as a part of Egypt. The covenant God made with Abraham (see Genesis 15:18–21) four thousand years ago contained a promise of land for his descendants through Isaac (see Genesis 17:19). God said this land would extend from the Nile River delta to the Euphrates River, and His promise was nearly fulfilled in David and Solomon's time.[11]

Today many nations of the world are attempting to restrict Israel to a small portion of God's promised allotment, while much of Islam seeks to remove Israel entirely from this land. Both attempts will ultimately fail because the Lord will fulfill His covenant to Israel just as He fulfilled His promise to David. No power on earth will be able to prevent it.

17

THE MONARCH'S
MISTAKES

Successful and prosperous times carry an unseen but potent danger. Our very successes and victories can lull us into a state of complacency, or we can allow pride over our accomplishments to take root in us or subconsciously pull us away from daily dependence upon the Lord. Little wonder then that Scripture contains a number of references admonishing us to be continually vigilant (watchful). Being in a tremendous Season of Blessing does not guarantee that we will be free from the possibility of making mistakes or falling into sin.

David's extraordinary and varied gifts and abilities were certainly demonstrated during this season. Unfortunately some of his failings were major ones, mistakes that would have a serious impact on his future.

A Wrong Choice

One of these failures seems very uncharacteristic of David. He was a good judge of people and almost always seemed to select the right person

176

for a major assignment—with one notable exception. David made Joab commander-in-chief of Israel's armies. Joab was a close relative, the son of Zeruiah, one of David's older stepsisters. He had joined himself to David during the fugitive years. The Bible pictures Joab as a man who had a few good traits. He was a brave and fearless warrior, a clever and canny general and a person who demonstrated his loyalty to David by a willingness to strongly confront the king on two critical occasions when David was in the wrong (see 2 Samuel 19:1–8; 24:1–3).

But these favorable qualities were greatly offset by a number of serious character flaws. The man was overly ambitious, extremely jealous of his position, vengeful, arrogant and insolent. He was the very antithesis of David. "David was all heart, and passion, and sensibility; while Joab was all self-will, and pride, and hard as a stone."[1]

Joab's selection is one of the paradoxes of Scripture. How could a man so filled with serious character flaws, a man who David sees as a continual thorn in his side, become the commander-in-chief of Israel's army? Simply because David made a rash and foolish promise. When he was besieging the Jebusites' stronghold at Jerusalem, he offered this promotion to whoever of his warriors could break into this fortress and overwhelm its defenders.[2] Did David make this spur-of-the-moment pledge because he was momentarily insulted and incensed by the taunts of the enemy who were saying even the lame and blind could defend their stronghold against David's attack? Possibly. If so the king's angry slip was a grievous one, and he would sorely regret it in later years.

Joab's promotion was particularly sad due to the fact that David had a number of highly qualified and brave warriors who would have been excellent candidates for this position. Most of them were probably men of honor and integrity. David could have had a problem trying to choose one man from a long list of capable candidates—military leaders who were men of exemplary character. Instead he allowed a hasty decision caused by a momentary surge of anger to dictate this important appointment.

This caution is not a blanket indictment against making hasty decisions. Many times circumstances may require us to take quick, on-the-spot action. During my days in the investment industry, for instance, I often had only a few seconds to determine whether or not to buy, sell or arbitrage certain securities. The more important the choice, however, the greater care is needed in making the decision.

Principle #10: **Avoid the tendency to make decisions in haste or anger.**

Correct selection of key personnel is the most critical factor in the future strength and success of any organization—whether a commercial business, a governmental entity or a church. In his book *Good to Great*, author Jim Collins offers an insight frequently overlooked by corporations. This advice would serve equally well for voters electing candidates for public office, as well as for those leading Christian organizations:

> The old adage "People are your most important asset" is wrong. People are not your most important asset. The *right* people are. Whether someone is the "right person" has more to do with character traits and innate capabilities than with specific knowledge, background, or skills.[3]

A Negligent Father

David's other failure involved his family. Second Samuel notes that he came to Hebron with two wives (see 2:2) but soon acquired four more (see 3:2–5). And after being proclaimed king in Jerusalem, he "took more concubines and wives" (2 Samuel 5:13–16; 1 Chronicles 14:3–7). Numerous children were fathered from these unions, but only the firstborn sons of the wives are listed in the text. Information about these women is scanty, and nothing is said about some of them.

The Bible does not provide us with any pictures of David's family life during the years when his children were being reared. We can, however, easily imagine the daily atmosphere in a palace filled with this many women and their offspring. In such close surroundings the rivalry between the wives and concubines was undoubtedly intense, and the children would certainly have picked up on their mothers' attitudes. Consequently the royal household must have been filled constantly with noise, bickering, arguments, accusations and petty jealousies. The daily (and nightly) aura of disorder and tensions would have tried the patience and wisdom of the Lord's godliest people. Remember that many of David's marriages were entered into for political reasons rather than romantic attraction. Under these circumstances each woman would naturally attempt to exercise influence over the king so he would favor her own children and nation when he made governmental appointments, promotions and foreign policy.

The likelihood also exists that the king was an absentee father for a couple of reasons. One was the incredible demand on his time and energy to manage and build his relatively small nation into the powerful kingdom he envisioned it could be. Scripture does not provide much detail about David's administration, but it does indicate that he delegated a number of the governmental and military responsibilities to his subordinates—with two notable exceptions. "Since no vizier (prime minister) is listed, we must assume David actively headed his own government."[4] In addition, 2 Samuel 8:15 says that he also acted as supreme judge over Israel, perhaps following the example of Samuel, the nation's last great judge. But the heavy military campaigning the king undertook yearly must have kept him away from Jerusalem for weeks at a time. The question arises as to how effectively David could have managed the government and still have seen to the well-being of his large family.

In the last analysis, though, even a very busy man with a demanding work schedule can carve out some amount of quality time to spend at home with his wife and children—if he really desires to do so. But David's home most likely did not provide the kind of convivial and restful surroundings a busy and burdened leader wanted and needed. If this assumption is correct, then here was another instance where a large collection of problems on the home front caused a man to escape them by spending an inordinate amount of time at the office.

FAILURE

The Season of Backsliding
(2 Samuel 11)

"God in His wisdom allows what His power could prevent."
—GRAHAM COOKE

18

THE TRAPS
OF TEMPTATION

King David was hot and uncomfortable as he lay on his bed that early evening in spring. The room seemed unseasonably warm to him, the atmosphere more like the torrid heat that summer would pour upon Jerusalem in a few weeks. He had been attempting to take a nap, hoping a short rest would refresh him after the long hours he had spent earlier in the day, plodding through the dreary routine of administrative duties. But the air in his bedroom felt muggy and close, like an unwanted blanket.

David knew it was useless to try sleeping under such conditions. He swung his feet to the floor and started toward the flat roof of the palace. It usually provided a more pleasant atmosphere late in the day, particularly when a cool evening breeze began to remove the day's oppressive heat.

The roof did indeed provide some relief from the hot, heavy air below. But his body still felt listless while his mind was restless, unsettled and filled with wandering thoughts and reflections. He had been having these same mental struggles for a number of days, and only now was he becoming fully aware of what was the real reason for this lethargy and the sense of unease gripping his body, mind and spirit. He was bored. Simply flat-out bored!

David was a man of action and always had been, even as a youth. When he entered his adult years, he looked forward to spring because it marked the end of the rainy season in the region of the Promised Land. That end allowed warfare against Israel's enemies to be resumed. The roads would once again be in passable condition, and an army on the march would be able to find food in the fields for themselves and for their horses and pack animals.[1] But with the onset of this spring he found himself relegated to the role of onlooker, an impotent spectator for the first time in countless years, watching while others were involved in the clash of battles that would determine his future and that of his nation.

When he had first made the decision to stay in Jerusalem and delegate the leadership of the army to Joab, the choice had seemed to be a wise one. After all, I've been engaged in battles and conflicts of one kind or another for over three decades, *David thought.*

Had he not, during the previous year, led his troops to a decisive victory over a formidable Syrian army which had been allied with the nation of Ammon, Israel's nearest and fiercest enemy? As a result of this battle—and an earlier one—all that remained for Joab was to defeat the now much-weakened Ammonite forces and capture their capital of Rabbah (2 Samuel 10:15–11:1). Certainly Joab and his men could do this easily enough, could they not? Just to absolutely ensure success, though, David had sent "all Israel," his entire army, to finish the conquest (11:1).

Everything had seemed to indicate that it was time for him to step aside. Of course, he would go to the scene of battle, as soon as the Ammonite army was defeated and Rabbah was ready to fall, and formally claim the victory for himself and his nation. Did he not deserve to enjoy a time of rest until then? Was he not entitled to enjoy the comforts of royal life, without the frequent interruptions calling him to charge out to another battle? Had he not endured the hard life of campaigning and the dangerous task of soldiering for enough years to fill two or three lifetimes?

Look at what he had accomplished for his nation since assuming the kingship! Israel's territories had been enlarged to the greatest extent in its history, and the land was secure and peaceful. The petty tribal quarrels and disputes had been stilled, so the nation was truly united and the people were experiencing greater prosperity than ever before. David himself was loved and honored throughout Israel and respected and feared in those nations and regions he had conquered.

(On looking back at this time, one historian remarked, "It seems safe to say that David was the most powerful and influential monarch of the entire Near East in his day."[2])

David thought to himself, Certainly my reasoning would have made sense to anyone who honestly evaluated the situation.

And yet none of these rationalizations could quell the discomfort and gnawing feeling in his spirit—the feeling that he was deluding himself and had taken a wrong turn. In this unsettled state of mind, Israel's king began to wander aimlessly about the roof of his palace.

David was so absorbed in his musings that he hardly noticed the quiet arrival of a soft, refreshing evening breeze. Occasionally he would glance idly down into the city of Jerusalem, spread out below the hill on which his palace stood. It was a sight he had looked at on many occasions, each time remembering with pride and satisfaction that he had captured this city, conquered its Jebusite stronghold and made it into Israel's spiritual and political capital. He had never grown tired of seeing the results of his many building projects and the restorations he had Joab perform in various neighborhoods.[3] Tonight, however, he was much more focused upon his inner thoughts than on these buildings and homes, until. . . .

His meandering gaze was sharply arrested as he caught sight of a woman, a remarkably beautiful woman, bathing herself in the enclosed courtyard of a house just below the walls of his palace. Though the daylight was fading, the oil lamps in the courtyard cast a warm, soft glow upon her. Their rays highlighted the glistening film of water on her skin, accentuating the voluptuousness of her naked body.

David stood transfixed, his eyesight bolted to her nubile form as she moved, turning and bending to sponge every surface of her body. He had known numbers of beautiful women. Even before he had left Hebron to go to Jerusalem and assume the rule of all Israel, David had acquired six wives. Then, as king in the succeeding years, he took several additional wives as well as an uncounted number of concubines. With his kingly position, a warrior reputation of heroic proportions, eloquent way with word and song and handsome features,[4] David undoubtedly projected an almost fatal attraction for scores of desirable young women who were quite willing to make themselves available to him.

But Bathsheba was not just any woman. The Bible says she was "very beautiful," and Youngblood points out that these two words:

> Translate a Hebrew phrase for people of striking physical appearance (e.g., Rebekah [Genesis 24:16, 26:7], Vashti [Esther 1:11], Esther [2:7] and . . . David himself [1 Samuel 16:12 where a cognate Hebrew expression is used]).[5]

If we put this phrase into modern-day layperson's language, Bathsheba was "drop-dead gorgeous," a "knock-out" with a "killer" figure.

David made no attempt to nip this temptation at its outset. Years later he would pen a line in one of his psalms, "I will set nothing wicked before my eyes" (101:3). This resolve to keep any visual temptation from invading his imagination would, sadly, come much too late for him to avoid the tragedies this desire and its accompanying sin would bring.

He was completely captivated by his ravishing vision. Her allure and beauty seemed to far exceed that of any of the women who peopled his harem. His thoughts surged quickly to the next obvious step—nothing less would do! He quickly strode back into the palace, accosted one of his personal servants and sent him to discover the identity of this beautiful, unknown woman. "She lives in a house just below the palace," he instructed the man, describing the exact location in terms of its relation to the place on the roof where he had been standing. The servant hurried off on his search while David fretfully paced the floor, eager for the man's return with the hoped-for information.

The servant soon came back, respectfully approached the king and quietly gave him the answer. But because he was concerned for his master's welfare, he skillfully wrapped his report with a soft and subtle warning. He had learned through years of experience the folly and danger of confronting or criticizing a powerful leader. He knew it was vital to give advice only when asked, and then always in a careful and deferential manner. But after having served in the royal household for some time, he felt he could surmise where the king's intentions were leading in this situation, so he politely replied, "Her name is Bathsheba. She's the daughter of Eliam and the wife of Uriah the Hittite."

In his mind, the servant added, Be very careful, my lord. She's a member of a noble family and is a married woman. Her husband is one of your trusted and loyal mighty men,[6] and so is her father.[7] Her grandfather is Ahithophel, your chief counselor![8]

The servant's information should have stopped David's carnal desire then and there. But the facts seemed, incredibly, to have no restraining effect on him at all. He certainly knew God had commanded, "You shall not covet . . . your neighbor's wife" (Exodus 20:17)[9], and understood that the punishment for adultery under Moses' law was death (see Leviticus 20:10). But this command and the accompanying threat of judgment were somehow brushed aside. Nor did he give any consideration to the corrosive impact such a deed would have not only on his relationships with Uriah, Eliam and Ahithophel but on his reputation and sacred responsibility to shepherd God's people as their king, priest and prophet.

His thoughts were entirely elsewhere. Bathsheba, of course, *he reflected. I've met her casually and briefly at a couple of the palace's social functions and do remember what an extremely attractive young woman she was. I just couldn't recognize her face at such a distance in the twilight.*

In these few seconds of reflection, his desire to bed this beautiful creature rose to a height that completely captured his mind, will and emotions. He summarily orders his servants to bring Bathsheba to him at once. Pride shows its evil face in David's actions as he ignores the servant's veiled warning, his own conscience and his knowledge of God's law. Why? Because he is the king, of course, and the cliché "Rank has its privileges" was probably in use long before David's time.

Lord John Acton, the English historian and moralist of the nineteenth century, coined the oft-quoted aphorism "Power tends to corrupt, and absolute power corrupts absolutely." This evil aspect of power infected Israel's king at that moment, and his behavior was that of a ruler who considers himself to be "above the law."

The young fugitive who twice refused to obtain the throne by putting a madman out of his misery had become a king for whom adultery—taking the wife of one of his loyal servants—was not sinking too low.

Scripture is silent concerning the conversation that occurred upon Bathsheba's arrival in David's bedroom. We can only speculate about her feelings at this moment. Was she experiencing great loneliness with her husband away at war and flattered to be called suddenly into the king's presence? Did David use his most persuasive words and his royal magnetism to overcome any protests the lady may have made? Second Samuel 11:4 simply ends with the terse report that they had sexual relations and afterwards she returned to her house.

This brief encounter undoubtedly provided both of them with a few moments of great pleasure. Let's be honest—sin does bring pleasure, and the Bible attests to this fact. Proverbs chapters 5 and 7 warn about the enticing and momentary gratification of illicit sex. According to Hebrews 11:25, Moses refused to be entrapped in Egypt by what Scripture calls "the passing pleasures of sin." The hidden hook in sin is revealed by the words "momentary" and "passing."

A mistake some parents make is the failure to acknowledge to their children that sinful activities can be very pleasurable at first. Drugs, alcohol and premarital sex all can, and usually do, offer enjoyment, excitement, thrills, a sense of freedom, wonderful "highs" and an escape from reality. But the so-called "benefits" of such activities are brief, momentary and limited. Then comes payback time. In the words of an old-time preacher, "There will come a payday someday."

19

THE SEEDS OF SIN

The question is sometimes asked, "Was it only David who was at fault?" The Bible's report of his liaison with Bathsheba is very brief, covering only three verses (see 2 Samuel 11:2–4), but it clearly places the blame on David: He saw, he coveted, he had her brought to the palace and he undoubtedly used his considerable charisma against any of her possible inhibitions.

All of these things are true, and yet it is worth remembering the saying "It takes two to tango." Bathsheba was by no means entirely innocent. To expose herself by bathing outside, albeit in an enclosed area, was a careless act on her part. She must have recognized—if she thought about it—that her courtyard could be seen from the palace roof, and roofs were normally used as porches in the Near East; being high enough to catch the breeze made them some of the few comfortable places to endure the summer heat.

This same kind of thoughtless behavior is especially prevalent among women today, including Christians. The first line of a Cole Porter tune of the pre–World War II era goes, "In olden days a glimpse of stocking was looked at as something shocking, now heaven knows, anything goes!" Anything does seem to go in the way some dress (or undress)

189

today, whether at the shopping mall, a concert, a sporting event, the local swimming pool or a beach.

One additional point should be noted about David and Bathsheba's brief union. Scripture gives no indication of his using any physical force to subdue her against her will. She most likely acquiesced to his seductive invitation and, in the process, she simply forgot God just as David had done.

Satan's Snare

It is extraordinary that a man with David's spiritual background could make this decision. Not only did he forget God, he gave no thought to the dangers to which he was exposing both himself and his nation. He was like an insect flying into a Venus-Flytrap, which is an unusual plant native to a small area of my home state of North Carolina. This flower attracts insects, inviting them to land on its petals, and then closes its leaves over the victims and digests them. Satan used the allure of sexual intoxication to entrap Israel's great and godly leader in a very similar way.

Several Old Testament passages warn about the amazing power of illicit sex to

- obliterate the believer's sense of God's presence,
- nullify the teachings of Scripture,
- warp our normal reasoning process almost beyond recognition,
- and overrule any concerns about the potential consequences of such actions,

but the first four verses of 2 Samuel 11 present the Bible's most graphic portrayal of the enticingly beautiful but deadly make-up of sexual temptation. A critically important moral from these few verses is "If it could happen to David, it could happen to any of us." The high-profile ministers and ministries that have fallen in recent years give sad testimony to this truth. In nearly every case such falls were caused not by alcoholism or financial improprieties or doctrinal aberrations but by man's inability to stand against sexual sin.

People down through the centuries have questioned and wondered at David's sudden and precipitous fall into gross sin. At this point in his life, then, many Christians would consider David a spiritual giant. But we know that outward appearances can be quite deceiving. A person's sharp, sudden fall into major sin almost always surprises people, especially if the person is a well-known and successful Christian minister or leader. But we would not be so astonished had we been able to more closely observe the person's life over a long period of time.

Such is the case with Israel's great king. The seeds which eventually led to his adultery with Bathsheba had been planted in his life many weeks, months and even years prior to his act. Most of these seeds had, sadly, been planted by David himself. His fall was not the result of "The devil made me do it." Satan certainly took full advantage of these seeds of sinful actions and mind-sets that David had allowed into his heart, but David alone was ultimately responsible for his sin.

What were these seeds and how did they lead this man of God to so quickly give in to temptation and, as we will discuss shortly, draw him into further abominable actions? They are the same kind of seeds that Christians, young or old, male or female, layperson or minister, are capable of planting in their own lives. The dangers of backsliding are always nearby.

Complacency

The first of David's failings was his unwillingness to continue faithfully fulfilling his duties and responsibilities. As chapter 11 opens we find the king displaying an attitude of complacency and self-indulgence. There is a striking contrast between where he is and where he should be. David is in Jerusalem while his army is fighting battles in a foreign land. Kings in this period were expected to lead their nations in warfare (see 1 Samuel 8:20). It was the season "when kings go out to battle," but David has given his general, Joab, the responsibility of commanding Israel's troops. The king is still a physically capable and even fearless leader, but he remains behind and sends the nation's able-bodied warriors ("all Israel") into battle. He is enjoying the comforts and safety of the palace while his troops daily face the discomforts and dangers of injury and death. The moral is clear. If David had been in his appointed place of leadership, this sinful episode would never have happened.

The Bible does not explain the reasons why David remained in Jerusalem, but various events recorded elsewhere in its pages allow us to make a conjecture. Both the Old and the New Testaments point out a sad fact: God's people often seem able to handle adversity much better than prosperity. The book of Judges offers a prime example of how God's people would become self-satisfied, materialistic and apostate whenever they enjoyed a long time of peace and prosperity. A number of the prophets—Isaiah, Hosea, Amos and others—confronted and warned their people for allowing times of "peace and prosperity" to breed spirits of pride, complacency, idolatry and spiritual emptiness in their hearts. The Laodicean church (see Revelation 3:14–22) is a sharp New Testament reminder of how riches can sometimes be dangerous commodities in our spiritual lives.

David seems to have fallen into this kind of mind-set. He had experienced a long period of unparalleled success in both the military and political areas and must have felt great satisfaction over his accomplishments since assuming the kingship. Did this cause pride to well up in him? Was the unending stream of military victories and political triumphs tempting him to believe he could do nothing wrong?

Then there was the matter of leisure time, an experience he had never known before. From his early shepherding years until the present, David had never been idle. He had always known and lived with pressures and stress from battles with wild animals and Israel's enemies, from living on the run as an outlaw, from the arduous task of training his fugitive army and providing for their households, from gradually winning the loyalty of Israel's twelve tribes and becoming their king, from the daily responsibilities of organizing and administering the people and affairs of his nation and from overseeing the affairs of the lands he had conquered. The situations that had caused him to cry out to God were now things of the past.

Reliance upon the Lord no longer seemed paramount in the day-to-day activities and decisions David faced. His actions reflected a strong belief in his own abilities. It seems that his pride brought him to the point where he said inwardly, *The wisdom and knowledge I've gained from my accomplishments will enable me to keep the kingdom running smoothly.*

Israel's king had fallen prey to a malady that became a contagion among scores of affluent and successful Americans in the latter decades of the twentieth century. This malady was *hubris*—an exaggerated self-confidence and pride in one's own abilities and accomplishments. Its signs were seen everywhere in the attitudes of business and political leaders, stock market investors and media and entertainment personalities.

David had, tragically, permitted himself to fall into this trap, "the pride of life" (see 1 John 2:16). Satan understands mankind's weakness. Lucifer, the "anointed cherub" who had fallen from his high position in heaven due to the sin of pride (see Isaiah 14:12), knows how to use pride to bring down God's servants. God promises He will not allow us to be tempted beyond our strength to withstand and overcome it, but also will provide us with a way of escape from it (see 1 Corinthians 10:13). But when this powerful sexual temptation struck David, he neither resisted nor turned to God for help to escape the temptation.

Compromise

David's second failing involved the seeds of moral compromise he had been planting in his lifestyle for many years. Moral compromise does not usually appear to us as gross sin or overt disobedience of God's Word. Instead we prefer to view it as merely a temporary or minor accommodation to the world's way of doing things. And so we turn a blind eye to certain questionable business practices in our jobs, to letting our children and teenagers go along with the crowd in order to be accepted by their friends and classmates and to entertaining ourselves with the parties, movies, television programs, music, magazines, etc., that the world deems popular and enjoyable. But despite its innocent appearance, moral compromise can dull our spiritual senses and make us vulnerable to temptation.

What was David's vulnerable area in moral compromise? Marriage! The Lord had laid down certain principles for Israel's kings in Deuteronomy 17:14–20, nearly four centuries before Saul, the nation's first king, came to the throne. He instructed a king not to "multiply" (that is, acquire, accumulate) for himself horses, wives or riches ("gold and silver"). David obeyed two of the three commands but violated the one carrying a specific, severe warning. Deuteronomy foretold that having many wives would cause David (and any other ruler) to turn away from the Lord—and it did!

Polygamy was permitted in the culture of David's time, but monogamy was the norm. The major reason was financial. A man had to be quite prosperous in order to afford more than one wife and, consequently, kings and the wealthy were the few men who had multiple wives and concubines.[1]

David undoubtedly had his choice of the finest women for his bed and was becoming a connoisseur of female flesh. He was also a man of strong passions, both good and bad. The range of emotions we see in his psalms gives testimony to this fact. Everything he did in life, he did wholeheartedly. These two aspects of David's makeup—his passionate nature and his practiced eye for the ladies—formed a very volatile mixture. Satan knew this and had probably been working carefully for a lengthy time to bring together the right temptation and setting to catch his hated enemy, Israel's great king.

Two other factors, however, also influenced the number of wives/concubines in his royal harem:

> The number of wives was a very concrete token of the power and wealth of the king. Another important factor was the need for establishing alliances. Marriage with the daughter of a foreign ruler was a political expedient that helped to cement relations between the two states.[2]

Why did David resort to this worldly expedient to establish and strengthen his political and commercial standing among the nations of the Near East? He knew that the Lord was providing him with His divine protection, deliverance, prosperity and a host of other blessings. In spite of his godly faith and trust, Israel's king succumbed to the ways of the world. One of the saddest commentaries on David's multiple marriages is found in 1 Chronicles 14:2–3. The text tells us David "perceived that the LORD had established him as king over Israel, for his kingdom was highly exalted because of His people," but continues, "then David took more wives in Jerusalem."

Before criticizing David too strongly for his willingness to adopt the world's methods, we ought to truthfully analyze how often we have given in to doing certain things the world's way while conveniently ignoring the Bible's teaching and the prompting of our consciences. Whatever our age, we, like our children, too often give in to peer pressure and try to justify it as they do by the rationalization "But everyone else is doing it."

Aren't you relieved how little others actually know of your sins and failures? Aren't we all glad that there are no "candid cameras" in our homes, recording all of our words and actions for the world to see? Swindoll offers a light but telling perspective on this point:

Personally, when I step into this chapter of David's life, I am forever grateful that God has finished writing Scripture. [David] sinned, but his sin was no greater than your sin or mine; ours simply have not been recorded for all to read.[3]

But where was the Lord when David was following the polygamous practices of heathen rulers? Why did He permit these kinds of unholy alliances to happen and not chasten and punish His chosen servant? The answer, of course, is that all of us were created as free moral agents. As a consequence, God's apparent lack of intervention was not due to His indifference toward David's polygamy nor to His excusing of the king's sin on the basis that he had been God's choice to be Israel's ruler.

Principle # 11: **The fact that God allows His people to behave in sinful or foolish ways does not mean that He approves of their sin or foolishness.**

One writer gives an apt warning on this matter: "We should never interpret the silence of God as the indifference of God. How easily we misinterpret divine patience as divine tolerance!"[4] Punishment would eventually come. David would finally pay for his polygamy. His collection of wives and concubines did probably enhance his reputation and power in the eyes of the rulers of other nations, but this prestige would prove to be ephemeral. None of us, including David, can flout God's Word indefinitely. The time will come when the sinful seeds we have planted will produce a bitter harvest.

A Problem with Sin

And so ended David's brief sexual encounter. "Just a one-night stand" goes a popular euphemism of today's society. "No big deal," you say? "It happens all the time in our modern world," you argue? The end of the matter? Absolutely not! This single act of adultery was the beginning and not the end of David's sin and troubles. The Bible is about to show us one of the often-forgotten but awesomely powerful aspects of sin.

Principle # 12: One sin often leads to more sins, particularly when a person attempts to cover up his or her initial wrongdoing.

A Change of Seasons

A number of days pass. The dreary palace routine continues. Unbeknownst to David, his Season of Blessing ended when he took another man's wife, but he is still bored and has almost forgotten his few moments of physical delight with Bathsheba. He also continues his pattern of forgetting God. There is no outward indication of any pangs of conscience and certainly no sign of any movement toward confession and repentance before God. (However, the next section will show David's true inner feelings as revealed in certain psalms he wrote.) David continues to backslide. This word probably sounds a bit strange to our modern ears, but it conveys a very significant truth for every born-again Christian. It is a derivation of a Hebrew verb which means "to turn" or "return."[5] Just as we can turn away from sin and toward God in repentance, we can turn away from God by backsliding, thereby returning to our sinful ways.

The torpor and boredom of this uneventful time are shattered suddenly and unexpectedly as this new season begins to manifest itself. It will last only about one year, but David will live in a hell of his own creation throughout this time. During these twelve months he will lead a double life. Outwardly he will appear to be the same strong, charismatic and God-anointed ruler Israel and the world had come to know over the past two decades. Inwardly, however, he will be consumed with guilt, suffering both physically and emotionally from the trauma of his evil actions, but still unwilling to face his Lord in confession and repentance.

20

THE QUICKSAND
OF A QUANDARY

The fateful day begins when a servant brings to David a private
message from Bathsheba. She informs him she is pregnant (see
2 Samuel 11:5). The king immediately recognizes that he, and
not Uriah her husband, is the father. Verse 4 tells us Bathsheba "was
cleansed from her impurity" when she came to David, indicating that
the bath she was taking when the king first saw her signified the end of
her menstrual period.[1]

With this totally unexpected development, the Lord provides David
with another opportunity to admit his sin before God and the people,
repent and seek forgiveness. Instead he begins to concoct a cover-up to
hide his guilt from every eye. Sin has sunk its talons deep into David's
mind and emotions, and he begins to react irrationally. We sometimes
read of a seemingly intelligent and sensible person who suddenly panics
under the stress of a momentary crisis and commits a rash and foolish act.
For David to do this seems almost unthinkable, but such is the power of
sin when we fail to confront it and confess it to the Lord; it can quickly
spread through our whole being and warp our thoughts and actions.

A Scheme to Hide Sin

David does not realize that he is stepping into a morass of sin that will pull him like quicksand ever deeper into depravity. The downward spiral begins when he sends a letter to Joab, ordering his general to have Uriah report to him in Jerusalem. When Uriah arrives the king makes a pretense of asking him for news of the battles against the Ammonites and their capital city of Rabbah. Then he tells this mighty warrior to go enjoy the comforts of his home and sends a gift of food with him, encouraging Uriah to take this opportunity to be with his wife. By this clever subterfuge David intends to ensure that Bathsheba's pregnancy will be attributed to her husband and not to him.

It is a very ingenious scheme—except for one thing he does not anticipate. Uriah refuses to go to his home but instead spends the night in one of the outer rooms of the palace. When the king discovers this and questions him, Uriah's answer shows him to be a man of loyal dedication and devotion both to God and to his calling as a soldier—the kind of warrior David himself had always been. He tells the king that he will not allow himself to enjoy the pleasures of home so long as the Ark of the Covenant[2] and Joab and the army are camped in tents on the battlefield.

David tries one more stratagem. He orders Uriah to remain in the palace an additional day, and then proceeds to ply him with food and drink so that the man becomes inebriated. By this tactic the king hopes to weaken Uriah's resolve and entice him to go home to his wife. But once again this faithful soldier chooses to spend the night in the quarters of the palace servants.

His well-planned schemes have failed and David has run out of options. Only one course of action seems left to him. Uriah must be killed. He writes a letter to Joab laying out a secret (and he thinks cunning) way for his army commander to have Uriah die in battle, and has this noble warrior unsuspectingly carry the letter himself.

What a horrible, hypocritical plan! Over three decades earlier King Saul had wanted to eliminate David as a rival to the throne. Saul disguised his intent by sending the young man on a suicide mission, asking him to kill one hundred Philistines as the bride-price to marry his daughter but secretly expecting him to die in the attempt. Now David repeats this same evil subterfuge.

A Slight Change in Plans

The Bible pictures Joab to be a very complex personality, as we saw in the previous section, and David understands quite well the ruthlessness and hardness of this man. All of Israel's other military leaders, David's mighty men, would likely have refused to be an accomplice to murder. But not Joab. Whyte says that Joab's "only virtue was a certain proud, patronizing loyalty to his king."[3] This loyalty combined with his cruel nature will enable Joab to carry out Uriah's assassination with no qualms or hesitation, and David knows it.

General Joab is no mindless assassin or "hit man," however. The king, in his haste and consternation, has ordered a faulty plan for Uriah's demise. David's instructions call for Uriah to be put at the front in a fierce battle and for Joab to then withdraw his soldiers so that Uriah will be isolated and killed by the enemy. As a seasoned military man, David's general immediately sees the flaw in the king's instructions. At the least, it will hurt the army's morale when they see his failure to support and aid one of their mighty warriors. More importantly, the *intent* to single Uriah out for death might well appear too obvious.

Instead Joab himself leads the troops into battle but assigns Uriah and some of the army to a place he knows will involve the fiercest fighting and present the greatest danger. Joab recognizes his own risk, both in the battle itself and in the change he has made to David's explicit instructions. It will mean the deaths of a number of Israel's troops along with Uriah because the army will advance close to the walls of the city, a very risky and hazardous maneuver in ancient warfare. But Joab is certain that this ruse will completely cloak David's plan to have the enemy kill Bathsheba's husband. To all appearances, the deaths of Uriah and the other valiant soldiers will be the unfortunate outcome that so often happens in warfare.

The scheme unfolds just as Joab has planned. The fighting is intense and some of Israel's bravest are killed along with Uriah. The general sends a messenger to David reporting on the outcome of the battle. As Joab had suspected, the king does become angry when he learns of the change in his original plan and the resulting deaths of some of his prized troops. Nearness to a town's fortified walls was a dangerous and foolhardy position for attackers. The defenders enjoyed a height advantage over the attackers and could easily hurl down arrows, javelins, large stones, firebrands and other missiles from their protected positions.[4] The king cannot understand why his instructions were not followed and why such unnecessary risks were taken with the army. Then the messenger finishes his report as Joab had instructed him by saying, "Your servant Uriah the Hittite is dead also."

All's Well That Ends Well?

David's surge of anger quickly disappears. "Shedding crocodile tears" is an old figure of speech. It means giving an outward show of sorrow over some unfortunate event in order to fool others, while rejoicing inwardly because it happened to someone you disliked or wanted to see punished. So it is with David. Upon hearing of Uriah's fate, he reacts with pious hypocrisy. No Pharisee in Jesus' time could have performed this role any better. He gives the messenger some comforting words to carry to Joab. The fact that Joab countermanded his orders and numbers of loyal soldiers were killed as a result suddenly becomes immaterial to the king. Uriah is dead and nothing else matters!

David is pleased. His cover-up has worked quite well. When Bathsheba learns of her husband's death, she mourns for him (see 2 Samuel 11:26), but the text is silent about any remorse she may have felt. When the prescribed period of mourning is concluded, David brings her to the palace and she becomes his wife. End of the matter? Case closed? Hardly! The closing sentence of chapter 11 contains a quiet but very ominous warning: "But the thing that David had done displeased the LORD." David is in the process of learning several hard, painful lessons concerning sin, lessons all Christians need to remember and follow absolutely—unless we want to encounter and live with the consequences of our failures like David will do.

The Lessons Begin

The first lesson can be abbreviated into a one-sentence principle:

Principle #13: Sin affects not only the sinner but others as well, because no one can sin in a void.

The world has been selling a certain kind of bromide in ever-increasing amounts over the past generation. This particular sedative not only sounds and looks appealing, it acts remarkably well in dulling our moral senses and silencing any warnings from our consciences. It is sold by leaders in the media, by teachers on our nation's campuses and by politicians trying to appeal to the growing numbers of an amoral electorate. It goes as follows: What's done in private by an individual or between consenting adults should be of no concern to anyone else.

This bit of worldly "wisdom" is a flat-out lie, although, as with many lies, this one appears reasonable, persuasive and enticing.

Some who are uneasy with this "new morality" may ask, "But what about the potential consequences?" The man and woman of the world have a ready answer for that question: "It is my life and I'm willing to pay any of the consequences from my actions." However, they fail to understand that these consequences are like ripples from a stone thrown into the placid waters of a pond. The fall-out from one's own sin too often extends to impact a number of other people.

Iverna Tompkins often tells her audiences, "You'll never pay it alone." For confirmation you can ask the family, friends and co-workers of any drug addict, AIDS sufferer, alcoholic, adulterer or slave to pornography. They are the innocent victims whose only fault was some sort of ordinary connection to the sinner.

David and Bathsheba's short time of illicit satisfaction is an excellent Exhibit A in the courtroom of God. We have already seen how their union led to Uriah's death and to those of several other Israelite warriors. But this tragedy is not the end of the consequences. Many more people will experience the evil results from this couple's liaison. A royal family will be torn apart, a nation will suffer civil war and the final years of a great king's reign will be tarnished forever—all the result of a single, private act between consenting adults.

Planting and Harvesting

The next lesson David will receive from the Lord is one of the most vital principles in all of Scripture. I have come to believe that it is perhaps also the most overlooked, particularly in today's supposedly "enlightened" society. This powerful truth is found in Galatians 6:7, and here is my way of phrasing it for our 21st-century ears:

Principle #14: Do not mislead yourself. You cannot fool God and make Him your puppet. Whatever you plant is what you will harvest.

We tend to think that planting and harvesting happen only on farms. The fact is that this principle is at work in the life of every person, in every occupation and in every action that we take.

The Seed Factor

It is important to watch what we plant, because in Galatians 6:7 God promises that we will *always* harvest just exactly what we planted. Everything produces after its own kind, as the first chapter of Genesis tells us. This law is so self-evident and simplistic that even young children recognize its validity. They know that a farmer who wants to raise corn will have to plant corn seeds in his fields. On a more mature level, students and workers realize that if they want to succeed in the classroom or in their chosen profession, they will need to invest effort, time and training in order to have the best chance of achieving their goals.

In the spiritual realm, however, this obvious truth is often ignored or rationalized away. Believers want occasionally to pursue activities that are not entirely legal or "right." Indulging in wishful thinking allows them to get past the law of sowing and reaping—or so they think. As a result, they cheat on their income taxes or on their spouses or on their employers—oblivious to the danger such sinful seeds are bringing on themselves and others.

I can understand how non-Christians can buy into this kind of thinking and behavior. But for a Christian to pay so little attention to this basic truth is foolhardy at least and tragic at worst. Large numbers of God's people today seem to be fulfilling the definition of a Christian given a century ago by Ambrose Bierce, an American journalist and writer. Bierce wrote, "A Christian is a person who follows the teachings of Jesus Christ, insofar as it doesn't interfere with his life of sin."

Why do numbers of people who claim to be truly born-again Christians fail to grasp the obvious truth of Galatians 6:7? First and foremost, many of them have a false image of God. It has been said that to a certain degree all of us make our own images of God, and these images make us. We, as a result, eventually become like the God we imagine. The problem arises when we refuse to properly receive and follow the revelation God has given us of Himself in the pages of Scripture.

In his provocative book *Ten Lies About God*, Erwin Lutzer entitles the first chapter, "God Is Whatever We Want Him To Be."[5] Having been raised in a culture that idolizes rampant individualism and secular humanism, people want a God who will help them toward their personal life goals. Since the God of the Bible is so holy and demanding, Lutzer says Americans go "god shopping," likening this activity to a "spiritual smorgasbord" where they can "find a deity that is best suited to their tastes. We prefer a God we can manage, not an omnipotent God, but an accepting deity committed to helping us fulfill our human potential."[6] Given this kind of philosophy, it is no wonder that so many of us ignore the warnings of Scripture and plant whatever seeds we feel will best suit our needs and desires at any given moment.

The Time Factor

I believe that the other main reason Christians think they can get away with disobeying God's Word is that they do not understand the role time plays in the principle of planting and harvesting. Your harvest will come only some time *after* you have planted. Just as a farmer plants his fields in the spring but does not bring in the harvest until late summer or fall, weeks, months or even years may pass before the bitter harvest of some sinful episode we planted in our lives finally arrives. During this time we often think or hope that these evil seeds will die in the ground and that our actions will never come to harm us or become known to others. One writer makes this telling observation:

> How easy it is to believe that if God's judgment isn't swift, it isn't coming. We think we are getting away with things when God is only withholding judgment while hoping for repentance on our part.[7]

The Bible is very explicit, though, and you can be certain of one thing—the harvest will arrive. God will see to that. These seeds *will* germinate and grow and begin to push up into the light of day, and the crop they produce will come to harvest time. When such time arrives, we will be forced to confront God's judgment and the grievous results of our sins. These confrontations will not, moreover, usually take place in some convenient private and surreptitious way but in the glaring and embarrassing light of public scrutiny.

The Multiplication Factor

Certainly the first two aspects of planting and harvesting should contain enough warnings to dissuade Christians from the temptation to plant wrong things—whether in their families, vocations, finances, friendships or entertainment. But it is the third fact about planting and harvesting that should give pause to any believer.

This third component can be simply stated as "You'll harvest *more* (and often much more) than you have planted." Once again, this is a truism of agriculture but an absolutely vital one for human existence. Mankind could not survive unless the seeds planted by farmers each year produced harvests sufficient in size both for present consumption and to provide seed for next year's planting.

Some of my family's relatives were farmers, and as a young boy I observed the planting of corn. Two or three kernels of corn would be planted in a small hole in the soil. Several weeks later, a stalk of corn would grow from these few seeds, and on that mature stalk would be anywhere from one to five or more ears of corn. Count the number of kernels on the next ear of corn on the cob you eat, and you will get a vivid illustration of the multiplication factor in planting and harvesting.

Now consider the application of the Galatians 6:7 principle to all aspects of human existence. God is both encouraging and warning us of an inescapable fact concerning the seeds we plant in our lives. On one side of this coin is the evil we are capable of doing and planting. Scripture promises, "Be sure your sin will find you out" (Numbers 32:23). The numerous instances in recent years of well-known individuals whose bright careers or ministries came to startling and tragic conclusions are testimony to this fact. Long periods of education, training and hard work, years of climbing the ladder of success, a lifetime of service and dedication to some good cause—all come crashing down because of one misdeed, one brief dalliance, one wrong seed planted years ago and almost forgotten. A valuable name and reputation are irreparably tarnished, lives are shattered and the course of a family or a ministry or an organization or a nation is diverted into tragic paths. Such will be the sad case with David. The sin of Israel's greatest king is one of the best examples in Scripture of how a single sinful indulgence can set in motion an avalanche of grief and disaster. His brief moment of passion will result in years of trauma for himself, for many of those he loves and for the nation he leads.

The other side of the coin, however, offers an incredible cornucopia of blessing for the obedient saints who love God's Word. David's life up to the point of his sin with Bathsheba is possibly the finest illustration in the Bible of how the Lord can and will bless a person whose heart is to serve Him above all else. Consider again David's journey. He went from an unknown shepherd boy raised in a dysfunctional family and living in a backwater town to becoming the mighty king whose exploits and wisdom propelled his tiny nation to heights we still remember and extol three thousand years later. The tiny seeds of faith and trust in God that the young boy first began to plant in the unpromising soil of the bleak hillsides of Judea continued over the next decades to produce a harvest of victory, accomplishment, fame and wealth almost beyond measure.

The Bottom Line

In his challenging book *How Now Shall We Live?*, Charles Colson makes a statement that may seem almost impossible at first glance, but which I think underscores the importance of Galatians 6:7. "Christians who understand biblical truth and have the courage to live it out can indeed redeem a culture, or even create one."[8]

I would add, "Or redeem their smaller units of a society—families, neighborhoods, churches, schools, businesses and local governments." Planting the right kind of seeds can make a profound difference in our lives and in the lives of those around us. Future harvests are awaiting each of us. The question is, What kind of crops will these harvests produce?

We are about to discover the bitter harvests awaiting David.

FORGIVENESS

The Season of Brokenness
(2 Samuel 12–20)

"When the doctrine of the love of God is not balanced with an understanding of the fear of God, error is the result. Likewise, when the fear of God is not balanced by the love of God, we have the same results."

—JOHN BEVERE

21

CONFRONTATION

The prophet Nathan's slow, labored walk reflects the heavy thoughts gripping his mind as he approaches the palace on this spring day. The rays of the early morning sun are already dispelling the night's chill and announcing the beginning of a pleasant and bright day, but Nathan is oblivious to the inviting scene around him. His mind is in the midst of a turmoil like he has never before experienced. He feels nearly overcome by a mixture of grief, concern, apprehension and fear.

The grief is the result of a fateful message God has instructed him to deliver to his friend David. The concern and apprehension come from uncertainty about the possible effect this message might have on the futures of the king and the nation. The fear is the product of his coming confrontation with a powerful monarch, a confrontation involving a stern censure from the Lord and a humiliating public exposure of the king's hidden sin.

None of the palace guards or staff question Nathan about the purpose for his visit or stop him from entering David's quarters. He is, after all, one of the monarch's closest friends and widely recognized as a mighty prophet. Both he and the prophet Gad serve as the king's spiritual advisors. But as Nathan *approaches the king's quarters, he finds himself wishing once again that the Lord had chosen Gad to deliver these distressing and dangerous words.*

Nathan knows why God has assigned this unpleasant task to him, however. The divine call started many months ago, when he began to receive the first quiet hints about some questionable events involving the king. His initial suspicions came from the whispered gossip and snatches of rumors he heard circulating among the palace staff. At first he had simply dismissed these words as idle speculation or fabrication, the kind of almost slanderous hearsay common to most organizations. As the weeks passed, however, Nathan sensed a divine prompting to investigate the matter.

But no matter how careful his probing, discreet his inquiries and astute his observations, Nathan knew that he absolutely needed God's revelation about the true nature of this matter. So he spent long periods of prayer and meditation before Him, and the Lord soon revealed and confirmed to His prophet the tragic extent and depth of David's sin. He moreover charged Nathan with the responsibility of confronting David, giving the prophet clear direction about when and where to confront the king, the words to speak and the method of presentation.

The prophet did not hesitate or delay but obeyed God's summons and set out for the palace. He knows that God has carefully and surely selected the moment, the message and the messenger.

(We have seen how the Lord divinely chose the time, the setting and the method of battle when David faced Goliath. Such is the case with this confrontation.)

David smiles warmly as Nathan enters the room. Very few people are allowed to so unexpectedly and freely enter the private quarters of the monarch, but the prophet is one of the select number. The two exchange pleasantries and sit down. Nathan begins to speak at once, and his opening statements sound to David as if the prophet is presenting an important legal matter for his consideration. The king assumes this case is before one of the courts and involves some difficulties which he, as the nation's supreme judge, will be called upon to rule.

Nathan conveys God's words in a skillful and penetrating story-like manner, causing David to be drawn like a wild creature into a well-baited trap. Nathan describes a situation involving two men, one very rich and the other quite poor. The rich man is visited by a traveling friend and, in the manner of Near Eastern hospitality, desires to provide his friend with a fine meal. Rather than kill an animal from his own extensive flocks for the meal, however, he takes the only animal of the poor man, a little ewe lamb who has become like the family pet.

As Nathan's narrative comes to a close, the king reacts in great moral anger against the greedy actions of the rich man, declaring that this person deserves to die. But since the theft of a lamb is not a capital crime, David invokes the command of Exodus 22:1, requiring the offender to repay four times over for the lamb he took.

David has, unknowingly, just passed sentence on himself. He does not realize that he has been ensnared until Nathan now springs the trap. The Bible contains a number of verses and statements so overwhelming in their divine and dramatic power that they are known and remembered even by numbers of people who rarely read the Bible. Genesis 1:1 and Moses' message from God to the pharaoh of Egypt, "Let My people go," are two examples. Nathan's pronouncement, "You are the man," belongs with them.

These four words slice into David's soul and spirit like a razor-sharp sword, a living illustration of the operation of God's Word as promised in Hebrews 4:12: "For the word of God is living and active. Sharper than any double-edged sword, it penetrates even to dividing soul and spirit, joints and marrow; it judges the thoughts and attitudes of the heart" (NIV). They come so unexpectedly and with such divine force that it takes several seconds for their full impact to register on the king's mind and conscience. Then the realization bursts upon his psyche. The deed is known! The awful hidden sins he has so cleverly buried have been resurrected for all to see, and the voice he is hearing is not Nathan's but God's!

David is too stunned to interrupt while Nathan presses on, delivering the full divine judgment. The prophet speaks in the first person, emphasizing that the words are not his but come directly from the Lord. In the manner of other Old Testament prophets, Nathan begins by recounting the many blessings David has received from God's hands over his lifetime. Then he tells how these blessings have been ignored or forgotten by David while His chosen king has entered into sin.

Nathan pronounces a three-part sentence, each one mirroring an aspect of David's sin. Since he had brought violent death upon Uriah, he will experience violence and bloodshed throughout the remainder of his life. The child who was conceived from this adulterous relationship will die. Evil will, moreover, be raised against him from his own family. And while David's initial sin of adultery was done in private and his murder of Uriah was performed surreptitiously, this violence and evil will be done openly so that the king is publicly humiliated.

David responds with the terse statement "I have sinned against the LORD." With these brief words he fully admits his guilt, offers no excuses or rational-

izations and humbly accepts God's judgment. This heartfelt admission enables the prophet to at once give the king a further word from God: "The LORD *also has put away your sin; you shall not die."*

Nathan reaches the end of his message. He has completed God's assignment and so he gets up and leaves as suddenly as he came. David remains seated as the prophet exits the room; he is fully absorbed in repentant reflection. Despite this public exposure of his sins and the penalties he will suffer because of them, he finds himself relieved and thankful as an amazing sense of deliverance and freedom sweeps through him. The enormous burden of sin he has carried for months is suddenly lifted from his inner being, and the cloud of unconfessed guilt that has separated him from the light of God's presence is blown away. The Lord has truly forgiven him and his sin is gone!

For the first time since the fateful evening with Bathsheba, David once more experiences the stirring in his spirit he had enjoyed in so many past times. He kneels in the middle of his room, reaching out to his God in humility, brokenness, contrition and gratitude, and the words start to come:

> Have mercy upon me, O God,
> According to Your lovingkindness;
> According to the multitude of Your tender mercies,
> Blot out my transgressions. . . .

Psalm 51

As David later continues to ponder the forgiveness granted him by the Lord, he will compose additional praises to His mercy and infinite love, such as Psalm 32.

The king realizes that, for the foreseeable future, he must face the consequences of his sinful actions. There will be no escape from that. He knows it will mean a time of tests and trials, a period different from the recent glorious past. But he takes consolation in the knowledge that his Lord will be with him through it all, just as He has been with him ever since those long-ago days in the solitary Judean pasturelands.

As David continues kneeling in prayer before the Lord, Nathan reaches his home and slumps wearily on a couch. He feels spent, spiritually and emotionally, but is still able to gather a few fragments of physical and inner strength to begin a prayer of intercession for David. His heart is heavily burdened for his beloved friend, the king. He perceives only too well the trials and tests awaiting David because of his sins.

At that very moment a palace servant approaches the king. The man is nervous and apprehensive because he carries a distressing message. Bathsheba's infant son has suddenly become seriously ill, and the king is urgently requested to come at once. David has been forgiven by God, but his Season of Brokenness has already begun.

22

HARD LESSONS

The memorable meeting between David and Nathan offers critical and much needed lessons for 21st-century Christianity, particularly for believers in the United States. The teachings we will examine once undergirded the values and beliefs of nearly all Christians in our nation. Today, however, biblical guidelines either are forgotten or only given lipservice. This development is the prime reason why the lifestyles of most people who claim to be Christians hardly seem to differ from the behaviors and attitudes of the general public.

Deadly Disrespect

The Lord through Nathan twice makes a profound indictment of David's sin (2 Samuel 12: 9–10) first by asking, "Why have you despised the commandment of the LORD?" and then by stating, "You have despised Me." The Hebrew word translated "despise" is defined as follows:

The basic meaning is "to accord little worth to something." While this action may or may not include overt feelings of contempt or scorn, the biblical usage indicates that the very act of undervaluing something or someone implies contempt. Thus David's adultery with Bathsheba is equated with contempt for the Lord and His word.[1]

If David could so flagrantly despise God and His commandments, can any of us think we are somehow immune from falling into the same behavior? It would seem so; based on my experience, Christians by and large question the idea that they could ever become guilty of despising God. The basis for such skepticism lies in the way we have allowed the world's viewpoint regarding truth to influence our attitudes and behavior. What is this viewpoint? It is the subtle but pervasive influence of moral relativism. Many Christians have been infected by this spiritual disease without their being aware they have contracted it.

The Trap of Moral Relativism

What exactly is moral relativism? It is the belief that there are no absolute moral truths, the conviction that everything in life is relative to the person and his own situation. So we are free to

Do whatever seems right, what feels good, what produces the least resistance, and what provides the greatest personal fulfillment. Each person thereby dictates the standards and principles that will rule his/her world, regardless of anyone else's standards and principles.[2]

The evidence of moral relativism is easy to spot. You will find it in expressions such as "I know what the Bible says but . . ." or "Everyone's doing it" or "Your personal choice is all that really matters."

This mind-set has grown to epidemic proportions throughout the Christian Church in America. A recent survey reported that only 32 percent of born-again Christians in the United States believe in moral absolutes.[3] In other words the majority of American Christians think there is no such thing as absolute truth. Given such statistics it is not difficult to explain how nearly one-third of born-again Christians say that cohabitation, gay sex and watching sexually explicit movies are morally acceptable, or why they have the same probability of divorce as non-Christians.[4] Let's be totally frank: Moral relativism is an abomination in the sight of God. One principle is clearly taught from the first book of the Bible to the last, Genesis to Revelation:

Principle #15: Ignoring the Bible's commands and teachings, or thinking we are free to change its meanings in order to satisfy our personal feelings and desires, is tantamount to treating our God with disrespect and even contempt.

The entire Bible is God's Word, and it gives us the absolute and unchanging standard of right and wrong because it is based upon His divine nature. It does not just *contain* God's Word, but it *is* His Word. This Word is moreover unchanging and eternal (see Isaiah 40:8; Matthew 5:18; 24:35).

Moral relativism is simply another attack upon God's Word, a warfare as old as mankind. The first battle was fought in the Garden of Eden when Satan threw doubt upon the Lord's command by saying to Eve, "Has God indeed said . . . ?" (Genesis 3:1). She succumbed to his temptation and decided to base her actions upon her personal feelings and desires. David fell into the same trap when tempted by the alluring sight of the naked Bathsheba. The end results in each instance proved disastrous.

The most serious danger facing both the true Church and America in the beginning years of the 21st century is not from terrorists, nor the Mideast crisis nor the tidal wave of drugs and pornography washing over the land. Our greatest threat comes from the growing popularity and acceptance of moral relativism. If this philosophy succeeds in capturing the minds of enough people, then the Church and our nation will experience times similar to those Israel underwent during the book of Judges when "everyone did what was right in his own eyes" (Judges 17:6; 21:25).

This period seems to be fast reappearing in America. The mind-set of moral relativism is already sending shock waves through our daily lives. Consider as an example the well-publicized revelations of financial chicanery at some of the largest American corporations. The disclosures surrounding Enron, WorldCom, Tyco and others have negatively impacted stock markets here and abroad and are altering the public's sense of trust toward business in general.

But why do we tend to be so surprised by these exposures? "[This] wave of corporate fraud did not emerge in a vacuum. It is in part a consequence of a society that refuses to recognize absolute standards of right and wrong."[5] The philosophy of moral relativism has been gradually permeating the lessons taught in our schools and colleges, the laws promulgated by our legislatures, the decisions rendered by our courts and the news and entertainment manufactured by our media. If no universal ground for morality exists, as the proponents of moral relativism contend, then the individual can choose and construct for himself or herself whatever system seems to best suit his or her personal preferences. The end result will be more Enron-type affairs in every area of our society.

The Crisis of Confrontation

We can learn from Nathan how to deal with others when differences, disagreements or disobedience come between us. These happenings will almost inevitably bring about some sort of confrontation, and confrontation is one of the most difficult tasks people face, especially those in leadership positions.

As a business executive I was occasionally required to severely reprimand or even fire my subordinates. This was one of the aspects of management I most disliked, but I knew it was a necessary component for properly leading any group or organization. Confrontation will always be a part of our lives, whether we are on the giving or receiving end of it. "Life without confrontation is directionless, aimless, passive. When unchallenged, human beings tend to drift, to wander, or to stagnate."[6]

Consider how vastly different David's life might have been had the Lord not sent someone to confront him. How might his hidden sin have exerted an increasingly corrosive effect upon his spirit, soul and body, drawing him into further acts of evil?

There is a tragic aspect to the United States' obsessive emphasis on political correctness, particularly as it applies to the tenets of moral relativism. It is the growing acceptance of the belief that we should never criticize or confront others for their lifestyle choices. (Of course, this stricture against confrontation and criticism often does not apply when dealing with born-again Christians, since this group is deemed by the political correctness police to be too narrow-minded in their beliefs.) The fruit of such *laissez-faire* morality is on public display every day, from the well-publicized lack of ethics among leaders in business and government, to the recreational use of drugs by all segments of society, the growing acceptance of pornography and violence in entertainment and the growing acts of random violence. The list goes on and on.

Even worse is the way confrontation between God and man has been nearly eliminated from the American consciousness. Consequently we frequently read or hear statements such as "If people are generally good during their lives, they will earn a place in heaven no matter what religious faith they follow." Many Christians are, sadly, not exempt from having a faulty concept of God and a gross ignorance of the Bible's teachings.

It is popular among believers to see God solely as a deity of love and mercy, an understanding and benevolent heavenly Being. The Bible, however, presents the Lord as perfect in all His moral attributes—love, mercy, justice, righteousness, holiness and faithfulness.[7] All of His attributes function together in perfect harmony. He truly is a God of love (see 1 John 4:8), but He is also a just and righteous God (see Romans 10:3) and so He must punish sins; otherwise He would not be true to all the aspects of His nature. There is no contradiction or tension in His character. Both the mercy and justice of God are declared and maintained in beautiful divine balance.

> If you think of God only as merciful, you'll find it easy to disobey his Word. You'll believe he esteems his warnings lightly, that he doesn't mean what he says.[8]

We must, as Christians, reflect this divine balance of loving justice. This requires us to have the right heart attitude, motive and concern for the people we confront. Christians have an all-too-prevalent tendency to confront each other in anger, haste, ignorance or prejudice. One Christian counselor cautions that:

> A context of caring must come before confrontation. A sense of support must be present before criticism. An experience of empathy must precede evaluation. A basis of trust must be laid before one risks advising. A floor of affirmation must undergird any assertiveness. A gift of understanding opens the way to disagreeing. An awareness of love sets us free to level with one another.[9]

Nathan exemplified these traits beautifully in confronting David, but he knew that he was literally taking his life in his hands when he faced the king. Even though he was speaking the truth in love, it was a hard, brutal truth and the prophet could not be certain how David might react. Nathan could not be certain that the king would not attempt some further evil to keep this matter hidden. But he had an assignment from God, and the fear of death was not going to keep him from following the Lord's directive.

Where are the Nathans in today's churches? They seem to have become a scarce commodity. Have today's Christian leaders been so seduced by the popular mind-set of political correctness that they have reduced biblical principles to the level of personal preferences? Has the modern emphasis on trying to be a "user-friendly church" caused pastors and elders to water down the Gospel message so no one will be offended (or convicted of sin)?

Inner Turmoil

We can learn from David the effect that hidden and unconfessed sin can have on the entire body. Our society attempts to convince people that the concept of sin is sadly quaint, an old-fashioned and outdated superstition and that absolute moral truth is a fantasy, the creation of narrow-minded religious zealots. The notions of sin, guilt and conscience are figments of unenlightened thinking. Such fantasies should have no place in the makeup of a well-educated and ambitious person living in our highly advanced Western culture. All lifestyles are equally valid, so self-fulfillment should be our goal. But we will not reach it unless we free ourselves from the stultifying perspective of some supposedly unchanging standard of right and wrong.

David would beg to differ with this viewpoint. During the year between his acts of adultery and murder and his confrontation with Nathan, the king lived in his own private hell. Outwardly he may have appeared to be the same strong, decisive and charismatic leader his nation had come to esteem and follow. Inwardly he suffered intensely, tormented and tortured daily by the remembrance of his sin and the knowledge that by it he had estranged himself from God.

How can we know this about David? Very simply: He tells us so in his own words. Psalms 32 and 51 were most likely written very shortly after his encounter with Nathan. He vividly describes throughout these verses his inner feelings and thoughts about the aftermath of this terrible episode. In Psalm 51, he acknowledges that he could never escape from the constant guilt of his sin (see verses 3–4). He further confesses that his sin was ultimately against God (see verse 4), and that it had taken away the joy he had always experienced with his Lord (see verses 8, 12).

He likens his inner anguish to a person suffering from broken bones (see 51:8) and aged and wasted bones (see Psalm 32:3). (Bones are referred to in various Old Testament passages as a symbol of the well-being and vitality of the entire person.) In Psalms 6 and 38, which some scholars believe were also written about the Bathsheba and Uriah event,[10] David further records how his outer and inner man suffered as a result of these hidden sins.

His experience is not unique. Scripture warns repeatedly about the consequences of sin, and Erickson holds a very insightful discussion about them, which I have condensed and paraphrased as follows:

- Sin has the power to enslave. One sin can lead to another, so it can become a habit or even an addiction.
- Continuing in sin produces insensitivity and causes a person to become less responsive to the promptings of conscience.
- There can develop an unwillingness to face the reality and the consequences of sin, resulting in a denial of sin by the use of positive language or relabeling. Sin becomes described as a matter of mere sickness, or deprivation or ignorance.
- Sin negatively affects a person's relationships by making him or her increasingly self-centered, more prone to reject authority and less able to love and empathize.[11]

True Repentance

Americans are becoming desensitized to genuine wrongdoing. Terms such as "right and wrong," "virtue versus evil" and "moral responsibility" hold little meaning for most people. In fact, words like *sin* and *repent* can even be an affront to the sensibilities of certain groups. Immediately after the 9/11 attacks, the United States seemed to be caught up in a new religious wave. But this wave appears quite similar to the description I once heard of the Platte River in Nebraska: a mile wide and an inch deep. One writer summarized our nation's spiritual shallowness with the title of his article—"America's New Religiosity: God Bless America, But Don't You Dare Tell Us to Repent!"[12] Colson makes a telling observation: "Typically, prison is the one place where I don't have to belabor the message of sin; it is the one biblical truth that men and women behind bars know well."[13]

David knew that he had sinned and understood that only an act of true repentance could gain him God's forgiveness and restore his broken relationship with the Lord. In Psalm 51, David recorded all of the elements of true repentance. Throughout this psalm, there is an underlying tone of genuine sorrow for the sins he has committed, a recognition that God ultimately is the one we sin against, a refusal to offer any excuses and an acknowledgment that true repentance demands a complete change of mind and a resolve to totally turn away from the sin and obey God.

What a contrast with the public confessions of wrongdoing we read about in the newspapers! Even Christians have a tendency to adopt a worldly and shallow form of repentance, thinking that a perfunctory belief in Jesus Christ and a brief, superficial prayer is all that is required. We seem to have little desire to demonstrate the honesty of our repentance by changing the ways we live. Bonhoeffer called this type of thinking and attitude "cheap grace."

> Cheap grace is the grace we bestow on ourselves. Cheap grace is the preaching of forgiveness without requiring repentance, baptism without church discipline, Communion without confession, absolution without personal confession. Cheap grace is grace without discipleship, grace without the cross, grace without Jesus Christ, living and incarnate.[14]

David was not a superman, merely a man flawed like any other human being. But he demonstrated the key quality God looks for in those who have a desire to be people after His own heart. This quality is daily submission to the Lord and a willingness to deal drastically with sin through the godly kind of confession and repentance.

Foster lists confession as one of the spiritual disciplines and writes, "The Discipline of Confession brings an end to pretense."[15] When David admitted to Nathan, "I have sinned against the LORD," he stopped pretending and found God's forgiveness and grace he so desperately needed. We need to follow David's example and not the world's brand of "confession."

The Inexorable Harvest

Here is another area where the theology of cheap grace has misled many Christians. Not only have they bought into the notion of some superficial form of repentance, they have blithely assumed that God's forgiveness means He has also removed any repercussions from their sins.

> *Principle #16:* **When we honestly confess our sins
> and truly repent, God promises to forgive us
> completely (see 1 John 1:9), but He does not remove
> the effects and consequences of our sins. We have to
> live with and through them.**

A close relative of my wife's led a dissolute existence for many years.
Then late in life he was miraculously and gloriously saved and filled
with the Spirit. This man became an active and valuable layperson in
a large, dynamic church, and faithfully witnessed everywhere about the
Good News of Christ's offer of eternal salvation. But his long years
of sinful behavior had taken their effect on his body. He lost a lung
and suffered from a variety of other ailments. Even though he led an
exemplary Christian life after his conversion experience, God did not
heal him from the physical consequences of his past life. A few years
later the ravages he had inflicted on his body took their deadly toll.
What you plant you will eventually harvest. It is sad that when this
happens most people are greatly surprised and want to blame God for
their circumstances.

David was about to enter into a series of bitter harvests. The wonderful
forgiveness he had received from the Lord had not eradicated the evil
seeds his actions had planted. Those seeds had germinated and were
beginning to produce fields full of disorder and death.

God Does Not "Play Favorites"

People often have serious questions and problems with the apparent
mercy God showed to David. Leviticus 20:10 orders the death penalty
for adultery. Why did God not demand this punishment for David? Was
the Lord "letting him off the hook," or was He showing favoritism to
the man He had chosen to be Israel's king? Neither! Schultz offers a
sound insight on this matter:

> After Nathan had exposed the sin of David, he proceeded to declare his
> sentence. It was not a sentence of death in the ordinary sense of the term,
> but it was a sentence of death in a sense even more difficult to bear.[16]

The remaining twenty years of David's life bear stark confirmation of this assessment. Israel's king would experience an unending stream of heartaches, humiliations and hostilities and a series of personal trag-edies, bringing him frequent times of misery during the remainder of his life.

Other people come down on the flip side, wondering at the final part of God's judgment. Nathan foretold that the child born from David's adulterous affair would die. It may seem unfair and even unjust that this little one should be punished because of David's sin. Such is our human reasoning. God, however, told David that his sin had enabled the enemy to blaspheme His name.

David will not die, but the son born to him will. "When David slept with [Bathsheba] and created new life, the woman did not belong to him but to Uriah. The child cannot belong to David."[17]

23

BITTER HARVESTS

The death of Bathsheba's infant son is the first tragedy to strike David, but it is only the initial stage of the Lord's judgment. More grievous events lie in store for him because the Lord has declared in 2 Samuel 12:10–12:

> The sword shall never depart from your house . . . [and] I will raise up adversity against you from your own house; and I will take your wives . . . and give them to your neighbor, and he shall lie with your wives in the sight of this sun. For you did it secretly, but I will do this thing before all Israel.

There are many bitter harvests contained in this short prophecy, harvests that will bring repeated miseries and remorse into the remaining years of David's life.

In reading over the events of these years, some readers might be tempted to criticize the Lord for being unduly harsh toward David. But these situations need to be viewed through the lens of God's Word. What really matters about sin is not what we or society think but what God thinks. Over the past two or three generations an amazing transformation has taken place in our culture. One writer observed the earlier stages of this trend:

The word "sin," which seems to have disappeared, was a proud word. It was once a strong word, an ominous and serious word. It described a central point in every civilized human being's life plan and life style. But the word went away. It has almost disappeared—the word, along with the notion. Why? Doesn't anyone sin anymore? Doesn't anyone believe in sin?[1]

God's Word contains some very blunt, uncompromising teachings on sin. The Bible tells us that sin, our sin, had separated each of us from God and doomed all mankind to eternal damnation. But "God so loved the world" He sent His Son, the Lord Jesus Christ, to bear the death penalty for our sins by dying in our place. The awfulness of sin can only be truly seen against the infinitely costly remedy God the Father used in order to redeem us from the ultimate consequences of our sin.

The Bible also teaches that we have responsibilities toward the blessings the Lord has given us. Before Nathan pronounces God's judgment he reminds David of the phenomenal blessings he has received from the Lord (see 2 Samuel 12:7–8), and God further says, "I would have given you much more!" David has allowed a momentary surge of sexual lust to blind him to the goodness of God.

Public Shame

And so the bitter harvests began to reach fruition—heart-wrenching adversities and trials David will undergo for nearly two decades. The first of these involves great personal embarrassment and humiliation, an enormous public shame that comes in two stages.

In our times sin in high places can be hidden for a while. Eventually, though, the truth breaks out in a tidal wave of newspaper headlines and special television reports. When this happens the culprit enlists a cadre of "spin doctors" in an attempt to minimize the shame and damage to himself.

David refuses to set this kind of shallow and morally shabby precedent. He actually helps to make the full extent of his sin become known by writing Psalm 51. He expresses in these verses his deep grief over the sin and gives spiritual insights, instructions and warnings to others so they might learn from the folly of his evil.

Remember that David's psalms were not his own private meditations and, therefore, meant strictly for his own personal edification. Nor were

they only compiled and distributed publicly many centuries later. Psalm
51 (as well as a number of other psalms) carries the superscription, "To
the Chief Musician." Why was this notation made a part of the psalm's
title? Simply because:

> The author of the psalm, usually David, put the psalm into the hands
> of the choirmaster with the intent and purpose that he might rehearse
> it with the Levitical choirs and so *introduce it to Israel for public worship*
> [emphasis mine].[2]

Imagine our own reactions if we discovered some of our most heinous
sins, ones that were private or known only to our spouses or closest
friends, suddenly being put into words and to music to be sung in the
Sunday morning service in our local church.

The fundamental aspects of true scriptural repentance remain the
same for us as they were for David. Sometimes godly repentance can
be done entirely in a private meeting between the contrite, broken and
repentant sinner and his Lord. Other times, however, repentance may
also require the sinner to seek forgiveness from others he has wronged.
Such is the case with David. Israel's king knows he has broken trust
with the nation God has called him to shepherd. So despite the personal
embarrassment, he recognizes the need to admit his wrongdoing before
the people, to let them know he has truly repented to the Lord and seek
to regain their trust in him as a godly ruler.

What a rare and astounding action for a great leader! It usually seems
that the higher a person's station in life, the more difficult it is for him
to honestly and openly admit to any personal wrongdoing. The reason
for this hesitancy is not hard to find. Pride is the obstacle that so often
keeps people from truly dealing with their sin. What some today are
calling repentance is nothing more than a form of regret, human sorrow over the fact that they have been caught and are concerned over the
embarrassment or hurt they might suffer because of their sin.

Involuntary Humiliation

David's humiliation is continued years later when his son Absalom
leads a well-planned revolt to seize the throne and kill his father. Shortly
after David and most of his supporters flee Jerusalem, Absalom and his
followers enter the city. One of his first acts is to ask Ahithophel, for-

merly David's counselor but now one of the rebels, for advice as to what should be the next step in their revolt (see 2 Samuel 16:20). Ahithophel counsels this rebel son to have sexual intercourse with the ten concubines David has left behind by putting up a tent on the palace roof and publicly taking each of these women into the tent.

> It was, according to Eastern ideas, the grossest insult that could be offered to a king, and that king a father, and it would prove the breach between David and Absalom was irreparable, that it was vain to hope for any reconciliation.[3]

The Valley of Violence

There are a number of clichés concerning the ways children mirror the attitudes and behaviors of their parents: "Like father, like son" or "The acorn doesn't fall far from the tree" or "He's a chip off the old block." David's children certainly fulfilled these old adages. Tragically they copied his sinful traits while seeming to ignore his good qualities.

David planted the violent murder of a loyal man. His harvest is a stream of violence erupting from within his own family. When God told David, "The sword shall never depart from your house," He was predicting severe and grievous events in the king's future life. The swords David faced until now have been on the battlefields, fighting against Israel's enemies. Now the warfare will take place in his own home.

Sexual Violence

The opening act of violence sets the stage for some later tragedies. The trend begins with Amnon, David's firstborn son and the heir-apparent to Israel's throne. Like his father with Bathsheba, Amnon finds himself consumed with lust for his beautiful half-sister Tamar, whose brother is Absalom. Second Samuel 13 details his sordid maneuverings to entice her into his bedroom. Once there he proceeds to rape her and then callously evicts her from his house, implying that she was at fault for the whole affair.

Tamar's future now has been irreparably ruined. As a virgin daughter of the king, she most likely would have been given in marriage to the son of a high official in Israel. Now she is forced to hide herself in Absalom's household, devastated and made desolate by this horrible experience (see verse 20); a young woman who will be deprived forever of the opportunity to enter into a choice marriage.

David soon learns of Amnon's despicable act and becomes "very angry" (verse 21). Then he does . . . nothing! Why does he take no righteous action, when the Law's punishment for such sin is clearly stated (see Leviticus 20:17)? What sort of message will the king's inaction send to Amnon, to the rest of his family and indeed to everyone who learns of this violation? Won't David's failure to punish Amnon be construed as indifference toward sin and appear to give license for others to act however they please?

Various suggestions have been offered by Bible commentators to account for David's lack of action. Some point to a phrase that was added to verse 21 in the *Septuagint*, a Greek translation of the Old Testament widely used in the three centuries before Christ. This addition states that David loved Amnon because he was his firstborn son. If so, such love was sadly warped. God's Word is clear: punishing (chastening) a child for wrongdoing is evidence of the parent's love and concern for the child's well-being.[4]

Another suggested explanation claims that David was inhibited from punishing his son because he had done even worse things in the incident with Bathsheba. The king may have recognized intuitively that

> Children take their cues from their parents—how honest they are, how they treat people, and what are their values and goals. The child assumes that it is all right to do what the parents do. When the model for the act has been the parent, it is hard to criticize the child.[5]

But the real fault seems to lie with David's failure to properly control and guide his family and to train his sons. This incident, along with at least three others in the coming years, reveals this great warrior and ruler of Israel to be a failure as a father. While the demands of the kingship on his time and energy obviously limited the hours David could spend in his household, Scripture indicates that he was negligent and even indifferent in ministering to his large family.

Violent Revenge

The next spasm of violence involves Absalom, David's second-oldest son,[6] and his reaction to Amnon's rape of his sister Tamar. He is infuriated by his brother's crime and seeks for an opportunity to avenge Tamar, eventually waiting two years for the right moment to retaliate. The nurturing of this murderous anger is demonstrated by his never speaking to Amnon during this time.

At last Absalom senses the perfect opportunity and concocts a devious plan to assassinate his brother. He arranges a celebration in connection with the annual shearing of his flocks and invites David to the feast. When the king politely declines, Absalom persuades him to let Amnon go in his place, and the king agrees. Here we see David's negligence. If he had truly been attentive to family matters, he would have been aware of Absalom's hatred for Amnon.

Absalom succeeds in killing Amnon, leading to another bitter harvest for David, this one being an estrangement between Absalom and himself. Absalom flees to the country of his mother's relatives and remains there for three years. During this time David takes no action either to pass judgment on his son for his murderous act or to forgive and recall him even though he "mourned for his son every day" (verse 37, KJV). David continues to be indecisive. "His love and his sense of justice find no place of reconciliation, so, torn between the two, he does nothing."[7]

Joab finally takes action and devises a ruse to convince David that he should allow Absalom to return to Jerusalem (see 14:1–24). But once his son comes back David refuses to see him for "two full years" (verse 28). The king and his son finally meet after a five-year hiatus, but the scene is brief and perfunctory, with little sense of true forgiveness and reconciliation on either part (see verses 29–33). So the stage is set for Absalom's final act of rebellion, the most grievous and terrible of David's bitter harvests.

The Violence of Rebellion

Treason! The word resounds with the discordant chime of betrayal. The name of Benedict Arnold lives in memory because of it, and the pages of history are filled with men who violated their sworn allegiances. Yet Absalom's treason is particularly despicable in that his treason is against a man who is both his own father and the Lord's chosen ruler.

Absalom begins at once to spin a deviously calculated plot that will require a lengthy period of time (four years)[8] before he is ready to strike. His methodology is an ominous presage of the tactics used by some

modern-day politicians. He begins by capitalizing on his appearance, and
the text indicates that he must have been an extremely handsome and
virile man (see 2 Samuel 14:25–26). He appears in public regularly with
an impressive retinue of chariots, horses and fifty attendants, projecting
the picture of a powerful leader and creating the clear impression that
he is indeed the heir apparent to the throne. Next he stations himself
early each day at the city gate, the place where law affairs and business
transactions are usually discussed and decided. He cunningly intercepts
those who are coming to Jerusalem with a legal matter they want the
king to judge, feigns a show of sympathy for the rightness of their cases
and deceitfully claims that David has not appointed any representa-
tives to hear their complaints.[9] Absalom never actually attempts to help
them with their legal problems, but craftily suggests how much better
the system of justice would be if he were in charge. This hollow show
of concern, phony sympathy and an adroitly suggested political solution
enable him to gain great popular support and allow him to lead a successful *coup d'etat* after only four years.

David seems, strangely and surprisingly, oblivious to what is happening, despite the length of time and public nature of Absalom's subver-
sion. The king, just like the people, is completely fooled by his son's
smooth words (see 15:7–9). Why? How could a man so blessed by God
be blind to what was taking place under his very nose? There are two
possible and plausible reasons, and each one offers a lesson for leaders
and parents today.

A Lesson for Leaders

The initial success of Absalom's rebellion seems, on the surface, quite
baffling in light of David's long and successful rule. How could so many
Israelites turn their backs on the God-anointed man who has led their
nation to its greatest heights and elect to follow a brash, inexperienced
upstart like Absalom? Some have conjectured that it might have been
the result of the king's deteriorating ability to rule and care for his people
during these latter years.[10] This decline may well have occurred to some
extent and been a factor in swaying people's loyalties. But an additional
explanation involves our human fickleness toward leadership in general.
The longer a person leads an organization, the greater seems the tendency

for people to magnify that leader's faults while diminishing or forgetting his accomplishments.

A classic example involves Great Britain's Winston Churchill, a man many consider the greatest statesman of the twentieth century. He became Prime Minister at one of the darkest moments in his nation's long history, the early stages of World War II. It seemed nearly certain that the little island nation would suffer defeat at the hands of Hitler's powerful armed forces. But through his incredible leadership and stirring speeches, Churchill saved his country, guiding it successfully through the long years of conflict. Shortly after the allied victory, however, he and his political party were soundly voted out of power.

How quickly people can forget! How often we become disillusioned with a leader because of our tendency to focus on his failures or become dissatisfied by thinking, "What has he done for me lately?" (The sudden and widely shifting results of the approval ratings for our key politicians demonstrate how abruptly the public's opinion can fluctuate.)

Perhaps David, like many leaders, had become so confident in the strength of his position and his lofty reputation that he felt untouchable by any possible stirrings of revolt. Perhaps he saw Absalom as a rebellious boy and not as a true threat.

A Lesson for Parents

Some parents turn a blind eye to their children's actions while others appear unwilling to be objective about the lifestyles of their offspring. The Bible gives us a number of examples of how *not* to raise children and, sadly, David's is one of them. Scripture admonishes us to talk plainly and regularly to our children about the love of God, His provision for us at the cross and the incredible and eternal advantages of living godly lives. We must never leave them to chance and the circumstances of life, hoping that they will automatically make wise choices now and in the future. My wife frequently counsels on family matters and offers the following advice to parents:

Learn to know your children. Become involved in their schools and leisure activities. Let them have their friends in your home so that you know what kinds of conversations and entertainments interest them. Influence their choice of clothing and how they decorate their rooms. You do not need to be on the attack for everything they do, but be prepared to reason with them and, if necessary, forbid their participation. The parent has a responsibility to stand in the way of a child's foolishness when that parent knows where certain activities will or may lead. While we often need to stand by and allow them to test their wings, we also need to be alert and ready to help them back on the right track. At other times we may need to be more directive and prevent their involvement in some activity we know will have certain lasting negative consequences. God will always be faithful to guide you if you honestly seek His wisdom in raising your children.

24

GRACE IN THE MIDST
OF A STORM

The Lord is allowing David to harvest the results of the wrong seeds he has planted earlier in life. He is not being unjust or cruel by permitting these things to happen, however. "God forgives the planting of the seeds of sin, but this does not necessarily prevent those seeds from growing into full maturity."[1] This mature harvest will be a means the Lord uses to chasten and discipline David. Hebrews 12:5–8 describes the "God-kind" of correction and how we should respond to it. Such discipline is not administered harshly but in divine love. God's goal is the ultimate well-being of His people.

A Hasty Exit

The train of events begins suddenly and proceeds swiftly (see 2 Samuel 15:13–23). David receives news of the revolt from a loyal, unnamed messenger who has correctly ascertained the probable size and danger of Absalom's following. The king reacts at once and plans to evacuate Jerusalem immediately. Somehow he feels unable to defend the city.

Whatever his reasons, the king and all those in his enormous household grab what items they can, hurriedly vacate the palace and begin the long trek eastward out of the city, up the Mount of Olives and along the road leading toward the Jordan River. The scene is a humiliating one for David, the powerful monarch, who is now reduced to a refugee fleeing for his life, burdened and surrounded with a large number of women and children as well as assorted members of the palace staff. The once-mighty ruler of Israel is walking along barefooted and weeping with his head covered, and all of the people accompanying him are doing likewise (see verse 30).

The Miracles Begin

Then the Lord begins to send His miracles into David's tragic situation. The first one involves David's friends. God has arranged for him to get life-saving support from a variety of people who are willing to hazard their own lives to join with him at this critical time. There is a contingent of six hundred fighting men, foreign troops who have been an integral part of David's forces since his fugitive years in the wilderness. Next is a soldier named Ittai, a Philistine. He has joined the royal forces only recently, yet he pledges to go with the king even though David offers to release him from his commitment. What a contrast these men present! Here are non-Israelites who remain steadfastly faithful to David while his own son is working for his overthrow and death.

Next come the priests, Zadok and Abiathar, carrying the Ark of the Covenant, but David tells them to take the Ark back into Jerusalem because he knows it belongs in the nation's capital city. His faith and trust are in the living God rather than in any superstitious belief about some magical qualities associated with this holy symbol (see verses 25–26). He does, however, instruct them to be his eyes and ears in Jerusalem and send information to him when Absalom and his forces take over the city (see verses 27–29).

Ziba, Mephibosheth's servant, arrives with a large supply of food, drink and animals for transportation. Some have questioned Ziba's motives, claiming that he probably brought these items to curry favor with David and to falsely accuse Mephibosheth of abandoning David, in the hope of gaining political power for himself. The fact remains, though, that this man proves himself loyal and helpful to the king at a crucial moment when many others are deserting to Absalom.

Several other people are also willing to risk their lives for David by getting secret messages to him concerning Absalom's actions and plans. They include two sons of the priests who act as messengers, an unnamed servant woman who brings needed information to the two messengers and an unknown man and his wife who hide the messengers from Absalom's servants. Finally, when David and his large company reach the Jordan River and cross over to safety, another group of men provide the weary, fearful refugees with a wide variety of food and other necessities. Each of these people fulfills the Bible's description of true friendship.[2] God has directed them into David's crisis at precisely the moment they are most needed. May we, too, find these kinds of friends in our moments of need!

Divine Deception

The second miracle arrives at the same time some bad news comes to David. He is told that Ahithophel, his brilliant counselor, has joined Absalom's conspiracy. His defection is a severe blow to David's cause, and the king is greatly grieved over this latest betrayal by a close and trusted friend. Many scholars believe David wrote Psalm 55 during these days, and claim that verses 12–14 refer specifically to Ahithophel. Despite his shock and sorrow David does not wallow in despair. Once again he immediately gives the matter over to God and prays, "O LORD, turn Ahithophel's counsel into foolishness" (verse 31). David is, in essence, asking for a miracle, because 2 Samuel 16:23 mentions how greatly this man's counsel is respected and followed. Baldwin explains:

> [Ahithophel's] advice was accepted with all the authority normally reserved for the word of God himself. Since both David and Absalom acted on his advice, he was virtually running the country.[3]

The Lord supplies His solution in the person of Hushai, one of David's close friends and a person the king has also turned to for counsel. His desire is to join David's cause, but the king wisely recognizes that Hushai can best serve him by returning to Jerusalem and acting as a spy in Absalom's court. So he gives Hushai some insightful instructions as to how he can ingratiate himself to his rebel son. In doing this David foresees that the man may have an opportunity to give advice to Absalom that might somehow offset the counsel of Ahithophel (see 2 Samuel 15:32–37).

The plan works to perfection as God divinely directs events. Hushai greets Absalom when he comes to Jerusalem and, by using flattering words (with a double meaning Absalom does not catch), wins over the rebel leader and gains entrance to his court. How ironic that David's son had used the same kind of vain and deceptive words to win over thousands of Israelites to his rebellion! Now he is unwittingly caught by someone else's flattering speech. Here is a further example of harvesting what you plant.

Absalom calls his leaders together almost immediately after settling into the capital. Ahithophel is, naturally, the first one asked for advice as the deliberations begin, and his two-part recommendation is a masterpiece of ruthless, ungodly wisdom and decisive, brutal action. If Absalom follows Ahithophel's proposed course of action, David will be killed, his supporters immobilized and the revolt will fully succeed.

Absalom and his leaders seem ready to adopt Ahithophel's plan. Then the Lord intervenes by putting a thought in the rebel leader's mind—to call for Hushai and ask for his opinion of the plan. He is brought into the meeting where Absalom quickly summarizes Ahithophel's advice and curtly asks Hushai's evaluation of it. David's friend has no time to ponder and consider his reply. Consequently the answer he gives is a remarkable demonstration of how the Lord can quickly and effectively impart wisdom to His people in critical situations.[4] Calling Ahithophel's plan "not good," Hushai proceeds with an artful mixture of past truths (David and his men are mighty, valiant warriors), spurious suppositions (they are like enraged bears and already are in hiding), inaccurate assessments (they are still capable of inflicting defeat on Absalom's forces) and fawning flattery (success will come if Absalom leads all Israel against David) to sway the minds of Absalom and his leaders (see 2 Samuel 17:5–14).

Absalom's pride is his Achilles' heel, and Hushai plays to it with consummate skill. Ahithophel's wise counsel is overridden by this God-anointed deception. All the rebels agree that Hushai's advice is better and they adopt his plan, thereby sealing the rebellion's fate and illustrating the truth of Proverbs 16:18: "Pride goes before destruction, and a haughty spirit before a fall." As one commentator aptly summarizes this episode, "It is with counsel as it is with many other things: what pleases best is thought best; solid merit gives way to superficial plausibility."[5]

"The Battle Is the LORD's"

God's third miracle for David is wrapped up in the battle itself, and the details are provided in 2 Samuel 18. It begins with the selection of the battle site. The king, with his long experience in warfare (and obviously aided by divine insight), chooses a location known as the Wood (or Forest) of Ephraim. This area lies a few miles east of the Jordan River, approximately halfway between the Sea of Galilee and the Dead Sea.[6] The terrain is mountainous and, in David's time, "was probably thickly wooded with oak, pine, cypress, arbutus, etc."[7] So the king entices Absalom and his army to fight in a location where the advantage lies with the loyal forces of David. Many centuries later the Duke of Wellington will draw Napoleon into battle near the little Belgian town of Waterloo because he knows that the ground will be particularly suited to the tactics he intends to use against the French army.

Absalom's forces probably outnumber his father's by a significant number,[8] but David does not consider this situation to be a serious obstacle for three reasons: First and most importantly, Jesse's youngest son has almost always faced battles against opponents who were stronger and more numerous than his own forces. He has absolute faith that God will give him this victory, too, and even instructs his leaders not to harm his son, fully expecting the young man to be captured by David's victorious troops.

Second, David knows that the rough, wooded terrain will impede the enemy's ability to use his numerical advantage. Under these conditions the skill, battle experience and courage of the individual warrior in David's army will outweigh his opponent's more numerous troops. Lastly, Absalom is not a warrior, nor has he experience in leading an army into battle. David's three generals are seasoned warriors and well schooled in the strategies and tactics of military leadership. So it is no surprise that when the tide of battle turns in David's favor, Absalom appears unable to rally his troops.

A Humiliating End

Thus it happens: Absalom suddenly finds himself confronted by David's warriors and attempts to evade capture. But while trying to ride his mule through the thick forest, his hair becomes caught in the low branches of a prickly oak tree. The mule gallops on leaving David's son hanging helplessly in the air. One of the soldiers sees Absalom's absurd predicament and rushes to tell Joab. The general berates the man for not killing Absalom then and there, but the soldier has heard David's command not to harm his son and tells Joab that he will not disobey the king's instructions.

Joab has no such qualms, however. Letting Absalom live, whether as a prisoner or an exile, may well pose an ongoing threat to the remaining years of David's reign and lead to further civil uprisings. So Joab is now willing to earn the king's wrath by killing this rebel son. He finds Absalom, thrusts some spears through his body and has a few of his soldiers finish the grisly task by hacking the body to pieces with their swords.

What an inglorious end for this proud, vain, ambitious and self-seeking son of David! First he is caught like a frightened animal in a hunter's trap. Then to be so mutilated by swords that his once-handsome features and virile body are unrecognizable when he is finally thrown into a pit in the woods! One commentator says, "This was God's judgment on the young man's vanity."[9]

Tough Lessons

The real measure of our spiritual strength and maturity can be accurately determined only during those times when the storms of life appear as though they are about to overwhelm us. Throughout these discouraging and dangerous days, David's whole demeanor shows him to be an Old Testament saint who lived by the New Testament precepts taught in Philippians 4:6–7.

David does not become angry or bitter toward the Lord and makes no attempt to manipulate Him, but he hopes that God will still find a way to show him mercy. By sending the Ark back to Jerusalem, he places his present difficulty and uncertain future in God's hands (see 2 Samuel 15:25–26). Shortly afterward he refuses to retaliate when a relative of Saul named Shimei verbally and physically abuses the king and his followers. Over four centuries ago, Madame Guyon wrote about adopting this kind of heart attitude: "You must utterly believe that the circumstances of your life, that is, every minute of your life—anything, yes, everything that happens—have all come to you by His will and by His permission."[10]

All Christians are like David since, no matter how godly we try to live, there will be times when God must discipline and chasten us as was mentioned earlier in this chapter. When my wife and I served as pastors, Christians would occasionally ask us for prayer and assistance because they claimed "the devil was attacking them" in a certain area of their lives. After counseling, however, we would often discover that they were simply undergoing corrective training and discipline from God. So let's not be too quick to blame our negative experiences and crises on Satan. We should guard against the urge to blindly rush in and try to extricate another Christian from some hard circumstances.

> We need to have a deep sense of knowledge that God is at work in people's lives through various crisis times and experiences, and we need to allow them to run their courses, so the purposes of God might be achieved. [Otherwise, we will] absolutely prostitute the purposes of God in that person's life.[11]

Awful Aftermath

The news of the army's victory and Absalom's death reaches David. The rebellion has been crushed, but the decisive battle cost the lives of twenty thousand men. Neither this triumph nor the deaths of so many warriors matters to David at this moment, for his son is dead and the king throws himself into a black hole of grief and despair. He completely ignores Absalom's deceptive and ruthless revolt, the grave dangers this attack presented to himself, his family and all his supporters and the commitment and courage of his loyal army. He withdraws from everyone, offers no thanks to his troops for their bravery and makes no attempt to assert his leadership over the nation. The king is so consumed by sorrow over his son's death that he is totally oblivious to the effect his reaction is having on others. Why?

Chafin says, "When we can't get over some loss, it is usually because there is a larger agenda than grief alone."[12] In David's case the agenda consists of his numerous failures and sins, beginning with the many wives and concubines he acquired all the way through his adulterous episode with Bathsheba, the murder of Uriah and his neglect of his family. David has recognized his errors too late to save his son, so now he has submerged himself in a spasm of self-recriminations and torment.

A Different Kind of Friend

Joab—rough, brutal and unfeeling Joab—will not allow the king to continue in his self-inflicted misery and isolation. He accosts David with blunt, uncompromising words and causes the king to see the potential disaster to himself and his people unless he puts aside his unhealthy grief and once again takes up the mantle of Israel's leadership (see 19:1–8). Joab indeed has some serious character flaws, but at this moment he is willing to face David's wrath. No wonder then that Swindoll makes the following assessment of Joab's action: "Joab was a friend to David. He cared enough to confront him. He cared enough to tell him the truth and prevent him from compounding the damage that already had been done by making an even greater mistake."[13]

David may have "hated Joab's guts," to use a coarse colloquialism. Nevertheless he was able to recognize the godly wisdom in the old general's harsh reproaches. Joab was certainly different from the friends who came to David's aid when he was on the run from Absalom, but he was still a friend to the king at this critical moment.

Most of us are familiar with the stereotype of the powerful leader who surrounds himself with people who will tell him only what he wants to hear. We call these followers "yes men," "flunkies" or worse. Before criticizing this kind of leader, consider one thing about our own lives: I wonder how often we, subconsciously perhaps, are willing to receive advice, counsel or correction only from those we consider "real" friends—people we genuinely like, persons we agree with and who always seem to agree with us. Would we be willing to receive a strong message from God if He sent it to us through a "Joab"?

And Life Goes On

David arises from his gulf of grief and returns to his kingly duties. The aging monarch will discover, however, that the remaining years of this Season of Brokenness will be difficult and depressing ones.

Some of his decisions (those involving Shimei, Ziba and Mephibosheth) will, unfortunately, be odd or even unexplainable, indicating the possibility of a slippage in David's previous ability to make wise and decisive choices. Most extraordinarily David appoints Amasa, the man who had commanded Absalom's forces during the rebellion, to the generalship of his army in place of Joab (see 19:11–13). We can only conjecture why David makes this astounding choice. Perhaps he wants to punish Joab for killing his son. Or perhaps he is trying to show Absalom's supporters that he will not take any revenge upon them. This attempt at change is, however, short-lived. Joab soon murders Amasa, and the king is once again forced to live with an army leader he fears and despises.

Through all these and other events, the wound in David's heart over Absalom's death will remain. It will be a constant reminder of his folly in letting the pursuit of sinful pleasure and neglect of his family lead to such a disastrous end. So the final years of his life, a time that might have been rich with honor, achievement and peace, will instead be covered with the ashes of ruined dreams and lost opportunities.

FINALITY

The Season of Begetting
(1 Kings 1:1–2:12; 1 Chronicles 22, 28, 29)

"Success is measured by generational transfer."
—BOB MUMFORD

25

GOD CHOOSES AGAIN

The old king presents a pathetic picture as he lies bedridden in his chamber. His once vigorous body is now almost drained of its physical prowess. His mind, will and emotions are pale shadows of his former self.

His condition, however, is not the result of the many years he lived as a fugitive or of the lengthy and frequent periods of campaigning and warfare he endured as king. None of these things—not even the stress and pressure associated with the daily demands of kingship—could have wreaked such havoc on David's body and soul. His enfeebled condition has been caused largely by the overwhelming tide of heartache, grief and guilt over his failure as a father and the unbelievably sinful actions of his eldest sons, Amnon and Absalom. He has just reached the age of seventy, but has declined so rapidly in body and mind that he appears much older and more infirm than his actual age would indicate.

His servants have brought a beautiful young woman to serve as David's nurse, hoping she will be able to help him regain some vitality. The younger David, under similar circumstances, would have quickly seduced this lovely creature and added her to his harem. Now he has become an impotent invalid, no longer capable of enjoying such pleasures, even when she lies next to him in bed.

David's mental decline is a more serious matter for the well-being of Israel. He has been losing touch more and more with the affairs of his kingdom. The palace staff is the first to notice their monarch's inability to stay involved with the daily business of governing, but others in the kingdom have also begun to recognize the signs of his decay.

The most critical concern, however, is the question of who will follow David as the next king. In the nations surrounding Israel, the eldest son of the reigning king would normally be expected to follow his father to the throne. Israel is a relatively new nation, though, and its rights of primogeniture (who should become the next ruler) are not very well defined. The general population is wondering about the how and who of the royal succession.

One person in particular has become keenly interested in this question: David's eldest remaining son, Adonijah. He, like his brother Absalom before him, is endowed with handsome features and an ability to promote himself and attract a following. He has heard rumors about his father having promised Bathsheba, Solomon's mother, that he has selected her son to succeed him as king. But David has done nothing about it since apparently making this decision,[1] so Adonijah is encouraged to take advantage of his father's ambiguous behavior. He has believed ever since Absalom's death that the kingship is rightfully his as the eldest surviving son, and that most of the nation considers him to be the heir apparent to the throne. Solomon is still a comparative youth after all, while Adonijah is a mature man of 35.[2]

But Adonijah knows that David might suddenly decide to keep his promise to Bathsheba by holding a public ceremony to anoint Solomon as king. He must strike quickly to gain the great prize. Following his brother Absalom's example, he first gathers an entourage—chariots, horses and men—to show his prestige and power. Then he persuades two of David's oldest associates, Joab and Abiathar, to join his plan. Finally he organizes a great sacrifice and feast just outside of Jerusalem and invites all of his brothers (except Solomon) as well as a number of David's other officials. By this maneuver Adonijah is formally claiming the throne for himself, and the people attending the feast give their approval by proclaiming, "Long live King Adonijah!"

At this critical moment the Lord has a man prepared to step forward boldly and thwart the enemy's plan. God is not about to allow His choice of Israel's king to be circumvented. So the prophet Nathan intervenes for the third time to bring David back to the path ordained by God.

Nathan quickly informs Bathsheba of Adonijah's coronation feast and then devises a plan for both of them to independently tell David what is happening. By this means each will confirm and reinforce the other's report and, hope-

fully, shock the king into filling the political power vacuum he has allowed to develop. Bathsheba goes first and asks David why Adonijah is proclaiming himself to be the new king when David has promised that Solomon would be his successor. She expresses the potential danger to both Solomon and herself if Adonijah succeeds to the kingship.[3] As soon as Bathsheba finishes speaking, Nathan enters and confirms what she has said. He adds that neither he nor Bathsheba, Zadok the priest, Benaiah the commander of the king's bodyguard nor even David himself has been invited to Adonijah's coronation.

An unbelievable change appears instantly in David's entire demeanor—a change that can be only attributed to God's divine intervention. His eyes, dull and lifeless moments earlier, now seem to flash with life and purpose. The weak and querulous voice suddenly recaptures its old timbre and force. The calendar is turned back twenty years and people again see the David they remember—the strong leader exhibiting quick thinking, godly wisdom and decisive action.

He begins by pledging to Bathsheba that he will this very day fulfill his oath to make Solomon king. Next he issues a series of stern orders that will completely undercut Adonijah's attempted rebellion. Zadok, Nathan and Benaiah are instructed to place Solomon on the king's royal mount and conduct him along with the loyal palace servants and guards to a sacred royal place outside Jerusalem. There Zadok and Nathan are to anoint Solomon and proclaim him king.

This procession naturally attracts a large number of Jerusalem's residents, who follow along. When the coronation takes place, all the people join together in noisy celebration proclaiming, "Long live King Solomon!" The crowd accompanies their new king back into Jerusalem with shouting, dancing and playing of musical instruments. Their enthusiastic behavior is so spontaneous and prolonged that the very ground seems to shake.

Their noise reaches the place where Adonijah and his supporters have gathered, and they wonder what might be happening back in Jerusalem. Just then a messenger arrives and informs them that their plan has failed. Solomon has been crowned king by David and his royal officials, and the people are giving their approval with a loud and jubilant celebration.

Panic immediately sets in. Adonijah's conspirators and all the guests rush from the feast, anxious to distance themselves from this aborted revolt and avoid the new king's wrath. Adonijah knows all too well what awaits him, so he hurries to the tabernacle in Jerusalem and seeks sanctuary at the sacred altar, begging the new king to show him mercy. His revolt has collapsed in a few moments, and Solomon will reign as God's choice for the next forty years.

What began only a few hours earlier as the actions of an old prophet, a middle-aged wife and a king near death has culminated in the victorious coronation of an incredible monarch. His wisdom will be renowned through the ages, and he will be used by God to author three books of the Old Testament. "Bold and courageous conduct on the part of a few, had an astonishing effect upon the many."[4]

Procrastination

David almost causes a disaster to his family and nation by default. For some reason he has procrastinated in publicly naming and anointing Solomon as his chosen heir to the throne. He could have firmly established his son's position and authority by having him serve as co-regent during his final years. Why has the king delayed when he knew from the time of Solomon's birth that the Lord loved this child and had chosen him to someday succeed his father to the throne?[5] Through his non-involvement and failure to recognize the imminence of his own death, David nearly allows man's appointment of leadership instead of God's.

Perhaps David was waiting for the "perfect time," or possibly he felt Solomon was not yet old enough to take on such responsibilities, or maybe David just wanted to rule by himself for a few more years. Whatever the reason, his delay opens the door for Adonijah's attempted palace coup. God comes to his rescue at what seems to be the very last moment, and the Lord's miraculous intervention prevents a political disaster which would probably have pushed Israel into a second civil war.

Before criticizing David, let's remember the times we have allowed ourselves to delay doing something we knew needed our immediate attention. An advertising slogan used by a sports-related company says simply, "Just do it!" Some of us might be helped by posting this little phrase as a reminder in our homes.

26

NEVER-ENDING
BLESSINGS

The word *beget* means to bring into existence. Just as a man and woman can beget a child, we can birth things into reality that will still be operative long after we have departed this earth. The aged King David is about to beget some profound things that will affect the course of Israel's history.

Two Kinds of Friends

One of the most difficult experiences a Christian ever deals with is having a close and trusted associate turn against him without warning or apparent reason. David faced this situation on at least two notable occasions. One occurred when Ahithophel, his wise friend and counselor, suddenly joined Absalom's rebellion. The second takes place during Adonijah's attempt to seize the throne: Joab and Abiathar, members of David's inner circle who have been with him since his fugitive days, decide to align themselves with Adonijah's cause.

The truth is that people will often disappoint us. Even those we consider the strongest and most dedicated born-again believers can fail us at certain times. No wonder the Bible warns us about where to place our ultimate trust:

> It is better to trust in the LORD than to put confidence in man.
>
> Psalm 118:8

God is not surprised when your best friend betrays you. If we continue to serve Him in trust and obedience, we will eventually discover that He has already prepared the remedy. When Ahithophel betrayed David, for example, God sent Hushai, whom He used to counteract Ahithophel's treachery. Likewise at this crisis in the Season of Begetting, the Lord comes to David's aid by replacing Abiathar the priest with Zadok the priest and Joab the military commander with Benaiah the military commander.

We have already seen Nathan's devotion to God and his holy boldness in confronting David. He continues his faithfulness at this decisive moment by enlisting Bathsheba's help in alerting the king to the danger that is about to topple his reign. Once again David is willing to receive the prophet's warning; God in His wisdom uses the only two people who could have persuaded David to take such immediate and powerful action.

Next we meet Benaiah. He is another of those minor Bible figures who appear suddenly at a vital moment to fulfill some special, God-ordained task. The Lord has been preparing this man, and has now placed him in exactly the right place and time to assist David and Solomon. But who is Benaiah? He is one of the mightiest of David's mighty men. Scripture records several of his extraordinary military exploits.[1] He has been serving as a general who commands one of the monthly courses of 24,000 troops.[2] At this time he is also in charge of the several hundred soldiers who comprise David's personal bodyguard.

How perfectly the Lord has arranged the situation! Although Joab is the commander-in-chief of the nation's entire army, he is preoccupied for the moment with Adonijah's coronation feast. His troops are scattered and not ready for immediate action. Benaiah's soldiers, on the other hand, are all on duty and ready to respond instantly to orders. Benaiah and the whole bodyguard are intensely loyal to David, so when the king commands him to accompany and protect Solomon throughout his coronation, Benaiah replies affirmatively and enthusiastically. No outside force is strong enough to oppose this dedicated warrior and his obedient troops. No one will be able to prevent Solomon's coronation.

Man's Way versus God's Way

During this Season of Begetting David experiences a blessing similar to the ones that God has performed for him in his past seasons of life. From his childhood years in Jesse's home until this season when his earthly life is drawing to a close, the Lord has constantly frustrated man's attempts to defeat David. His father and older siblings sought to keep him as the low man on the family's totem pole. Saul tried to kill him to prevent his becoming king. The Philistines made numerous attempts to defeat him. Absalom connived to overthrow and murder him. Adonijah now plots to usurp the throne and deny David's choice of a successor. Every one of these men has two things in common: They all were actually fighting against God's plan, and they all failed.

There is an old saying, "Man proposes but God disposes." A similar thought is repeated twice in the book of Proverbs (see 14:12; 16:25) and can be paraphrased as follows: "There is a road before each of us that may seem like the right way to go, but it eventually will lead us to death."

Do we realize at this very moment that God has a specific plan for each of us? Do we realize how much better and greater His plan is than ours? Jesus came to give us abundant life (see John 10:10), and God promised through Jeremiah the prophet (see 29:11) that His thoughts are to give us a future and a hope. If we put aside our plans and fully cooperate with His plan, no power in heaven or on earth will be able to defeat it.

David's life provides numerous illustrations of this divine truth. Time after time we read of David's cry to the Lord for help as he recognized his own limited abilities compared to the infinite, miraculous power and grace of the Almighty. Time after time we read of God's answer.

27

DAVID'S LEGACY

A legacy is something handed down to a person from one of his predecessors or from the past. This word is not often used today. The phrase "last will and testament" is the usage we are more familiar with. We also tend to think of a person's last will and testament in terms of material things—money, investments, property and so on. The Bible makes no reference to David's last will and testament. Nevertheless he does leave Solomon a tremendous tangible legacy: the rule of the powerful, prosperous and peaceful kingdom of Israel.

The Real Owner

King David in his seventieth year has become one of the world's wealthiest men, not merely for his time period but for all ages of history. Yet despite the almost incalculable wealth he controls, it does not control him. (Can we imagine any of today's richest families giving billions of dollars to a project for the Lord, as David did?) The king is able to do this with a glad and willing heart because he knows the true source and giver of all things. Read his prayer in 1 Chronicles 29:10–19, paying particular attention to verses 14 and 16. David enunciates an important spiritual principle in this passage.

> *Principle #17:* **Everything we have comes from God, so we are not the owners of the things we possess but merely the stewards.**

A steward is a person who manages and cares for another's property. The relationship, therefore, of men to worldly property is analogous to the role of temporary stewards, whose privilege is that of managing and of rendering back to God what is already His own.[1]

David recognizes that no person can boast in how his own human abilities have enabled him to gain his wealth. David knows the teaching of Deuteronomy 8:17–18: It is God who gives us the power to gain wealth. Centuries later Paul will remind us of this fact in 1 Corinthians 4:7 when he writes that all we have (including our personal giftedness) comes from the Lord and will eventually be returned to Him since He is the owner.

Statistics reveal that only a minority of Christians tithe. One reason people often give for not tithing is their belief that it is an Old Testament command. They believe that, because Christians are no longer under law but under grace, we do not have to tithe. This rationale is dead wrong. Scriptural stewardship is the reason, the foundation, for the doctrine of tithing.[2] All our wealth and other possessions really belong to God. He allows us to use them throughout our lives, only requiring us to give Him a small portion (the ten percent tithe) of the whole to which He is entitled. When we tithe we are acknowledging His full ownership of all things in our lives.

Another Kind of Inheritance

In addition to the physical kingdom of Israel, David passes on to his son a great intangible legacy that, in certain ways, is even more significant than the kingship. One part of this intangible legacy is a spiritual heritage.

In a manner reminiscent of Joshua's final words to the children of Israel in chapters 23 and 24 of the book of Joshua, David charges Solomon to wholeheartedly obey the Lord by keeping His commandments. He reminds the new king that living and ruling according to God's Word (the Law of Moses) will bring him and his nation the Lord's blessings and benefits. If Solomon faithfully follows these instructions, then God will fulfill the promise He gave to David through Nathan (see 2 Samuel 7:11–17).[3]

This is not the first time, however, that David counsels Solomon on spiritual matters. While David failed miserably to give any parental discipline and moral training to his other sons, he seems to have treated this boy far differently and to have been concerned about his spiritual upbringing.

> This is where Christian men have fallen short. They have become so wrapped up in the world that they have neglected their highest call-ing—the spiritual development of their children.[4]

Consequently some of Solomon's proverbs (such as 4:3–9) come from the instructions he has received from David and his mother, Bathsheba.[5]

A Mission from God

The other portion of David's intangible legacy involves the Temple. His great dream and desire has always been to construct a magnificent edifice for the Lord, whom he acknowledges "has redeemed my life from every distress" (1 Kings 1:29). God's will for David, however, is differ-ent. In 2 Samuel 7 Nathan first tells David that the Lord has selected someone else to be the Temple's builder. This builder is a son who will be born to David, the son God names Solomon. David himself testifies to this in 1 Chronicles 22:6–10 and 28:2–6.

So Solomon is given the divine calling for this mighty project. The Lord's decision must be a difficult one for David to accept, but accept it he does—not grudgingly or in a resigned manner but wholeheartedly and joyfully. First Chronicles 22 and 28–29:20 record his charge and instructions to Solomon and the nation's leaders, but it also reveals the king's personal feelings.

A Helping Hand

David does much more than simply encourage Solomon to undertake this project with courage and faith. David has already acquired the land on which the Temple will stand.[6] He has spent years collecting the enormous amount of materials his son will need, as well as organizing the workforce and the Temple ministries. The Bible does not record precisely when the king began the process of preparation, but it most likely occurred in the latter stages of his reign, possibly after the time of Absalom's rebellion.[7] The amount and value of the materials he bequeaths from his own private treasury are astounding. The gold he gives amounts to approximately 3.5 million ounces, while the silver totals well over 8 million ounces.[8] The boy who began life as a poor, obscure shepherd has become a powerful ruler who has amassed an almost incalculable amount of wealth. What a testimony to God's mighty ability and grace!

David also provides Solomon with highly detailed plans for the Temple, its furnishings and its personnel. The king acknowledges that he has received these plans by divine revelation, and he gives them all to his son; nothing is held back. Next he assembles all the nation's leaders and commands them to cooperate fully with Solomon, reminding them that the peace and prosperity Israel is now enjoying are blessings from God. In addition David's example of abounding generosity inspires the leaders (and later the people) to give willingly and abundantly to this work. A wise leader models the correct behavior for his followers, never asking them to do something he is not prepared and willing to do personally. The amounts gathered from this combined "fund-raising" are astounding and guarantee that this building will truly be one of the ancient world's greatest wonders.

David, Solomon and the whole assembly gather together the following day to praise and worship the Lord by offering thousands of animal sacrifices, and to celebrate His goodness toward Israel by holding a great feast. At this time they anoint Solomon again and proclaim him king, since this "great public assembly and the thousands of sacrifices would have been impossible in the context of the [earlier] ceremony."[9]

When God Says No

What happens to our attitudes toward God when our prayers do not appear to be answered in the manner and timing we want or expect, when our hopes and dreams never come to reality and when we struggle with difficulties and sorrows while others always seem to live the good life? Are we prone to become angry and bitter toward Him? Or do we hide our feelings behind a superficial smile, telling everyone, "The Lord knows best," while all the time our inner being is in the midst of a huge spiritual sulk?

Let's learn from how David responds when the Lord selects Solomon to build the Temple. The king remembers the great things God has enabled him to do rather than dwelling on the one dream he will not be allowed to accomplish.

Unfinished Business

David was a mighty man of God, but he was still a man who was capable of lapses into sin (as in the Bathsheba episode, or in his years-long failure to properly train and discipline his sons). He made other mistakes, errors not discussed in this book. One of the most serious was his ill-advised census of Israel and Judah (see 2 Samuel 24).

Here is one of the few times David proves to be unteachable. In taking the census (something God warned Israel's kings not to do), he rejects the wise counsel of Joab, possibly due to the already strained relationship between the two men. His sin brings God's judgment on the whole nation. When David recognizes and repents of his wrong action, he purchases the site where God's Temple later will be erected as a part of his repentance.

While David is leaving a great legacy to Solomon and the nation, he also leaves some nasty unfinished matters, a legacy of errors needing to be put right. One of these problems is Joab, who remains unpunished after murdering Abner and Amasa, countermanding David's orders in killing Absalom and joining Adonijah's attempted coup. The other unpleasant matter concerns Shimei, the man who cursed David but whom the king later reprieved. Now David instructs Solomon to have both of these men executed.

Why did David fail to take action against them earlier? A likely answer in Joab's case is David's own complicity in arranging the death of Uriah, which prevented him from meting out justice when Joab committed murder. The king did not punish Shimei immediately because David was struggling to reunify the nation after Absalom's rebellion and did not want to alienate Shimei's tribe, the Benjamites.

Solomon's coronation changes things dramatically. David knows that both Joab and Shimei have independent and rebellious spirits. This means that either of them could be hostile to Solomon's reign and his efforts to maintain the nation's unity. Consequently David signs their death warrants "for the good of the state," as one commentator remarks.[10] Even so David's procrastination in dealing with these men now leaves Solomon with the unpleasant responsibility of correcting his father's mistakes.

The Greatest Failure

The saddest and most unfortunate of David's legacies to Solomon was his failure to obey God's Word regarding marriage. Deuteronomy 17:17 forbids a king from taking many wives "lest his heart turn away [from following the Lord]." David's godly counsel to Solomon while the boy was growing up and his final instructions to obey fully the Law of Moses,[11] never had the desired effect. Why? Because David himself disobeyed God's command by marrying eight wives and having numerous concubines. After growing up in this kind of environment, it is no wonder that Solomon later took seven hundred wives and had three hundred concubines.[12] Nor is it surprising that some of them succeeded in turning him toward the worship of false gods.

The parental aphorism "Do as I say, not as I do" will not have the hoped-for effect on children. They are too wise, too "street smart" to follow such counterfeit counsel. They will ultimately copy our behavior, not our words.

Our Unfinished Business

What unfinished business would be left behind for our families and loved ones to confront if we were to die suddenly? During my years in the investment and commercial banking industry, I was surprised to discover how many people either failed to write a will or failed to have an earlier will updated to reflect the family's present situation. Larry Burkett offers sound advice on this matter:

> To die intestate (without a will) is to allow your state to draft your will for you! You might not agree with the decisions of your state regarding your property, your furnishings, and most of all, your children's destiny (if you and your spouse die at the same time), but you can do very little about it if you die without a will. Stewardship for the Christian is being accountable . . . for what happens to your resources in the future.[13]

There are many other ways we could leave behind a mess for our loved ones to clean up if we were suddenly to depart this earth—a monumental pile of unpaid bills and a dearth of ready cash, a basement or an attic full of junk we have never used, a lack of proper record-keeping, failure to educate a spouse on how to handle certain financial problems and so on. I believe giving careful thought to this matter right now would enable us to spot many of these potential messes.

Let me give a suggestion from an idea my daughter and her husband use in their daily lives, because it can be applied just as well in this area. They have two small children, both still in diapers. Between caring for these babies, the requirements of his job (which often involves travel and long hours) and their active involvement in a local church, it would be easy for their home to resemble a war zone, with clutter, disorganization and dirt everywhere. To combat this tendency, they have adopted a simple motto around their house: "No evidence!" Each one has agreed to do his or her part in keeping their living quarters neat and clean, so one spouse does not have to pick up after the other. This means

- If you dirty it, clean it;
- If you take it out, put it back;
- If you open it, close it;
- If you lose it, find it;
- If you break it, fix it;
- If you mess it up, straighten it out.

Adopt this mind-set and be determined to leave no evidence of a mess in your personal and family affairs, so that when you die, no one will have to spend time and money cleaning up or trying to solve the problems you have left behind.

Passing the Mantle

So David dies and is buried in the city that he made into Israel's spiritual and political capital. This youngest son of Jesse has exercised a phenomenal influence over his nation ever since that fateful moment when the stone from his shepherd's sling felled the mighty Goliath. He has excelled as a great warrior, general, statesman, administrator, his country's "sweet psalmist" and spiritual leader. He will remain Israel's ideal king down through all the succeeding centuries.

Now his son Solomon must take up his mantle and follow this outstanding ruler to the throne. But Solomon is a young man of whom the Bible gives no mention regarding his abilities and gifts. Even David said he was "young and inexperienced" (1 Chronicles 22:5). In the world's eyes, his rise to the throne might seem to be questionable. Solomon does have one qualification, though, and it is a critically important one: He is God's choice to succeed David as the nation's king, and this is the only qualification that really matters.

28

LEAVING OUR LEGACY

What sort of a legacy will each of us leave behind? In the previous chapter I warned against burdening our loved ones with a mess that we did not clean up ourselves. But there is more to a person's legacy than leaving one's financial and personal affairs in good order. How will we be remembered by our family, friends, co-workers and neighbors? Will our descendants even be able to recall our names, much less our reputations and accomplishments? The answers to these questions will largely depend upon the attitudes and behavior we project throughout our lives.

We may be sincere, born-again believers who regularly pray, read our Bibles, attend church services and tithe. We may shun society's philosophy of success at any price, its desire for an abundance of material things and the live-for-today mentality. We may dutifully avoid the world's other temptations—illicit sex, drugs, alcohol and so on. But if our general dispositions are critical, rigid, self-centered and unhappy, neither our words nor our brand of Christianity will have a positive effect on those around us.

Whether we like it or not, we influence others and, in turn, are influenced by them. Americans, highly individualistic, often overlook the powerful influences of others. The Bible clearly gives social influence proper credit.

Repeatedly in the Old Testament, believers are told to avoid the evil influences of the world, yet influence others to enter the kingdom of God.[1]

While our entire lives will have an effect upon the way we are remembered, it is oftentimes our final years that others will recall most vividly. My father-in-law was an alcoholic during much of his adult life and suffered some major disappointments in his business career. Then he was gloriously saved at the age of sixty, and the Lord led him and his wife into a quarter-century of active ministry. Both were involved in volunteer work for their church and other Christian ministries. In addition he became quite accomplished as a Gospel magician, performing "magic" tricks to illustrate and teach various Bible truths—the need for salvation, the pitfalls of a sinful life, the truth of Scripture and so on. People of all ages enjoyed his unique ministry; he always carried some balloons in his pockets and would make balloon animals for the youngsters wherever he went. He was a modern-day Pied Piper for Jesus. As his reputation grew, he received invitations to perform his Gospel magic in many non-church settings, including several public schools. It was always the Gospel he presented, not some watered-down, insipid and politically correct message. I never saw him give a performance without teaching some basic scriptural truths and explaining simply and powerfully the way of true salvation.

When he died, his long years of alcoholism were almost forgotten by those who knew him. Most people remembered the dramatic life change he underwent after becoming a Christian, his devoted service to the Lord and his church and the joyful, optimistic spirit he projected to everyone, whether on stage or off. He was a "walking epistle," and his legacy illustrates how God's marvelous touch can enable even our later years to be the most fruitful and productive of our entire lives.

A Common Problem

Even strong and mature Christians are subject to disappointments and failures, or to becoming unhappy and resentful when they occur. While these things can and do strike people at any age and station of life, such happenings become particularly difficult to accept when we have planned and striven so hard to achieve our dreams. An attitude of disappointment is often more noticeable in older persons, even in "senior saints," because the more we age, the greater grows our realization that many of our dreams and goals will never be fulfilled. A congregation can find itself with a few caustic, critical and complaining seniors who vent onto the church their frustrations over life's disappointments. Their litany of complaints about what the church does wrong can range from the loudness of the worship service and its lack of hymns to the supposed dearth of real "spirituality" in the youth ministry to the temperature in the main sanctuary. Sometimes the longevity and past service of discontented seniors can exert an influence disproportionate to their numbers.

A Scriptural Antidote

The Bible offers considerable insight on how Christians are to avoid or overcome the spiritual and emotional setbacks every one of us will encounter. Trying to distill all of these teachings and instructions into a few pages is an impossible assignment. But I have found the following three steps to be helpful in dealing with these situations in my own life:

Step One: Do not permit the world's value system to control your life.

One of my favorite Old Testament Scriptures for this step is Psalm 1. Verse one of this psalm exhorts us to avoid the mind-set ("counsel") of the world, its way of behaving ("path") and its attempt to get us to join with them ("seat") when they are actually the enemies of God ("scornful"). An excellent New Testament passage is 1 John 2:15: "Do not love the world or the things in the world." Jesus also spoke a strong warning about the world's values when He said, "For what is highly esteemed among men is an abomination in the sight of God" (Luke 16:15).

Step Two: Avoid comparing yourself with other Christians.

This is really a continuation of step one. Since we are to reject the world's system of measuring success, our level of spiritual obedience and achievement is determined on God's scale of values. The parable of the talents (a measurement of money) in Matthew 25:14–23 is instructive on this matter: One man is given five talents to manage and another only two. The man with five talents invests them and gains five more; the man with two talents invests them and earns an additional two. Jesus gives the exact same commendation and reward to both men because each one has used his talents to their fullest.

The lesson from this parable is clear: We may never be called and equipped for some public ministry. But if we obediently and faithfully serve the Lord with the "talents" He has given us, even if they seem small and insignificant, our heavenly reward will be as great as those who have been given powerful, high-profile assignments. The Lord places His approval on His people's willingness to serve, not on the amount of "talents" He gives them. (See Matthew 20:25–28.)

Step Three: Be willing to serve like David did, laying groundwork for the future.

Some Christians are called to be trailblazers and pioneers. Just as the early settlers of the United States went out into the wilderness to clear the land and establish farms and towns, these people faithfully and obediently serve the Lord by laying foundations for the spiritual growth and ministry of others. I have heard many people in ministry testify that their parents provided them with the strong Christian upbringing that was instrumental in leading them into the successful ministries they presently have.

A Word for Seniors

At this time in life, senior church members ought to be serving as "spiritual grandparents" by helping and encouraging those in the congregation who are young in age or in the Lord. My wife and I are both "senior saints" and grandparents, and so we are experiencing the ways most grandparents respond to their own grandkids. Even though it is hard on our aging bodies, we gladly put up with the physical discomfort and get down on the floor to play with our little ones. We will sit for many minutes reading simple storybooks to them or helping them with their little projects. We will gladly revise our schedules to act as babysitters so the parents can go to adult functions. Even as they grow into their teenage years, we seldom begrudge them our time, attention, comfort or money. We pray for them, send them birthday and Christmas cards, call them on the telephone, carry their pictures in our wallets and purses and brag on them to our friends.

So why can't we be more understanding about the church's "kids," whether they are youngsters chronologically or in their Christian development? Never forget that these younger and newer Christians are the generation that will carry on the Church's work and mission long after we are gone. Unless Jesus returns soon, most of us seniors will shortly be enjoying the first moments of an eternity filled with perfect peace, happiness and fulfillment. So let's not complain and grumble about the changes currently taking place in Christian music and our church services. Let's work with, encourage and support the younger generation, and leave them with a solid, godly legacy to build upon.

A Word for Everyone

Chafin offers a thoughtful admonishment to Christians on this matter of legacy:

The world has too many people who won't plant trees unless they are going to be around to eat the apples. The church needs more people who are planning and praying with the future needs of the church in mind. There are many things we would like to do and can't, but all of us can be a part of laying the foundation for the future of our children.[2]

I leave you with the same question I used at the start of the chapter: What sort of a legacy will each of us leave behind?

EPILOGUE

L et's roll."

These were the last words that anyone still living heard Todd Beamer say. He made the call to a GTE Airfone operator from United Flight 93 on September 11, 2001,[1] after being on the line for fifteen minutes. Todd presumably called to get word about the hijacking to authorities. He told her that "we're going to do something" and asked her to give a message to his wife. "I know I'm not going to get out of this," he said. Then he uttered those final words. The operator heard screams and a scuffle before the line went dead.

The terrorists apparently intended to drive the airliner into the U.S. Capitol in Washington, D.C. Instead the plane crashed and blew up in a Pennsylvania field. The actions of Todd and the other courageous passengers involved in the revolt against the terrorists saved the lives of many innocent people.

Todd's last two words struck an immediate and responsive chord in people throughout America. Neil Young, a rock musician, wrote a song eulogizing these brave people and titled it "Let's Roll." Those two words became a catchphrase in the new war against terrorism.

Todd's wife, Lisa, has, however, put a truly thought-provoking meaning to the little phrase:

> "Let's roll" is not a slogan, a book, or a song; it is a lifestyle. A lifestyle Todd and I began together . . . and one my children and I will carry on. Each time I hear those words, Todd's voice calls out once again to the children and me, letting us know it is time to set out on another adventure. Our journey is different now, but it is still one of hope, faith, and a knowledge of our ultimate destination.[2]

The Bible records that David lived this kind of lifestyle throughout the spiritual seasons he experienced. The psalms he composed vividly express his deep personal beliefs, his godly hope and faith (trust) in the Lord and his understanding that God would fulfill His promises to him.[3]

David had flaws, as is the case with every human being, and Scripture does not gloss over his sins and failings. Certain episodes in his life are a study in contradictions because his actions sometimes denied his convictions.

But despite his sinful backsliding and fleshly mistakes, David exemplified numerous godly qualities, traits that endeared him to the Lord and brought him the title, "a man after [God's] own heart." He demonstrated a lifelong spirit of humility, for example, and was as teachable when he was king as he had been as a youth. These two attributes are very rarely seen in powerful and famous people!

David did not allow his intimate relationship with the Lord and his giftedness as a psalmist to birth a sense of pride and spiritual superiority in him. Nor did he let his tremendous leadership abilities, immense popularity or the trappings of wealth and privilege cause any lasting defilement in his life or in his love and commitment to God. David understood the truth God spoke to him through the prophet Nathan: "And I have been with you wherever you have gone, and have cut off all your enemies from before you, and have made you a name like the name of the great men who are on the earth" (1 Chronicles 17:8).

David lived with the constant knowledge that God was indeed his *Jehovah Jireh*, "the Lord who will provide." I believe this is why he was never hesitant to repent when confronted, either by his conscience or by other people, about the sin in his life. He did not look for excuses or make rationalizations when convicted of sin.

David's life contains a final, often-overlooked aspect, a "secret" which helps to explain how an obscure shepherd boy could rise to such heights of accomplishments and lasting fame. This simple but profound secret was his all-consuming desire to be with the Lord (see Psalm 27:4). David demonstrated this desire by his willingness to cooperate with God no matter what spiritual season he found himself in at the time. In short he made full use of the most valuable resource the Lord gave him—the same resource God provides for each of us—time.

Most people think about resources in terms of the wealth and assets they have accumulated (or are trying to get), or their knowledge and experience, or the health they enjoy, or their physical abilities, popularity, good looks and so forth. But without the resource of time, we cannot utilize any of these other resources. Time is a unique resource because it cannot be saved. (When we speak about "saving time," we are really referring to using it more efficiently.) Neither can time be measured, because none of us knows precisely how much time we have been allotted by God. No wonder, then, that the Bible contains numerous verses reminding us about the brevity of life and exhorting us to make the most of the time we have been given right now.

The season that my wife and I were in when I began this book is finally coming to an end after nearly four years. While we are not sorry to see it go, we both acknowledge that "we wouldn't have wanted to miss it for the world"—as the saying goes. God appointed this time to impart some life-changing lessons and wonderful revelations into our lives, spiritual deposits that have caused us to grow and mature, divine dealings He will use as we enter into our next spiritual season. However it may appear to us at first glance, we know that our coming season will be exactly the right one for us.

Each one of you, my readers, is in a specific, divinely determined time, a personal spiritual season at this exact moment. How are you responding? Are you cooperating with God or complaining to Him? Do you comprehend the importance of living daily for His values, or are you wrapped up in striving for the goals of pleasure and money, in serving the gods of this world? Are you making every day count toward your eternal destiny, or are you living by the philosophy of "Never do today what you can put off until tomorrow"?

I urge each person who reads this book to follow David's example. None of us may ever attain great things in the world's eyes, but that is not really important on the scale of eternity. True success is obeying His call and giving it our best.

Let's agree with God's plan and adopt a lifestyle that gives Him the freedom to act whenever and however He chooses. Let's live for Him, knowing that none of our obstacles, battles and trials are too great, or our lives, abilities and opportunities too small. Let's allow Him to bring us to and through His divinely determined times, those spiritual seasons He knows are best for us. Let's always remember that He truly is "the God of the Impossible."

Let's roll!

PRINCIPLES

1. God is the controller of all things, and we are to live our lives in the recognition that He has a specific time, plan and purpose for every one of our life experiences and accomplishments.

2. Incomplete or partial obedience is disobedience.

3. The Foundation Season is the first and most important of all our spiritual seasons.

4. Relationship precedes leadership in the Kingdom of God.

5. Be extremely careful never to take any of the glory that belongs to God nor to misrepresent it.

6. Our response to God's dealings with us will determine our degree of spiritual growth and maturity.

7. There is no such thing as standing still spiritually. Either you are growing in Christ or you are backsliding.

8. God's blessing does not automatically and immediately follow God's calling.

9. "The spiritual leader and the servant leader are synonymous. The Church is an organism, the Body of Christ; but it is also an organization, and organizations require proper servant leadership."

10. Avoid the tendency to make decisions in haste or anger.

11. The fact that God allows His people to behave in sinful or foolish ways does not mean that He approves of their sin or foolishness.

12. One sin often leads to more sins, particularly when a person attempts to cover up his or her initial wrongdoing.

268

13. Sin affects not only the sinner but others as well, because no one can sin in a void.

14. Do not mislead yourself. You cannot fool God and make Him your puppet. Whatever you plant is what you will harvest.

15. Ignoring the Bible's commands and teachings, or thinking we are free to change its meanings in order to satisfy our personal feelings and desires, is tantamount to treating our God with disrespect and even contempt.

16. When we honestly confess our sins and truly repent, God promises to forgive us completely (see 1 John 1:9), but He does not remove the effects and consequences of our sins. We have to live with and through them.

17. Everything we have comes from God, so we are not the owners of the things we possess but merely the stewards.

ABBREVIATIONS

BRO	Barna Research Online
CBL	*The Complete Biblical Library: The Old Testament*
CBL:HED	*The Complete Biblical Library: The Old Testament Hebrew-English Dictionary*
EBC	*The Expositor's Bible Commentary*
ISBE	*The International Standard Bible Encyclopedia*
MOT	*Mastering the Old Testament*
TDNT	*Theological Dictionary of the New Testament*
TOTC	*Tyndale Old Testament Commentaries*
TSC	*Times Square Church Pulpit Series*
TWOT	*Theological Wordbook of the Old Testament*
WBC	*Word Biblical Commentary*

Notes

Prologue

1. The following list includes some of the books I found particularly helpful:

- Gregory A. Lint, exec. ed., The Complete Biblical Library: The Old Testament (Springfield, Mo.: World Library Press).
  - Samuel J. Schultz, *1 Samuel*, Vol. 6, 1998.
  - W. G. Blaikie, *2 Samuel*, Vol. 6, 1998.
  - F. W. Farrar, G. A. Lint, W. E. Nunnally, *1 Kings*, Vol. 7, 1997.
  - Andrew MacLaren, *Psalms*, Vol. 10, 1996.
- Frank E. Gaebelein, gen. ed., The Expositor's Bible Commentary (Grand Rapids: Zondervan Publishing House, 1992).
  - Ronald F. Youngblood, *1 & 2 Samuel*, Vol. 3.
  - Richard D. Patterson and Hermann J. Austel, *1 Kings*, Vol. 4.
  - J. Barton Payne, *1 Chronicles*, Vol. 3.
- Lloyd J. Ogilvie, gen. ed., Mastering the Old Testament (Dallas: Word Publishing).
  - Kenneth Chafin, *1, 2 Samuel*, 1989.
  - Leslie C. Allen, *1, 2 Chronicles*, 1987.
- D. J. Wiseman, gen. ed., Tyndale Old Testament Commentaries (Downers Grove, Ill.: Inter-Varsity Press).
  - Joyce G. Baldwin, *1 & 2 Samuel*, 1988.
  - Donald J. Wiseman, *1 & 2 Kings*, 1993.
  - Martin J. Selman, *1 Chronicles*, 1994.
- Charles Swindoll, *David* (Dallas: Word Publishing, 1997).
- R. Laird Harris, Gleason L. Archer, Jr. and Bruce K. Waltke, eds., *Theological Wordbook of the Old Testament* (Chicago: Moody Press, 1980).
- Gregory A. Lint, exec. ed., The Complete Biblical Library: *The Old Testament Hebrew-English Dictionary* (Springfield, Mo.: World Library Press, 2000).

- Geoffrey W. Bromiley, *Theological Dictionary of the New Testament,* abridged in one volume (Grand Rapids: William B. Eerdmans Publishing Co., 1985).
- Geoffrey W. Bromiley, gen. ed., The International Standard Bible Encyclopedia, rev. ed. (Grand Rapids: Wm. B. Eerdmans Publishing Company, 1992).

2. Genesis 50:22–26.

3. Luke 2:41–52.

4. Brennan Manning, *Abba's Child* (Colorado Springs: NavPress Publishing Group, 1994), 109.

Chapter 1: Types of Seasons

1. George Barna and Mark Hatch, *Boiling Point* (Ventura, Calif.: Regal Books, 2001), 56.

2. Walter C. Kaiser, Jr., *Ecclesiastes: Total Life* (Chicago: Moody Press, 1979), 11.

3. Ibid., 41.

4. E. F. Harrison, ed., *Baker's Dictionary of Theology* (Grand Rapids: Baker Book House, 1983), 215.

5. Kaiser, *Ecclesiastes,* 61.

6. Some critics may contend that Ecclesiastes 9:11–12 refutes this argument because the KJV and other translations say, "Time and chance happen (to all humans)—no matter how fast, strong, wealthy, or wise they may be." However, Solomon's point is that the issues of life are unpredictable and the mere possession of these talents does not ensure success in this life. (See J. Stafford Wright, "Ecclesiastes," in *EBC,* 5:1183–84.) Also, the Hebrew word translated "chance" (*pega*) carries the added meanings "event" or "occurrence."

7. Leonard J. Coppes, "*et*, Time," *TWOT,* 2:1650. Also *CBL:HED,* "eth, Time," 6496.

8. Coppes, 1650. Also *CBL:HED,* "zaman, To be appointed," 2248.

9. Charles Bridges, "Ecclesiastes," *CBL:OT,* 11:324.

10. Henry T. Blackaby and Claude V. King, *Experiencing God* (Nashville: Broadman & Holman Publishers, 1994), 5.

11. Brennan Manning, *Lion and Lamb* (Grand Rapids: Chosen Books, 1986), 26.

12. David Wilkerson, "That Which Is Spiritual Cannot Be Duplicated," *TSC,* 10 April 2001.

Chapter 2: Natural Seasons and Spiritual Seasons

1. There are numerous verses testifying to God's desire that all His people would know His will. A few examples are John 7:17; Ephesians 5:17; Colossians 1:9; and 1 John 2:17.

2. Wilkerson, *TSC.*

3. Frances Mayes, *Under the Tuscan Sun* (New York: Broadway Books, 1996), 64.

4. Ecclesiastes 2:24; 3:12–13, 22; 5:18–20.

5. John 16:33. See also Jesus' repeated exhortation to the seven churches in Revelation to be overcomers (2:7, 11, 17, 26; 3:5, 12, 21).

6. Charles Colson, "Salad-Bar Christianity," *Christianity Today,* 7 August 2000, 80.

7. The Lord is a holy and righteous God who must judge and punish those who are willfully and incorrigibly sinful and wicked. One agent of His judgment can be the forces of nature (as seen in the flood or the destruction of Sodom and Gomorrah, and that will be seen in the future events depicted in Revelation). God can also use people and nations as His agents. The children of Israel fulfilled this role when they conquered the Promised Land and destroyed much of the grossly immoral Canaanite civilization. Similarly, "the Amalekites were utterly depraved [and] they desired to destroy Israel. [Their] total destruction was necessitated by the gravity of their sin [and] their hateful act toward God's people and plan." See Norman Geisler and Thomas Howe, *When Critics Ask* (Wheaton, Ill.: Victor Books, 1992), 161.

8. John Wright Follette, *Arrows of Truth* (Springfield, Mo.: Gospel Publishing House, 1969), 9.

9. George Will, "Court Veers Into Dangerous Territory," *Charlotte Observer*, 4 June 2001.

10. *Charlotte Observer*, 10 June 2001.

11. David Wilkerson, "The Sound of His Voice," *TSC*, 4 March 2002.

Chapter 3: God's Choice

1. See 1 Samuel 7:16.

2. Was Samuel remembering back to the time when, at the Lord's instructions, he anointed Saul—a man who had all the visible attributes people tend to associate with a strong, impressive leader?

3. The genealogy in 1 Chronicles 2:13–15 lists a total of only seven sons for Jesse (David the youngest being the seventh). Youngblood (*1 & 2 Samuel*, p. 684) reconciles the difference by this analysis: "All things considered, it may be best to assume that one of David's seven older brothers died without offspring and is therefore omitted from [this] genealogy." Also see Payne, "1 Chronicles," in *EBC*, 334.

4. Some commentators believe it was a secret anointing. Schultz disagrees. "Whereas a prophet might have a private call from God, a king needed more than an inner voice. He needed to be confirmed by witnesses that he had been anointed as king." See Schultz, *1 Samuel*, 155.

5. Chafin, *1, 2 Samuel*, 134–35.

Chapter 4: Foundation Building

1. Millard J. Erickson, *Christian Theology* (Grand Rapids: Baker Book House, 1990), 967–968.

2. See 1 Samuel 13:14; Acts 13:22.

3. George Barna, "Annual Study Reveals America Is Spiritually Stagnant," *BRO*, press release of 5 March 2001. Barna reports "born-again Christians" were 41 percent of the adult population. "They were defined in these surveys as people who said they have made a personal commitment to Jesus Christ that is still important in their life today and who also indicated they believe that when they die they will go to heaven because they had confessed their sins and accepted Jesus Christ as their savior."

4. Ibid.

5. Charles Colson, *The Body* (Dallas: Word Publishing, 1992), 33.

6. Ibid., 282.

7. "Building Big Skyscrapers," *Public Broadcasting System Online*, notes on program of 17 October 2000.

8. Osmosis is the movement of a liquid solvent through a semi-permeable membrane into another liquid solution. This process is essential for the life of plants, animals and humans, because it enables them to absorb water and nutrients into their systems. Some Christians act as if their mere presence in a "religious" setting will set off a kind of spiritual osmosis and allow them to absorb all of the spiritual content of the event without any effort on their part.

9. Jack McCallum, "The Spirit of '76," *Sports Illustrated* (19 March 2001), 55.

10. Jim Cymbala, *Fresh Power* (Grand Rapids: Zondervan Publishing House, 2001), 171.

Chapter 5: Time for School

1. Jacob's wife Rachel died on their journey toward Bethlehem (called Ephrath in those days) while giving birth to Benjamin, her second son (see Genesis 35:16-20). The traditional location of her burial tomb is marked by a little white dome just north of Bethlehem, according to Robinson and Winward, *In the Holy Land* (Grand Rapids: Wm. B. Eerdmans Publishing Co., 1968), 44. The book of Judges contains three brief mentions of the town (12:8–10; 17:7–9; 19:1–2, 18). It also is the setting for the exquisite love story of Ruth and Boaz, David's paternal great-grandparents.

2. Yohanon Aharoni, *The Land of the Bible* (Philadelphia: The Westminster Press, 1979), 215.

3. Kurien Thomas, *God's Trailblazer* (Pant Nagar, Bombay—400 075, India: GLS Press, 1986).

4. Some of the better-known verses include Psalms 138:6 and 147:6; Proverbs 3:34 and 15:25; Isaiah 57:15; Matthew 23:12; Luke 14:11 and 18:14; James 4:6–10; and 1 Peter 5:5–6.

5. Fred H. Wight, *Manners and Customs of Bible Lands* (Chicago: Moody Press, 1978), 148.

6. Richard Foster, *Celebration of Discipline*, rev. ed. (San Francisco: HarperCollins Publishers, 1988), 96.

7. Baldwin, *1 & 2 Samuel*, 268. See also A. A. Anderson, *2 Samuel*, Word Biblical Commentary, gen. eds. David A. Hubbard and Glenn W. Barker (Dallas: Word Books, 1989), 11:223.

8. Ray Mossholder, "Raising Children," *Marriage Plus Seminar* (Chatsworth, Calif.: Ray Mossholder Ministries).

9. 1 Chronicles 27:18 does state that the head of the tribe of Judah during David's reign was "Elihu, one of David's brothers," but the text is unclear. Payne *(1 Chronicles*, 431) suggests that this could have been either an unnamed brother, or a relative, or possibly a variant for his oldest brother, Eliab.

10. Three of David's key warriors were Joab, Abishai and Asahel, the children of his half-sister Zeruiah (see 2 Samuel 2:18). They must have been fairly close to David in age. Abishai accompanied David when he spared Saul the second time (see 1 Samuel 26). Additionally, all three brothers are shown to be mature soldiers in David's army shortly after he was anointed king in Hebron at the age of thirty (see 2 Samuel 2). And Amasa, who later became the head of Absalom's rebel army, was the son of David's other half-sister Abigail.

11. Foster, *Celebration*, 97.

12. John N. Oswalt, "*batah*, Trust in, feel safe be confident," *TWOT*, 1:233.

13. Donald J. Wiseman, "*hasa*, Seek refuge, flee for protection," *TWOT*, 1:700.

14. Wight, *Bible Lands*, 162.

15. From telephone conversation on June 4, 2001, with Mark Jones, biologist with the North Carolina Wildlife Resources Commission.

16. Rick C. Howard, *The Finding Times of God* (Woodside, Calif.: Naioth Sound and Publishing, 1988), 47.

17. Jamie Buckingham, "Leader Traits," *The Spirit-Filled Life Bible*, gen. ed. Jack W. Hayford (Nashville: Thomas Nelson Publishers, 1991), 1600.

18. John C. Maxwell, *Developing the Leader Within You* (Nashville: Thomas Nelson Publishers, 1993), 98.

19. See Psalms 23:1 and 80:1; Isaiah 40:11; Jeremiah 31:10; Ezekiel 34:11–24; John 10:11–16; and 1 Peter 2:25 and 5:4.

20. Phillip Keller, *A Shepherd Looks at Psalm 23* (Grand Rapids: Zondervan Publishing House, 1970), 35.

21. Paul L. Garber, "Sheep; Shepherd," *ISBE*, 4:463–64.

22. Maxwell, *Developing the Leader*, 35.

23. J. Barton Payne, "*tamam*, Integrity, be complete," *TWOT*, 2:2522.

24. John Maxwell, *The 21 Irrefutable Laws of Leadership* (Nashville: Thomas Nelson Publishers, 1998), 188, 190.

25. Mark Oppenheimer, "Salvation Without Sacrifice," *Charlotte Observer*, 30 October 2000.

26. The theme of "waiting upon God" is found in at least nine of David's psalms: 25, 27, 37, 52, 56, 59, 62, 69 and 145.

Chapter 6: Dreams and Remembrances

1. Youngblood, *1 & 2 Samuel*, 3:696.

2. Doug Hood, "Ask the Rainmaker," *Entrepreneur* (September 2000), 50.

Chapter 7: God's Instructions

1. George A. Turner, *Historical Geography of the Holy Land* (Grand Rapids: Baker Book House, 1973), 189, 268. The Elah Valley where David confronted Goliath "has several prongs, one of which extends almost to Bethlehem. [So] David could have reached the site [of the battle] from his home in Bethlehem in a half-day's downhill journey."

2. Ralph Gower, *The New Manners and Customs of the Bible* (Chicago: Moody Press, 1987), 135–36.

3. Brennan Manning, *Ruthless Trust* (San Francisco: HarperCollins Publishers, 2000), 3.

4. Marshall Shelley, *Well-Intentioned Dragons* (Dallas: Word Publishing, 1985), 11.

5. Ibid., 37.

6. Manning, *Lion and Lamb*, 6.

7. David and Pat Alexander, *Eerdmans Handbook to the Bible* (Grand Rapids: William B. Eerdmans Publishing Company, 1973), 105.

8. Victor H. Matthews and Don C. Benjamin, *Social World of Ancient Israel, 1250–587 BCE* (Peabody, Mass.: Hendrckson Publishers, 1993), 218-19.

9. Following are two of several sources that attest to this practice:
   - Leon J. Wood, *A Survey of Israel's History*, rev. ed. (Grand Rapids: Zondervan Publishing House, 1986), 207.
   - William Sanford LaSor, David Allen Hubbard and Frederic William Bush, *Old Testament Survey* (Grand Rapids: William B. Eerdmans Publishing Company, 1982), 239.

10. Alfred J. Hoerth, Gerald L. Mattingly and Edwin M. Yamauchi, eds., *Peoples of the Old Testament World* (Grand Rapids: Baker Books, 1994), 239.

11. Gary R. Collins, *Christian Counseling*, rev. ed. (Dallas: Word Publishing, 1988), 82.

12. Ralph H. Alexander, "*yad*, Hand, power," *TWOT*, 1:844.

13. A. F. Rainey, "Valley of Elah," *ISBE*, 2:49.

14. John N. Oswalt, "*kabod*, Glory, be heavy, great," *TWOT*, 1:943. See also "kavodh, Glory, heaviness," *CBL:HED*, 3638.

15. See Isaiah 43:7 and 48:11.

16. John Bevere, *The Fear of the Lord* (Orlando, Fl.: Creation House, 1997), 9.

17. Howard, *Finding Times*, 153.

Chapter 8: The Battle

1. These coats of mail were also called "scale armor." "The coat was made from hundreds of small metal plates arranged like fish scales and sewn to a cloth or leather cloak." R. K. Harrison and Edward M. Blaiklock, "Arms & Weapons," *New International Dictionary of Biblical Archeology*, gen. eds. Harrison and Blaiklock (Grand Rapids: Zondervan Publishing House, 1983), 70.

2. In 1 Samuel 21:9, for example, David said of Goliath's sword, "There is none like it."

3. Ralph W. Klein, "1 Samuel," *WBC* (1983), 10:176.

4. Frank G. Slaughter, *David, Warrior and King* (Cleveland: The World Publishing Company, 1962), 95.

5. A person hit by such a powerfully thrown and well-aimed stone (or a bullet) normally would fall backwards. But Goliath fell forward, just as the idol of the pagan god Dagon did when the Philistines placed the captured Ark of the Covenant in his heathen temple (see 1 Samuel 5:4). Dagon could no more stand against the ark of almighty God than Goliath could stand against His representative, David. And in both instances, the idol and Goliath had their heads dismembered, a fitting climax demonstrating the impotence of the Lord's enemies and His infinite superiority.

6. Youngblood, *1 & 2 Samuel*, 703.

7. Saul's statements in verses 55–58 inquiring who David was may seem contradictory since in chapter 16:17–23 we are told that David served for a time in Saul's court as a minstrel and his armor-bearer. This difficulty can be readily explained because David had only shown his musical talents during this time, while his triumph over Goliath kindles Saul's interest in him as a warrior. So the king wanted to learn as much about him as possible. Also, it would not be unusual for a busy leader like Saul to take little notice of the many members in his entourage. See the following two sources for further commentary on this and other seemingly contradictory and difficult Bible passages:

- Gleason L. Archer, Jr., *Encyclopedia of Bible Difficulties* (Grand Rapids: Zondervan Publishing House, 1982), 175.
- Geisler and Howe, *When Critics Ask*, 164.

8. The false and scurrilous claim that the relationship between David and Jonathan was a homosexual one will be discussed in detail in the next section.

Chapter 9: Our Thoughts versus God's Thoughts

1. Manning, *Ruthless Trust*, 6.

Chapter 10: The Start of God's Lessons

1. Howard, *Finding Times*, 7.
2. Geoffrey W. Bromiley, "*kairos*," *TDNT*, 389.
3. Follette, *Arrows of Truth*, 9.
4. See Genesis 18:14; Jeremiah 32:27.

Chapter 11: When the Going Gets Tough

1. Howard, *Finding Times*, 101.
2. Archer, 179–80. How can evil come from our good God? Archer replies by pointing out Saul's past sinful behavior pattern. "By these successive acts of rebellion against the will and law of God, King Saul left himself wide open to satanic influence—just as Judas Iscariot did after he had determined to betray the Lord Jesus. Although he was doubtless acting as an agent of Satan, Saul's evil bent was by the permission and plan of God."
3. When Samuel anointed David, the text tells us, "The Spirit of the LORD came upon David from that day forward." David himself acknowledged God's daily presence in his life, particularly in the psalms he composed, such as Psalm 23:4 ("For You are with me"). God Himself testified to this fact saying, "I have been with you wherever you have gone" (2 Samuel 7:9). And people often recognized the Lord's presence and anointing upon David (see 1 Samuel 16:18; 18:12; 25:28–31; 2 Samuel 7:3; etc.).
4. Louis Goldberg, "*sakal*, Wisely," *TWOT*, 2:2263.
5. Psalm 59 is the first of fourteen carrying headings or titles which connect them with events in David's career. The others are Psalms 3, 7, 18, 30, 34, 51, 52, 56, 57, 60, 63 and 142. Fifty-nine other psalms carry some note saying in effect they were written by David. Maclaren, Kidner and Longman note that David's authorship of the psalms bearing his name have frequently been challenged but conclude in their estimation that David indeed wrote those psalms the titles ascribe to him. See:

- MacLaren, 706–7.
- Derek Kidner, "Psalms 1–72," *TOTC*, 33-4.
- Tremper Longman III, *How to Read the Psalms* (Downers Grove, IL: Inter-Varsity Press, 1988), 38–9.

6. Bromiley, "The OT Term *berit*," *TDNT*, 157–58.

7. For a good insight into the "gay Christian" movement and a discussion of how best to respond to their arguments, see Bill Shepson, "Can Christians Be Gay?" in *Charisma* (July 2001), 38–44.

8. Schultz, *1 Samuel*, 179. "The Hebrew word *ahev* used for 'love' involves a personal commitment of self in the purest and noblest intentions of trust and obedience toward God (cf. Deut. 6:4–5; 10:12f). It is not used to express homosexual desire or activity; the Hebrew word *yadha* used in the sense of 'having sex with' in Gen. 19:5 is never used in Jonathan-David relationship. The word 'love' also had political overtones in diplomatic and commercial contexts used in a treaty or covenant relationship (cf. 1 Kings 5:1)."

- Youngblood, *1 & 2 Samuel*, 706. "The verb *ahev* ('love') is not used elsewhere to express homosexual desire or activity, for which the OT employs *yada* ('know'), in the sense of 'having sex with' (Genesis 19:5; Judges 19:22). The latter verb is never used of David's relationship with Jonathan."
- (Also see *CBL:HED*, "*ahev*, To love," 154, which lists the 206 Old Testament occurrences of this verb, and discusses the various ways it is used.)

9. Tom Houston, *King David, Lessons on Leadership* (MARC Europe, 1987), 43.

10. H. Newton Maloney, "Mad; Madness; Madman," *ISBE*, 3:211–12.

11. Donald R. Bowes, "Cave," The Zondervan Pictorial Encyclopedia of the Bible (Grand Rapids: Zondervan Publishing House, 1976), 1:769.

12. William Sanford LaSor, "Adullum," *ISBE*, 1:58.

13. John E. Hartley, "*masoq*, Distress," *TWOT*, 2:1895.

14. Milton C. Fisher, "*nasha*, Lend on interest, usury," *TWOT*, 2:1424.

15. Victor P. Hamilton, "*mar*, Bitter," *TWOT*, 1:1248.

16. Maxwell, *Devloping the Leader*, 113, 116.

17. See 2 Samuel 23:8–39 and 1 Chronicles 11:10–47.

18. Aharoni, *The Land of the Bible*, 307.

19. Shelley, *Dragons*, 148.

20. See Leviticus 19:16; Proverbs 11:13; 18:8; 20:19; 1 Thessalonians 4:11; 1 Timothy 5:13; James 3:6. The word "talebearer" in the KJV and NKJV means a gossiper or slanderer.

21. John Bevere, *Under Cover* (Nashville: Thomas Nelson Publishers, 2001), 100.

22. Barna and Hatch, *Boiling Point*, 238–40.

23. Ibid., 235.

24. Bevere, *Under Cover*, 135.

Chapter 12: His Priceless Providence and Protection

1. Gower, *Customs of the Bible*, 143.

2. See Proverbs 14:17 and 25:28, two verses that counsel about the need for self-restraint.

3. Youngblood, *1 & 2 Samuel*, 3:753.

4. Ibid., 3:758.

5. Swindoll, *David*, 111.

6. The Hebrew word translated "strengthened" is in the *hithpael* stem and, while it can be translated in various ways, it is usually rendered with this meaning. See the following sources:

- Carl Phillip Weber, "*hazaq*, Become strong, strengthen," *TWOT*, 1:636.
- John Joseph Owens, Analytical Key to the Old Testament (Grand Rapids: Baker Book House, 1992), 2:267.
- *CBL:HED*, "*chazaq*, To be firm or strong, to grasp," 2480.

7. Howard, *Finding Times*, 131.

8. Henri Nouwen, quoted by Brennan Manning in *Abba's Child*, 21.

9. Paul D. Meier, Frank B. Minirth, Frank B. Wichern, Donald E. Ratcliff, *Introduction to Psychology and Counseling*, 2nd ed. (Grand Rapids: Baker Book House, 1991), 208.

10. Judy Keen, "President's Faith Is a 'Great Comfort' to Him," *USA Today*, 18 May 2001.

11. G. Lloyd Carr, "*shalom*, Peace," *TWOT*, 2: 2401.

Chapter 13: A Moment of Crisis

1. This passage is from Psalm 69:1–4, one of the many Davidic psalms that has no heading connecting it with some event in his career. Nonetheless, it could have been composed at this time since it so powerfully reflects David's hope and trust in his God during times of great crisis.

2. J. Barton Payne, *The Theology of the Older Testament* (Grand Rapids: Zondervan Publishing House, 1962), 48.

- Cornelis Van Dam, "Urim and Thummin," *ISBE*, 4:957–58.
- At this critical time David sought God's assistance and guidance by means of a peculiar Old Testament practice. While Bible scholars have a number of unanswered questions regarding the actual description and method of use of these objects, certain things about them generally are agreed upon. The Urim and Thummin were probably two gemlike stones which the High Priest carried in the pouch of his breastplate, a piece of linen attached to his vest (called an ephod). In seeking to ascertain God's will on a given matter, they were either cast like modern dice or drawn out of the pouch, thereby giving a yes or no answer.

3. There is an important point to remember about David's use of such a means of divine guidance at this particular time. The Bible records only one other instance where he sought God's guidance through the operation of the Urim and Thummin (see 1 Samuel 23:9), although there are at least two other occasions when Scripture mentions David's questions to the Lord and His answers in a way that indicates the Urim and Thummin were being used (see 2 Samuel 2:1 and 5:19). Even so we must remember that David had no access to this method during his early shepherding years when he confronted lions and bears and faced endless days and nights of solitary existence. What he did have was his growing awareness of and relationship with the Lord. And later, when Samuel anointed him in Jesse's home, "the Spirit of the Lord came upon David from that day forward" (1 Samuel 16:13). So

when he faced Goliath, successfully fought battles for Saul, spent years eluding capture by this mad king, gathered together and trained the core of what was to become his mighty army, learned the principles of leadership and trust in the Lord, it was the Holy Spirit alone who guided, protected and empowered David.

4. The Bible offers several illustrations of this truth. The most outstanding one is found in Luke 2:1–7, where the census decreed by Caesar Augustus caused Joseph and Mary's baby to be born in Bethlehem. Other instances involve the great Persian king Cyrus, whom God used to effect the return of the Israelites from Babylon to the Promised Land (see Ezra 1:1–4), and the Assyrian monarch Tiglath-Pileser who was employed by God to manifest His wrath in the judgment on the Northern Kingdom of Israel (see Isaiah 10:6). See also Proverbs 16:9 and Jeremiah 10:23.

5. Baldwin, *1 & 2 Samuel*, 168. This scholar points out that the word "twilight" in verse 17 of some translations has the sense of "dawn" as in Job 7:4 and Psalm 119:147.

6. The Hebrew day began at sunset. Thus, the phrase "the evening of the next day" in various translations refers to the end of that day of battle which had begun at dawn.

7. David Chadwick, *The 12 Leadership Principles of Dean Smith* (New York: Total Sports Illustrated, 1999), 2.

Chapter 14: Putting God First

1. Schultz, *1 Samuel*, 319.

2. See also Proverbs 20:24; 21:2; and Jeremiah 10:23.

3. John Phillips, *Exploring the Psalms* (Neptune, N.J.: Loizeaux Brothers, 1988), 1:188–89.

4. Patrick Morley, *The Man in the Mirror* (Grand Rapids: Zondervan Publishing House, 1997), 224.

5. 1 Samuel 18:12, 14; 2 Samuel 5:10 and 7:9; 1 Chronicles 17:8.

6. Chafin, *1, 2 Samuel*, 247.

7. 1 Chronicles 16:39.

8. Wilhelm Lotz, M. G. Kyle, Carl E. Armerding, "Ark of the Covenant," *ISBE*, 1:292.

9. See Schultz, *1 Samuel*, 359. He writes, "The punishment may seem hard for an offense which was ceremonial rather than moral; but in that economy, moral truth was taught through ceremonial observances, and neglect of the one was treated as involving neglect of the other."

10. A few other examples are Psalm 119; Isaiah 40:8; Matthew 24:35; Hebrews 4:12.

11. Swindoll, *David*, 153.

12. Judson Cornwall, *Worship as David Lived It* (Shippensburg, Pa.: Destiny Image Publishers, Inc., 2000), 14.

13. Foster, *Celebration*, 160–61.

14. See 2 Samuel 5:11; 1 Chronicles 14:1.

15. Chafin, *1, 2 Samuel*, 282.

16. The other two occurrences are in 2 Samuel 12 and 1 Kings 1.

17. For example, when the Jewish nation was divided after Solomon's death into the Northern Kingdom (Israel) and the Southern Kingdom (Judah), several of the Northern kings suffered violent overthrows, including Elah and Zimri (see 1 Kings 16) and Joram

(see 2 Kings 9). Also the great Assyrian king Sennacherib was killed by two of his own sons (see 2 Kings 19).

18. Judson Cornwall is one of several writers in recent years who have advocated this discipline. In his book *Praying the Scriptures* (Lake Mary, Fl.: Creation House, 1988), he writes the following on page 185: "As we introduce the written word of God into our praying, we not only discover the Father's will; we declare it. Our prayer rises above pleading to proclaiming, and this excites our spirits. We recognize that we are no longer repeating our own words. We are saying the very words of God who wrote the Scriptures. We have ceased originating the message and have become messengers for Almighty God as we proclaim His will to the entire spirit world."

Chapter 15: The "God Kind" of Kindness

1. K. Weiss, "*chestotes*, Goodness, Kindness," *TDNT*, 1320–22. See also:
   - "*chrestos, chrestotes*," *The Complete Biblical Library: The New Testament Greek-English Dictionary*, exec. ed. Ralph W. Harris (Springfield, Mo.: The Complete Biblical Library, 1991), 5378–79.

2. Youngblood, *1 & 2 Samuel*, 854–55. He explains the apparent contradiction between Joshua 15:63 and Judges 1:8: "Jerusalem was the name for the Jebusite settlement on two hills, one of which was heavily defended and was located in the southeast sector of the city, while the other consisted of unprotected open country located in the southwest." The Judges verse refers to the Israelites' conquest of the open area of the Jerusalem settlement while the Joshua verse refers to the fortified citadel which the Jebusites were able to hold until the time of David's successful attack.

3. Aharoni, *The Land of the Bible*, 292.

4. R. Laird Harris, "*hesed*, Kindness," *TWOT*, 1:698. This scholar believes the King James translation of "lovingkindness [is] not far from the fullness of the word." He opines other meanings can include "steadfast love, unfailing love, loyalty."
   - *CBL:HED*, "*chesedh*, Grace, steadfast love,*" 2721. "The most important way this word is used is in the theological context of describing a characteristic of God himself. [It] is one of the most important theological terms in all Scripture, giving an insight into the very essence of God."

5. Examples include Psalm 102:26–27; Malachi 3:6; Hebrews 13:8; and James 1:17.

6. R. Bultmann, "*eleos*, Mercy," *TDNT*, 222–24. This Greek word carries much of the same meaning as the Hebrew *hesed*.

7. J. I. Packer, *Knowing God* (Downers Grove, Ill.: InterVarsity Press, 1993), 132.

8. Schultz, *1 Samuel*, 389.

9. Chafin, *1, 2 Samuel*, 292–93.

Chapter 16: Blessing, Warfare and Work

1. Verses include 2 Corinthians 10:4; 1 Timothy 6:12; 2 Timothy 2:3; James 4:7; 1 Peter 5:8.

2. Chafin *1, 2 Samuel*, 272–73.

3. Genesis 15:18. Later Scriptures confirm this "covenant of land" God made with Abraham including Exodus 23:31; Numbers 34:1–15; Deuteronomy 11:24; Joshua 1:4; 1 Kings 4:21.

4. Much of this ancient Philistine enclave is a part of the so-called Gaza Strip of the present day. Moreover, God had promised the Israelites all of the land occupied by the Philistines (see Joshua 13:2–3), a promise that the Jewish nation has never fully appropriated.

5. Hoerth, Mattingly, Yamauchi, *Peoples*, 241.

6. Anderson "2 Samuel," 146; Payne, *1 Chronicles*, 398; Youngblood, *1 & 2 Samuel*, 921.

7. B. J. Beitzel, "Zobah," *ISB*, 4:1203–4; Hoerth, Mattingly, Yamauchi, *Peoples*, 215–16.

8. Kenneth O. Gangel, *Feeding & Leading* (Wheaton, Ill.: Victor Books, 1989), 31, 57.

9. John Bright, *A History of Israel*, 3rd ed. (Philadelphia: Westminster Press, 1981), 204. The author also notes, "David's empire, though by our standards not large, was by ancient ones of quite respectable size. His domain lacked but little of being the equivalent of Egyptian holdings in Asia in the heyday of the Empire."

10. Ibid., 206.

11. Stanley Horton, "Genesis," *CBL:OT*, 1:129.

Chapter 17: The Monarch's Mistakes

1. Alexander Whyte, *Bible Characters* (Grand Rapids: Zondervan Publishing House, 1977), 304.

2. Read both 2 Samuel 5:8 and 1 Chronicles 11:6 for a complete report of this incident.

3. Jim Collins, *Good to Great* (New York: HarperCollins Publishers, 2001), 64.

4. Bright, *History of Israel*, 205.

Chapter 18: The Traps of Temptation

1. Youngblood, *1 & 2 Samuel*, 928.

2. Eugene H. Maly, *The World of David and Solomon* (Englewood Cliffs, N.J.: Prentice-Hall, Inc., 1966), 78.

3. See 2 Samuel 5:9 and 1 Chronicles 11:8.

4. 1 Samuel 16:12.

5. Youngblood, *1 & 2 Samuel*, 929.

6. 2 Samuel 23:39 and 1 Chronicles 11:41.

7. 2 Samuel 23:34.

8. 2 Samuel 15:12.

9. J. Barton Payne, "*hamad*, Desire," *TWOT*, 1:673. The Hebrew word translated "covet" refers to an "inordinate, ungoverned, selfish desire."

Chapter 19: The Seeds of Sin

1. Gower, *Customs of the Bible*, 63.

2. Maly, *The World of David*, 80–1.

3. Swindoll, *David*, 179.

4. Erwin W. Lutzer, *Ten Lies About God* (Nashville: W Publishing Group, 2000), 55.

5. Victor P. Hamilton, "*shobab*, Backsliding," *TWOT*, 2:2340.

Chapter 20: The Quicksand of a Quandary

1. Youngblood, *1 & 2 Samuel*, 930.

2. The Ark of the Covenant accompanied Israel's army into battle on at least one earlier occasion (see 1 Samuel 4:3) and also had been carried around Jericho prior to this city's destruction.

3. Whyte, *Bible Characters*, 303.

4. K. N. Schoville, "Siege, Siegeworks," *ISBE*, 4:504–5.

5. Lutzer, *Lies About God*, 1.

6. Ibid., 5.

7. Judson Cornwall, *Forbidden Glory* (Hagerstown, Md.: McDougal Publishing, 2001), 29.

8. Charles Colson, *How Now Shall We Live?* (Wheaton, Ill.: Tyndale House Publishers, Inc., 1999), 477.

Chapter 22: Hard Lessons

1. Bruce K. Waltke, "b*aza*, To despise, disdain, hold in contempt," *TWOT*, 1:224.

2. Barna and Hatch, *Boiling Point*, 78–80.

3. George Barna, "Americans Are Most Likely to Base Truth on Feelings," *BRO*, Press release of February 12, 2002.

4. George Barna, "The Year's Most Intriguing Findings," *BRO*, press release of December 17, 2001.

5. Timothy Lamer, "Reaping the Whirlwind," *World*, 20 July 2002, 14.

6. David Augsburger, *Caring Enough to Confront* (Ventura, Calif.: Regal Books, 1982), 51.

7. Erickson, *Christian Theology*, 265.

8. David Wilkerson, "The Belly of Hell: The Consequences of Disobedience," *TSC*, 6 May 2002.

9. Augsburger, 52.

10. H. C. Leupold, *Exposition of Psalms* (Grand Rapids: Baker Book House, 1989), 307-8. Phillips, *Exploring the Psalms*, 49–50 and 289.

11. Erickson, *Christian Theology*, 615–19.

12. Dr. James White, "America's New Religiosity: God Bless America, But Don't You Dare Tell Us to Repent." Received from personal friend via e-mail, October 2001. No source given.

13. Colson, *How Now Shall We Live?* 191

14. Dietrich Bonhoeffer, *The Cost of Discipleship* (New York: Macmillan Publishing Co., 1963), 47.

15. Foster, *Celebration*, 157.

16. Schultz, *1 Samuel*, 413.

17. Youngblood, *1 & 2 Samuel*, 946.

Chapter 23: Bitter Harvests

1. Karl Menninger, *Whatever Became of Sin?* (New York: Hawthorn Books, Inc., 1973), 14.

2. Leupold, *Exposition of Psalms*, 9.

3. Schultz, *1 Samuel*, 469.

4. See Proverbs 13:24; 22:15; 23:13; 29:15, 17; Hebrews 12:5–8.

5. Chafin, *1, 2 Samuel*, 319.

6. David's second-born son, Chileab (see 2 Samuel 3:3, who is called Daniel in 1 Chronicles 3:1), apparently died at an early age. Thus, Absalom, the third-born son, becomes David's eldest living son upon the death of Amnon. See Youngblood, *1 & 2 Samuel*, 830. Also Farrar, Lint, Nunnally, *1 Kings*, 13, and Patterson, Austel, *1 Kings*, 29.

7. Baldwin, *1 & 2 Samuel*, 252.

8. Schultz, *1 Samuel*, 449. "The Hebrew text states that it was 'at the end of forty years' that Absalom struck the final blow. The reading of some manuscripts is more likely to be correct: 'at the end of four years' ('forty' is the plural of 'four' and thus, essentially, the same word)."

9. This last contention is a complete fabrication. 2 Samuel 8:15 and chapter 14 as well as 1 Chronicles 18:14 indicate the king was available for any Israelite who needed his ruling.

10. Chafin, *1, 2 Samuel*, 330; Youngblood, *1 & 2 Samuel*, 989.

Chapter 24: Grace in the Midst of a Storm

1. Cornwall, *Worship*, 111.

2. Proverbs 17:17 says, "A friend loves at all times." John 15:15 pictures the close relationship between Christ and the believer by His use of the figure of friendship.

3. Baldwin, *1 & 2 Samuel*, 265.

4. See Exodus 4:12; Matthew 10:19–20; Luke 12:11–12 and 21:15.

5. Schultz, *1 Samuel*, 475.

6. W. D. Mounce, "Mahanaim," *ISBE*, 3:222–23.

7. A. Denis Baly, "Forest of Ephraim," *ISBE*, 2:119–20.

8. Although exact numbers are not given, two verses indicate the probable large size of Absalom's following and forces. 2 Samuel 15:13 states, "The hearts of the men of Israel are with Absalom." And in 17:11, Hushai advises Absalom to fully gather all Israel "from Dan to Beersheba" before confronting David.

9. Schultz, *1 Samuel*, 487.

10. Madame Jeanne Guyon, *Experiencing the Depths of Jesus Christ* (Gardiner, Maine: Christian Books Publishing House, 1975), 32.

11. Howard, *Finding Times*, 5.

12. Chafin, *1, 2 Samuel*, 356.

13. Swindoll, *David*, 249.

Chapter 25: God Chooses Again

1. Bright, *History of Israel*, 210. Also refer to Roddy Braun, "1 Chronicles," in *WBC*, (1986) 14:288. This commentator contends that the statement in 29:22 indicating David had

Solomon anointed as king "a second time" in order to defeat Adonijah's attempt at usurpation "appears to be an addition to reconcile the passage with 23:1, adjudged above to be a later insertion. This deletion is further suggested by its omission in some manuscripts."

2. Farrar, Lint, Nunnally, *1 Kings*, 17. Also see Eugene H. Merrill, *Kingdom of Priests* (Grand Rapids: Baker Book House, 1987), 279. This writer believes, "Solomon was about fifteen years younger then Adonijah." Payne, *1 Chronicles*, 411, opines that Solomon was about twenty at this time.

3. Wiseman, *1 Kings*, 70. "A usurper would be expected to eliminate all rivals with their families."

4. William G. Blaikie, *David, King of Israel* (Minneapolis: Klock & Klock Christian Publishers, Inc., 1981), 364.

5. See 2 Samuel 12:24; 1 Chronicles 22:9–10; and 28:5–7.

Chapter 26: Never-Ending Blessings

1. See 2 Samuel 23:20–23; 1 Chronicles 11:22–25.

2. See 1 Chronicles 27:5–6.

Chapter 27: David's Legacy

1. Payne, *Theology*, 434.

2. Ibid.

3. "Wrong doing on the part of David's successors will not lead to the end of the dynasty, but only to corrective, parental discipline from God." Iain W. Provan, "1 and 2 Kings," in *New International Biblical Commentary* (Peabody, Mass.: Hendrickson Publishers, 1995), 32.

4. Paul D. Meier, *Christian Child Rearing and Personality Development* (Grand Rapids: Baker Book House, 1977), 92.

5. Robert L. Alden, *Proverbs* (Grand Rapids: Baker Book House, 1988), 45.

6. See 2 Samuel 24:18–25 and 1 Chronicles 21:18–22:1.

7. Merrill, *Kingdom*, 277.

8. See Edward M. Cook, "Weights and Measures," *ISBE*, 4:1054. These amounts may seem incredible to our modern eyes, but Payne offers an enlightening and plausible explanation. See Payne, *1 Chronicles*, 412, note 14.

9. Selman, *1 Chronicles*, 261.

10. Provan, "1 and 2 Kings," 34.

11. See 1 Kings 2:1–4 and 1 Chronicles 22:11–13.

12. See 1 Kings 11:3.

13. Larry Burkett, "Wills & Trusts," *Financial Freedom Library* (Chicago: Moody Press, 1992), 7–8.

Chapter 28: Leaving Our Legacy

1. Meier, Minirth, Wichern, Ratcliff, *Introduction to Psychology*, 165.

2. Chafin, *1, 2 Samuel*, 283.

Epilogue

1. Lisa Beamer, *Let's Roll!* (Wheaton, Ill.: Tyndale House Publishers, Inc., 2002), 214.

2. Ibid., 312.

3. Numerous psalms of David deal with these three things, so only a few examples are given in this footnote:

- Hope—38:15; 39:7; 131:3.
- Faith (Trust)—25:2; 31:1; 56:3, 4, 11.
- Understanding of God's ultimate plan—23:6; 57:2–3; 138:7.

Thomas A. Vaughn graduated Phi Beta Kappa from the University of Missouri, where he subsequently obtained a master's degree in finance. He earned a Chartered Financial Analyst certification and served nearly three decades in the commercial and investment banking industries in a variety of assignments, including as manager of several mutual funds and president and CEO of a commercial bank.

Tom and his wife, Jane, enrolled in the Assemblies of God Theological Seminary, where he graduated with a master's from the Bible and theology department (named outstanding student in his class). For the past twelve years he and Jane have served in active ministry. He spent six years as executive pastor of a large church in the Chicago suburbs and two years pastoring a small pioneer church in North Carolina.

Now retired from full-time pastoring, Tom and Jane write, teach and lead Bible studies and prayer meetings. They have three children and three grandchildren and moved recently to the Phoenix area.